COWLES FOUNDATION
FOR RESEARCH IN ECONOMICS
AT YALE UNIVERSITY

MONOGRAPH 25

COWLES FOUNDATION

For Research in Economics at Yale University

The Cowles Foundation for Research in Economics at Yale University, established as an activity of the Department of Economics in 1955, has as its purpose the conduct and encouragement of research in economics and related social sciences with particular emphasis on the development and application of logical, mathematical, and statistical methods of analysis. The professional research staff have, as a rule, a departmental appointment and some teaching responsibility.

The Cowles Foundation continues the work of the Cowles Commission for Research in Economics founded in 1932 by Alfred Cowles at Colorado Springs, Colorado. The Commission moved to Chicago in 1939 and was affiliated with the University of Chicago until 1955. In 1955 the professional research staff of the Commission accepted appointments at Yale and, along with other members of the Yale Department of Economics, formed the research staff of the newly established Cowles Foundation.

A list of Cowles Foundation Monographs appears at the end of this volume.

Bank Management
and Portfolio Behavior

Donald D. Hester

James L. Pierce

New Haven and London, Yale University Press, 1975

Library of Congress catalog card number: 74-78472
International standard book number: 0-300-01716-2

Set in Times Roman type
and printed in the United States of America by
The Murray Printing Co., Forge Village, Massachusetts.

Published in Great Britain, Europe, and Africa by
Yale University Press, Ltd., London.
Distributed in Latin America by Kaiman & Polon, Inc., New York City;
in Australasia and Southeast Asia by John Wiley & Sons Australasia
Pty. Ltd., Sydney; in India by UBS Publishers' Distributors Pvt., Ltd.,
Delhi; in Japan by John Weatherhill, Inc., Tokyo.

Contents

List of Figures and Tables

FIGURES

TABLES

Acknowledgments

We have incurred many intellectual debts while preparing this monograph, and considerable financial assistance from various organizations made the whole project feasible. No acknowledgment can adequately express our gratitude for the help we have received.

Planning of the monograph began in the fall of 1963 when both writers were staff members of the Cowles Foundation for Research in Economics at Yale University. That organization provided the essential stimulating and supporting environment which permits large research projects to be envisioned and executed. In later years Pierce moved to the Board of Governors of the Federal Reserve System, and Hester moved to the University of Wisconsin. The project could not have been completed without the encouragement and help flowing from these institutions as well.

At Yale James Tobin, William Brainard, David Cass, James Friedman, Tjalling Koopmans, Susan Lepper, Marc Nerlove, and Henry Wallich contributed by providing many helpful criticisms of our project. At Wisconsin our thanks go especially to Arthur Goldberger, who commented on a late draft of this monograph in considerable detail. D. L. Brito, Donald Nichols, and Guy Orcutt also made some very useful suggestions in Madison. Elsewhere, we are very grateful to Stephen Goldfeld, who critically read the entire manuscript. Leonall Anderson, Richard Beals, Karl Brunner, Michael Farrell, Lyle Gramley, George Hancs, Elmer Harmon, Saul Klaman, and Peter Tinsley all commented on individual chapters either informally or at professional meetings where preliminary versions were read. We are also indebted to Edward McKelvey for correcting two mathematical slips in chapter 3.

The acquisition of data required the assistance of many individuals who worked at the Board of Governors of the Federal Reserve, the Federal Reserve Bank of Boston, and the National Association of Mutual Savings Banks. The Computation Center of Massachusetts Institute of Technology contributed computer time that was used to condense, code, and sort deposit data about individual banks which were retained on punched cards at the Boston Federal Reserve Bank. The Yale University Computer Center made similarly important contributions.

Research reported in the following pages was in large part financed by grants from the National Science Foundation to the Cowles Foundation (GS-1212) and to the University of Wisconsin (GS-2305). During the 1967–68 academic year Hester was given a critically important release from teaching responsibilities at Yale in the form of a Ford Foundation Faculty Fellowship in Economics. The Federal Reserve Board has made an important financial contribution to this project as well in the form of computer, secretarial, and other support consumed by Pierce.

A group of very loyal and careful research assistants also played a major role in this undertaking. We especially wish to thank John Jeavons, Bill Manne, Richard Nelson, and Richard Zimmer at Yale; Harvey Gram, John Jurewitz, Robert Thayer, and Michael Vogt at Wisconsin; and Jacqueline McDaniel, Barbara McFadden, Bonnie Garrett, and Arnita Ficklin at the Federal Reserve Board. Valuable editorial suggestions were made by Karen Hester and by Mary Ann Graves. The manuscript was typed more than once and with remarkable accuracy collectively by Glena Ames, Linda Bielski, Mary Flaherty, and Amanda Slowen.

Finally, we would be remiss if the probing questions of faculty and students at Wisconsin, Yale, and about thirty other universities where chapters were presented in seminars were not gratefully acknowledged.

BANK MANAGEMENT AND PORTFOLIO BEHAVIOR

CHAPTER 1

Introduction

The banking industry is the largest financial intermediary in the United States capital market. Given its prominence, surprisingly few quantitative studies of the portfolio behavior of individual banks and the industry at large have been reported in the economic literature. The purpose of this monograph is to provide a microeconometric analysis of portfolio behavior and earnings by commercial and mutual savings banks. The results are shown to be of value in constructing an aggregate model for the analysis of systems of commercial and mutual savings banks.

The first section of this chapter provides a brief review and critique of existing theories of bank portfolio behavior. Section 2 summarizes the major findings of the present analysis, and section 3 presents a chapter outline of the monograph.

1. Studies of Bank Portfolio Behavior

Until quite recently, descriptions of bank portfolio behavior failed to exploit the rich analytical apparatus that has been developed to understand the profit-maximizing firm. Instead, bank decision making was characterized by a number of rules of thumb derived from a combination of environmental factors such as random deposit and loan fluctuations, legal constraints, and established banking lore. The major analytical premise of this monograph is that bank behavior can be better described by developing a framework that synthesizes the environmental and profit-maximizing approaches.

Roland Robinson's [1962] insightful analysis is an excellent example of the traditional banking approach. Robinson sought "to describe methods of achieving the most profitable employment of commercial bank funds consistent with safety" [p. 4]. For him, these methods essentially consist of setting and following a hierarchy of priorities in the employment of bank funds. The priorities, in descending order, are: (1) legally required reserves, (2) secondary reserves, (3) customer credit demands, and (4) open-market investments for income.

According to Robinson, an individual bank is assumed to view the volume of its deposits as exogenous. The interest rate paid on deposits, implicitly for demand and explicitly for savings and time balances, is not viewed as a decision variable for the individual bank. Given the volume and composition of its deposit liabilities, the bank makes a sequence of decisions concerning the composition of its portfolio. First, the bank meets its legally required reserve commitments. Second, it determines the size of its secondary reserve holdings; these reserves consist of liquid short-term assets. The demand for secondary reserves arises out of possible but unforeseeable cash drains associated with deposit losses and loan requests. The decision to hold secondary reserves is assumed to be made independently of prevailing and expected future interest rates. Third, the bank meets its customers' credit demands. If any funds remain, it makes long-term security purchases. This fourth decision is considered to be purely derivative: "When a commercial bank has provided the liquidity needed for safety and has satisfied in full the local customer demand for loans, it can enter the investment market with any remaining funds" [p. 17].

While this framework provides many insights into bank motives for holding various assets, it does not indicate how a bank optimizes when deciding whether or not to shift funds from one asset to another; marginal analysis plays no part in traditional banking analysis. What if strong loan demand causes a bank to exhaust its slack resource, investments? Robinson did not explain how banks do or should allocate scarce funds. Because rates of return do not enter the analysis, there is no way for loan customers to bid funds away from the portfolio of reserve assets. Clearly, the priority concept requires modification if it is to form a reliable base upon which to build.

Hodgman [1963] attempted to remedy some of the shortcomings of traditional banking theory. Using interviews and surveys, he sought to gain insights into bankers' attitudes toward such factors as long-standing deposit customers, the size and composition of their loan and security portfolios, and the adequacy of their capital and surplus. His most significant contribution was the customer-relation hypothesis in which the opportunity cost of a loan to a bank is a function of the average size of the customer's deposit balance and the length of time he has held an account in the bank. Thus, in Hodgman's view, banks are concerned not only with the composition of their asset portfolios but also with the relationship between deposits and loans over time. Deposit balances become endogenous; the customer relation gives banks a strong reason to lend to customers with large balances.

Hodgman's work is useful for understanding such aspects of contemporary banking as prime rate conventions and compensating balance requirements. He recognized the possibility of bank optimization, but unfortunately he failed to follow this lead. Banks are still assumed to be concerned about such constructs as maximum loan-deposit ratios that are apparently independent of interest rates.

Both Hodgman and earlier students of banking institutions combined a loosely specified objective function with a set of legal and administrative constraints to obtain decision rules for bankers. Chambers and Charnes [1961] improved upon this informal traditional analysis by suggesting a linear programming framework. By introducing interest rates in an objective function and by viewing the hierarchy of traditional decision rules as constraints, they produced a model of bank behavior that is consistent with both traditional theory and the maximization of bank profits. However, in their model the existence or absence of uncertainty is of no consequence. This feature is a serious shortcoming because avoidance of risk is one of the promising theoretical candidates for explaining portfolio diversification.

The importance of random deposit variations for the determination of a bank's optimum portfolio was first suggested by Edgeworth [1888]. Some seventy years elapsed between the publication of Edgeworth's study and the explicit introduction of uncertainty into models of bank portfolio selection [Porter, 1961].

Porter applied an inventory model to describe bank portfolio behavior under uncertainty.[1] The results from his application of inventory theory to banking are impressive; his model includes market imperfections, asset transactions costs, and uncertain future deposit flows and market yields. Porter's model suggests that a bank that maximizes expected profits will generally hold a diversified portfolio in an uncertain world.[2] He also demonstrates that if bank profits are a random variable, that is, determined by the joint probability distribution describing deposit flows and asset yields, then profit maximization, "liquidity," and "capital certainty" are insightful constructs for modeling bank behavior.

Because of its inventory-theoretic roots, this approach has been particularly useful in describing bank demand for excess reserves and other liquid assets. Later work by Orr and Mellon [1961], Morrison [1966],

1. An early precedent for applying inventory theory to monetary problems was reported by Baumol [1952]. For influential studies of optimal inventory behavior see Arrow, Harris, and Marschak [1951] and Karlin [1958].

2. A bothersome feature of static profit maximization in the absence of uncertainty is that optimal portfolios contain only the highest yielding asset.

Charnes and Thore [1966], and Poole [1968] clearly suggests the theoretical importance of uncertainty, transactions costs, legal and administrative constraints, alternative rates of return, and attitudes toward borrowing in explaining bank demand for secondary reserves.

The insights into bank behavior provided by these authors serve to pinpoint the deficiencies in the earlier money supply theory.[3] That theory indicated that with fractional reserve requirements the commercial banking system would expand its deposit liabilities by some multiple of an initial increase in the level of reserves. The size of the multiplier was determined by drains into Federal Reserve Banks, as well as by losses into the public's hoard of currency. Drains of reserves into desired excess reserve holdings and additions to reserves through bank borrowing from the Federal Reserve received little attention in the discussion of credit multipliers.

The deficiencies of the earlier approach are well documented.[4] The reserve multiplier is an ex post equilibrium relation, not a behavioral relation. Structure is to be found in the specification of such relations as a bank's demand for excess reserves or demand for discounts from the Federal Reserve. Brunner [1961] has developed a detailed analysis of the supply theory of money based upon an aggregation of such structural relations for individual banks. Direct derivations of money supply functions from aggregative structural models have been provided by de Leeuw [1965]; Goldfeld [1966]; and Modigliani, Rasche, and Cooper [1970].

Another approach to the question of bank portfolio optimization under uncertainty stems directly from Markowitz's [1959] pioneering study of efficient portfolio selection and from Tobin's [1958] paper on liquidity preference. Their portfolio approach assumes that an investor's utility function is quadratic in the rate of return. A portfolio is efficient if it is impossible to increase its expected rate of return without raising its risk (variance). The problem of portfolio selection is one of maximizing expected utility subject to the trade-off between risk and rate of return available from the set of efficient portfolios. This maximization for the "risk averse" investor will usually imply the selection of a diversified portfolio.

These methods have been applied to the problem of determining a bank's optimal portfolio by Pierce [1964 and 1967] and by Kane and Malkiel [1965]. Banks operate in a world in which asset rates of return

3. For an example of this theory, see Chandler [1964, chap. 5].
4. See Tobin [1963] for a general criticism of the approach and Meigs [1962] and Morrison [1966] for explicit criticisms of the lack of behavioral relations in textbook treatments of the problem.

are not known with certainty and in which return-risk characteristics differ among assets. Further, bankers are likely to be risk averse, either because their objective functions are convex in discounted future net income or because influential depositors and regulatory authorities induce them to act as risk averters. The application of the theory of portfolio selection to banking can yield precise statements about asset substitutions that banks will make in response to changes in expected rates of return and/or risk.

The strength of this portfolio balance approach lies in its explicit allowance for risk aversion and in its computability. The approach has important deficiencies as well. The results are sensitive to the specification of the utility function, and stochastic deposit flows cannot be handled as easily as with the inventory approach. Perhaps its greatest deficiency is that investors often do not have the detailed information about individual assets that the theory requires. Further, a bank chooses from a large set of assets with characteristics that cannot be uniquely mapped into the mean-variance rate of return space. The existence of such asset characteristics as loan maturity and borrower guarantees suggests that banks are concerned with many more dimensions of assets than simply the first two moments of the single period distribution of rates of return. Hodgman's [1963] description of the customer relation and Hester's [1962] analysis of the bank loan-offer function stress the complexities of bank asset selection.

The theories of bank behavior that have been discussed so far describe static equilibria; they do not describe the rate at which a bank moves from one position of portfolio equilibrium to another. In recent years several studies have appeared that analyze how a bank adjusts its portfolio through time.

The first such study [Meigs, 1962] argued that the rate at which a bank adjusts free reserves to their desired value is a function of the gap between desired free reserves and their actual value. In this model desired free reserves are determined by market interest rates. A different approach to bank dynamics is provided by Morrison [1966] in his study of bank liquidity preference. Morrison argued that excess reserves and other liquid assets are held as a buffer to avoid asset transactions costs stemming from unforeseen, transitory deposit shocks. A bank's demand for liquid assets is hypothesized to be inversely related to the predictability of its future deposit flows. Morrison also asserted that bank demand for loans and other illiquid assets is related to permanent (expected) deposit levels and is independent of transitory deposit variations. He assumed that a bank forms its expectations concerning permanent deposit values from a sequence of past deposits. This expectational scheme imparts a distributed lag structure to the adjustments of the bank's portfolio in response to an unforeseen, yet permanent, increase in its deposit liabilities. Finally, Charnes and Littlechild [1968] reported an application of chance-constrained programming techniques to banking that seems to yield a similar distributed lag adjustment pattern.

Empirical studies of bank behavior presented by de Leeuw [1965], Goldfeld [1966], Teigen [1964a, 1964b], Hendershott [1968], and de Leeuw and Gramlich [1968] all assumed that banks pursue a policy of trying to close the existing gap between desired and actual stocks of assets at a constant rate. This assumption of a simple stock-adjustment relation is frequently used for reasons of statistical expediency. It is disappointing to observe, however, that large differences in estimated speeds of portfolio adjustment are obtained by these investigators.[5] Studies by Rangarajan and Severn [1965], Bryan [1967], Mundlak [1961], and Zellner [1968] suggest that the simple stock-adjustment model is not appropriate when applied to aggregate data.

None of the studies discussed in this section provides an explicit analysis of the influence of costs of rapid adjustments on optimal rates of portfolio adjustments and/or on the final equilibrium portfolio composition. In making a decision concerning the rate at which its assets change through time, a bank must weigh the income foregone as a result of adjusting slowly against the costs avoided by reducing rates of portfolio adjustments.

Eisner and Strotz [1963], Lucas [1967], Gould [1968], and Tinsley [1971] derive expressions for optimal rates of adjustment of a firm's capital stock in their studies of investment behavior. In their studies the optimal rate of investment is determined by the penalty costs associated with rapid plant expansion as well as by the size of the gap between desired and actual capital. Their approaches are quite similar in spirit to the analysis of dynamic adjustment to be presented in chapters 2 and 3.

2. SUMMARY OF ANALYTICAL RESULTS AND POLICY CONCLUSIONS

A major achievement of this monograph is the demonstration that it is possible and practical to obtain direct estimates of dynamic portfolio adjustments for both commercial and mutual savings banks from cross-section data. The time path of adjustment of an asset in response to a deposit shock differs according to the asset being considered. These estimated response paths in general correspond to a priori expectations.

5. A brief survey of some of these results is provided in chapter 4.

Banks that were particularly profitable during the sample period had asset adjustment paths much more like those predicted by the theoretical model than did other banks.

Additional important results are:

1. Demand deposits of individual commercial banks are very predictable using a simple autoregressive scheme. Commercial bank time and savings deposits and mutual savings bank deposits are also predictable but to a lesser degree.
2. An adaptive-expectations model of bank portfolio selection that utilizes deposit forecasts is not as successful in explaining portfolio selection as is a model that utilizes actual deposit histories.
3. Estimates of asset rates of return and liability costs have been obtained from cross-section data.

Some informative results are obtained by aggregating the cross-section results to construct banking systems. It is not sufficient to know the parameters of the portfolio adjustment model for an individual bank in order to analyze dynamic system effects; it is also necessary to establish the pattern and timing of payment flows among the banks in the system. Results for several alternative systems are obtained, and these suggest that macro-studies have been right for the wrong reasons. The banking system does respond to variations in monetary policy with a long lag. This lag is not so much the consequence of long lags in adjustment for individual banks as it is the consequence of the banking system requiring a long time to establish equilibrium following a shock. The results obtained here do suggest, however, that most macroeconometric studies have tended to overestimate the length of adjustment lags.

Some interesting policy conclusions are suggested by the analysis in this monograph. First, there are relatively long lags in the adjustment of the banking system's portfolio to policy shocks. Second, the lags are not as simple as those frequently presented in the literature. Interpretation of observed changes in the banking system's portfolio can be quite intricate. Results reported in later chapters indicate, for example, that banks place a larger percentage of a deposit inflow in short-term government securities in the short run than they do in the long run. Observed short-term variations in bill holdings may, therefore, provide little information concerning the relative tightness of the banking system's portfolio. Banks may be currently shifting out of bills not because they have experienced an increase in loan demand but simply because they previously received a deposit inflow.

Third, the pattern of payment flows among banks is crucial for understanding the bank aggregation process. In order to predict aggregative behavior, these flows must be reckoned with. The results also indicate that the introduction of financial intermediaries, such as mutual savings banks, need not appreciably lengthen the lags of monetary policy.

3. OUTLINE OF THE MONOGRAPH

Chapters 2 and 3 develop the portfolio selection model to be estimated in later chapters. Chapter 2 presents the assumptions that underlie the model. A bank's objective function, its activities, the legal and technical constraints under which it operates, the type of risk and uncertainty it faces, and its costs of portfolio adjustment are discussed in detail.

Chapter 3 contains a number of theoretical models of bank portfolio behavior that differ in underlying institutional assumptions. These models suggest that a very strong case exists for expecting lagged portfolio adjustments by banks to deposit inflows. In subsequent chapters this hypothesis is tested by studying two distinct empirical formulations. The first, the "input-output" model, assumes that banks do not forecast future deposit flows. In this model, costs of portfolio adjustment lead to a relation between the history of a bank's deposit flows and the current composition of its portfolio. The second version is an "adaptive-expectations" model which assumes that banks use their previous deposit histories to forecast future deposit flows. In this model, costs of portfolio adjustment lead to a relation between current portfolio composition and a history of *forecasts* of the current value of deposits.

Chapter 4 discusses problems and techniques of estimating the structures of the two portfolio adjustment models as well as a model for deposit forecasting. The chapter also contains a description of a method for estimating interest rates and costs experienced by banks. Chapter 5 provides a detailed discussion of the data used in the estimation of the several models.

Chapters 6 through 9 report the estimated structures of the models for commercial and mutual savings banks. An empirical analysis of bank interest rates and costs is provided in chapter 10. Chapter 11 reports a normative analysis that relates bank profitability to portfolio adjustments.

Chapter 12 describes a series of macro-simulation experiments designed to measure the impact of monetary policy on bank portfolio choices. Several different aggregation assumptions are used to obtain portfolio adjustments for the banking system from the micro-results. Aggregate systems containing both commercial and mutual savings banks are considered.

CHAPTER 2

Underpinnings for a Theory of Bank Behavior

The principal determinants of behavior by an economic agent in classical economic theory are (1) his objective function, (2) his set of available actions (activities), and (3) restrictions imposed on his activities by technology, market prices, and laws and/or regulations. In the observable economy (4) uncertainty, man-made or natural, and (5) time-consuming institutional frictions also importantly influence firm behavior. The first five sections of this chapter interpret each of these factors for the cases of a commercial bank and a mutual savings bank. The sixth summarizes a set of assumptions that will form the basis for a theory of portfolio behavior. In chapter 3 models are developed, and their properties are exhibited with simulation studies.

1. A BANK'S OBJECTIVE FUNCTION

In this section it is especially important to consider commercial and mutual savings banks separately. After a heuristic survey of firm decision structures, this dichotomy will be strictly observed.

a. Firm decision structures

An individual is in *control* of an organization or a decision process if he is free to make decisions that maximize his objective function. An *organization* consists of a set of decision-making individuals joined by some legal instrument. The "tightness" of a decision maker's control varies widely within an organization. Thus, a person who approves or rejects loan applications is in control if he maximizes his function when deciding upon loans, but he does not necessarily determine policies for the bank at large. The chairman of a bank's board of directors, on the other hand, generally cannot take time to evaluate individual loan applications, but he and his board do establish policy guidelines.

An individual's *power* within an organization is indicated by his ability to make it behave in harmony with his preferences or objective function. If all individuals in an organization have identical goals, then it is a team;

11

in such circumstances the measurement of power within an organization is not interesting. Very small financial institutions (surely all one-man organizations) may behave as teams, but larger institutions such as the banks studied in this monograph are likely to exhibit pronounced non-team behavior.

All large firms have elements of nonteam behavior, which are evidenced in the managerial scramble for promotion. Also, Berle and Means [1933] and Baumol [1967] have convincingly argued that firm behavior is more likely to respond to managerial rather than to ownership interests and that these two groups have different goals. Most previous studies have viewed a banking organization as a team that serves ownership interests.

Few financial organizations are tightly controlled because decision makers face quite heterogeneous problems. A controlling element cannot afford the enormous sums necessary to enumerate exhaustive rules for its agents. Typically a controlling element itself cannot efficiently make the large number of decisions that must be made.[1]

These remarks suggest that the objective function of a bank is likely to have other arguments than just the discounted stream of expected future net income. Indeed, it is possible that the objective function may vary considerably from bank to bank depending upon the strength of different competing factions within the organization. However, in the absence of any compelling evidence to the contrary, this study will assume that the objective function is the same for each commercial bank in the study. Similarly, each mutual savings bank is assumed to have a common objective function, which may differ from that of commercial banks. These assumptions are introduced to limit the scope of the present investigation; they deserve further study.

It remains to suggest what arguments are likely to appear in a typical commercial bank's and a typical mutual savings bank's objective function. The magnitudes of weights on different arguments in the functions are not known a priori, and little evidence is available to suggest them.

b. Commercial banks

Stockholders of commercial banks are likely to be concerned principally with earning a high rate of return on their shares. This return may be accepted in the form of either dividends or stock-price appreciation. The determinants of the choice between paying dividends and retaining earnings in order to increase stock prices are not easily identified with

---

1. This point appears to be supported by at least one study of relatively centralized banking; see Hester [1964].

observable operating characteristics of banks. In general, growing net income and assets are commonly believed to be positively related to rates of return on stock, however realized.[2] To the extent that technology is embodied, growing firms will tend to have more efficient facilities and, ceteris paribus, higher profits. Therefore, rapid bank growth and high and rising net income are important to ownership interests.

Bank management, qua management, is likely to be concerned principally with its remuneration and the prestige and social status that attach to its positions. Top corporate executive salaries have been found to be closely correlated with firm sales [McGuire, Chiu, and Elbing, 1962]. Baumol [1967, p. 47] also observes that certain honorific executive associations place considerable weight on corporate sales when selecting members. Therefore, it appears that management as such will strive for high and rising firm sales (or assets, in the case of banks).

Personal income tax schedules tend to distort the form in which executives receive compensation. Stock options and other similar plans that utilize the capital-gains loophole are likely to reduce conflicts of interest between management and stockholders. Tax laws also induce management and directors to obtain compensation in totally or partially tax-exempt forms, such as by locating offices in elaborate, expensive buildings.

Management is also concerned with job stability; mobility tends to be limited for managers. This immobility reflects the fact that their salaries would tend to exceed their marginal productivity for some years if they were transferred to a new position. Job stability can be insured by avoiding failures that are conspicuous to stockholders and the investing public. Thus maintaining market shares, avoiding widely publicized losses, and smoothing out year-to-year fluctuations in net income are very important objectives of management.

Some other individuals, perhaps large stockholders or members of the bank's board of directors, have an interest in directing bank services to their other business holdings at less than market prices. Thus, loans carrying less than "prime" interest rates, small compensating balances, high fees for services rendered, and so on should be observed when such interests are strong. This behavior does not lead to obvious conclusions about the appearance of a bank's portfolio, although it is likely that bank profits will suffer if such interests are strong.[3]

2. See, for example, Baumol [1967], Modigliani and Miller [1958], and Nerlove [1968].

3. Recent extensive conversions of bank charters to the one-bank holding company form are likely to alter extensively the objective function for banks. At the time of this writing the effects of these changes are not foreseeable.

c. Mutual savings banks

Mutual savings banks are directed by a different set of controlling interests, in part because owner-stockholders do not exist. A remarkable feature of mutual institutions is that while they are formed by having the public subscribe *savings deposits*, which are temporarily nonwithdrawable, they generate an autonomous undistributed *surplus* (net worth) which is controlled de facto by management and by directors who are not necessarily depositors. This surplus was earned by investing depositor funds prudently and profitably; when depositor funds are withdrawn, the surplus reverts to the bank in a manner that is best viewed as legalized expropriation of savings.

The purpose of this subsection, however, is not to question the fairness of or the justification for existing mutual institutions, but rather to suggest what objectives these institutions may have.[4] De facto control of surplus (net worth) by management and/or the board of directors does not suggest that banks will wish to maximize the rate of return from these funds. Unlike stockholders in commercial banks, these groups cannot directly appropriate return for their own use through payment of dividends or realization of capital gains. Therefore, an important inducement for seeking high and rising net income and deposit growth is not present in mutual savings banks.

Management in mutual banks is likely to seek high remuneration and therefore will desire large and growing firm size. Managers also will be fearful of job market imperfections and will attempt to avoid conspicuous losses or failures. As in the case of stockholder-owned enterprises, managers of mutual organizations will attempt to obtain tax-exempt remuneration, perhaps through the use of elaborate office facilities. Similarly, nonmanagement directors will attempt to exact interest rate and/or other concessions for their own business interests.

In conclusion, differences in the objective functions of the two types of banks are expected to be observed because of legal differences in the bargaining power of potential controlling groups. Mutual organizations should be less interested in high and rising net income and somewhat less interested in sales growth than should stock-chartered organizations. Mutuals should be relatively more concerned with maintaining stability and in supporting activities that lend prestige to management. Given these

4. Such questions have been raised, at least implicitly, by previous studies of the savings and loan industry. See Shaw [1962], Jolivet [1966], Nicols [1967], Scott and Hester [1967], and Hester [1967].

differences, if the two types of organizations should coexist in a single market with identical legal restrictions, their behavior should differ.[5]

2. THE SET OF BANK ACTIVITIES (VARIABLES)

Banks, like most commercial enterprises, make many decisions every day. The decisions involve personnel, salaries, lending terms, asset diversification, public relations, trust department policy, underwriting, and so on. Of these decisions, few are well documented or observable by outside investigators; published summary data about bank behavior reflect a large number of individual decisions. Theories of a bank's behavior that are to be subjected to empirical verification must imply the existence of relations among reported variables. The scope of the theory in this monograph will arbitrarily be limited to a specification that yields hypotheses about variables recorded by certain bank regulatory agencies or trade associations and available for use by the present investigators. These variables are listed in chapter 5.

It is convenient to view all bank variables as flows. Banks are principally engaged in providing the service of intermediation by directing flows of funds from lenders to borrowers. Therefore, in this monograph the stock of an *asset* will be assumed to be uniquely associated with a flow of services that the bank controls through lending and investing decisions. A *deposit liability* is associated with a flow of services, and it is basically controlled by depositors. The control by banks and depositors is not tight; for example, banks occasionally experience losses through defaults and frauds, loans are sometimes unexpectedly renewed, and depositors sometimes temporarily relinquish control of their deposits when they commit their funds to a bank for a fixed period. Nevertheless, as a first approximation, it seems useful to view banks as attempting to select assets in order to maximize their objective function subject to externally determined deposits.

This formulation is highly simplified and misses many important aspects of bank behavior. Thus, compensating balances, negotiable certificates of deposit, long-maturity term loans, lines of credit, and revolving credit arrangements do not naturally fit into this formulation. Similarly, the very appealing notion of a long-term customer relationship [Hodgman, 1963] and the intricate bilateral determination of lending terms [Hester, 1962] are not readily incorporated in this framework. The omissions are necessary if the analysis is to be tractable. An effort is made

---

5. This appears to be the case in the savings and loan industry [Hester, 1967].

in this and the next chapter to suggest how such omissions are likely to affect relationships in the model.

While flow variables may be measured continuously or discretely, in practice all financial flows are recorded over discrete time intervals. Often flows are not measured directly; their magnitudes must be inferred from net changes in stock variables between two dates. Such measurements are appropriate only if a theory suggests that inflows and outflows have symmetric effects on and/or are symmetrically affected by other variables in the system. An important assumption in the present monograph is that no loss of information is experienced by studying net inflows.

Individual assets or liabilities are distinguished in theory because they have differing characteristics that make them imperfect substitutes.[6] The major characteristics of interest to banks and to most other investors are an asset's (1) liquidity, (2) reversibility, (3) predictability of rate of return, and (4) divisibility.[7] These characteristics in turn can be mapped into observable asset characteristics such as maturity, coupon, yield, taxability, collateral, credit rating of issuer, convertibility, subordination, call privileges, face amount, and associated brokerage fees.

Table 5-1 in chapter 5 indicates that commercial bank asset data available for this study are classified primarily according to (*a*) maturity, (*b*) insured or federally guaranteed status, (*c*) the existence of secondary markets, and (*d*) collateral. This breakdown of bank assets will prove very convenient for testing a number of important hypotheses. Commercial bank deposit data are classified both by ownership (public, private, or foreign), and by what reserve requirement applies. As is evident in table 5-3, mutual savings bank data are available in less detail than commercial bank data but available data do permit tests of a number of hypotheses.

In addition to assets and liabilities, other variables and functionals appearing in the subsequent theory are (1) interest rates, (2) cost schedules for acquiring and disposing of assets, (3) advertising and promotional rates, and (4) other schedules of costs and revenues that are incurred while servicing portfolios. They are assumed not to be affected by a bank's

6. Almost all individual financial instruments are unique in some respect. It is unrewarding to study assets at a level of disaggregation which requires that within each category only homogeneous elements are present.

7. This list of asset characteristics was originally suggested by James Tobin in the second chapter of his unpublished manuscript about monetary theory. The measurement of liquidity was subsequently reinterpreted by Pierce [1966] to apply specifically to the case of a commercial bank. Briefly, a perfectly liquid asset is an asset that can be sold at its full realizable value the moment a decision is made to dispose of it. A perfectly reversible asset can simultaneously be purchased and sold without cost to the transactor. An asset with a perfectly predictable rate of return has a sure rate of return. A perfectly divisible asset is one that can be purchased or sold in arbitrarily small amounts.

behavior. The cost schedules for acquiring or disposing of assets are assumed to be decreasing functions of the length of time between the date a decision is taken to acquire (or dispose of) an asset and the actual acquisition (or disposal) date; they are discussed extensively below. For simplicity, banks are assumed to believe that the set of interest rates and functionals will remain stationary at their observed levels.

3. CONSTRAINTS: LEGAL AND TECHNICAL

a. Legal and supervisory

Since the Depression banks in the United States have been tightly regulated and examined by one or more supervisory agency. These include the Board of Governors of the Federal Reserve System, the Office of the Comptroller of the Currency, the Federal Deposit Insurance Corporation, the Anti-Trust Division of the Department of Justice, and state banking commissioners.

Regulatory standards vary considerably among these agencies and across different groups of banks under a given supervisory authority. For example, branch banking is typically allowed on the East and West coasts, but not in the Midwest. Multibank holding companies are legal in some states, but not in others. States like California permit statewide branch systems, whereas New York discourages money market banks from moving upstate. Merger criteria appear to vary among federal supervisory agencies [Hall and Phillips, 1964].

Similarly, reserve requirements on deposits differ between classes of Federal Reserve System member banks. State banking commissioners impose different effective reserve requirements on nonmember banks than are established by the Federal Reserve. Commercial banks, mutual savings banks, and savings and loan associations have quite different implicit and/ or explicit reserve requirements on substantially identical liabilities.[8]

Also lending (discount window) practices of individual Federal Reserve Banks are likely to vary considerably among districts. Mutual savings banks chartered in different states have quite different lending and investing powers. From these observations it is clear that empirical verification

8. A number of volumes prepared for the Commission on Money and Credit report facts about variations in regulatory standards across intermediaries. See in particular the monographs prepared by the American Bankers Association [1962], the National Association of Mutual Savings Banks [1962], and Leon T. Kendall for the United States Savings and Loan League [1962]. See also the *Report of the Committee on Financial Institutions to the President* [United States Government, 1963] and the *Report of the President's Commission on Financial Structure and Regulation* [United States Government, 1971].

of a theory of portfolio behavior should be performed using a sample of relatively homogeneous banks regulated by a single set of supervisory agencies.

The prime institutional restriction on bank portfolio behavior is that a bank be prepared to honor requests by demand depositors for currency or check withdrawals up to the amount of their balance without notice. In practice, banks attempt (but do not promise) to meet such demands from their regular savings account depositors as well. These institutional features together with information about the distribution of deposit shocks and the costs of disposing of assets are hypothesized in this monograph to be important determinants of both the equilibrium portfolio mix and the rate of adjustment to this mix.

Reserve requirements administered by the Federal Reserve System are another important institutional restriction. They limit the percentage of bank assets that may be held in noncash form and, correspondingly, restrict bank net income. They are related to the restriction in the previous paragraph, since they diminish the maximum percentage of noncash assets that must be liquidated for each dollar withdrawn. Increases in reserve requirements cause banks to hold higher percentages of their assets in the form of cash; the effect of these increases on the distribution of funds among noncash assets is a matter of controversy.[9]

Legal restrictions apply to a large number of other aspects of bank portfolio behavior. For example, commercial banks are not allowed by law to (1) invest in common stock of nonbank enterprises, (2) lend more than 10 percent of their own capital account to any single borrower, (3) pay interest directly on demand balances, (4) lend more than trivial amounts to their own officers, (5) underwrite corporate debt or equity instruments, (6) charge interest rates higher than legally established usury ceilings, and (7) open or close branch offices without prior agency approval. The United States Treasury requires that all deposits of funds in tax and loan accounts be secured by approved liabilities of the government or its agencies. These regulations effectively prohibit a number of otherwise attractive portfolios and therefore tend to impede banks from maximizing their objective function. They also serve to limit the power of those individuals who control banks and specifically to ban some forms of managerial remuneration. On balance, regulations probably lower bank profits, strengthen the hand of ownership interests relative to management, and force banks to have portfolios that lessen the probability of bank failure.

---

9. See Aschheim [1959] and the subsequent extended controversy appearing in the *Economic Journal*. See also Brainard and Tobin [1963].

Frequent bank examinations by supervisory agencies also greatly affect bank behavior. A bank examiner may criticize banks for realized losses, unsound lending practices, inadequate capitalization, ineffective internal controls, excessive loan specialization, poor or incomplete records on outstanding loans, and other shortcomings. The possibility of unannounced examinations forces bankers to keep considerable documentation about their portfolio and creditors continuously on file. While detailed documentation (data processing and information retrieval) is common in financial institutions, examinations doubtlessly increase data processing burdens in banks. Therefore, bank examinations will cause an increase in costs for banks, a reduced frequency of bank irregularities and failures, and a smoothing out of fluctuations in loans and other assets requiring extensive data collection and analysis.

b. Technological and accounting

Technological constraints are analogous to those encountered in the theory of the production function. With a given set of inputs, such as labor, building, computer time, and telephoning, it is assumed that a set of maximal obtainable outputs exists for the firm. By identifying output with intermediation services, these constraints serve to introduce the notion of capacity restrictions on the rate at which banks can transmit deposit inflows into illiquid, risky credit outflows.

Accounting constraints refer to identities such as the conditions that the sum of a bank's assets must equal the sum of its liabilities and net worth or that a bank's receipts must equal the sum of its expenses and net income. These identities will be explicitly imposed in this monograph.

4. RISK AND UNCERTAINTY

It is correct but nonilluminating to observe simply that bank performance is sensitive to the values of a number of important random variables. It is important to analyze carefully the nature of risk and uncertainty in banking. In this section assumptions about the underlying stochastic processes for bank deposits, repayment flows, capital structure, and rates of return are stated and interpreted. Finally, a brief discussion of bank uncertainty about national economic events and central bank policies is presented.

a. Deposits

Data about the stock of a commercial bank's demand deposits are available in a disaggregated form according to whether the deposits are controlled by the United States government, banks, or other individuals, partnerships, and corporations. In subsequent chapters, which analyze bank portfolio behavior, it is assumed for simplicity that these three types of deposits can be aggregated for an individual bank without loss of information.

A second assumption concerns the relationship between demand and time deposit inflows to a commercial bank. In order to avoid an extremely ill-structured estimation problem in later chapters, it is necessary to assume that time sequences of demand and time deposits for a commercial bank are independent. Some indirect evidence supporting this assumption is reported in chapter 8.

Intertemporal fluctuations in the level of demand deposits at individual commercial banks have been studied by a number of investigators.[10] The following results have been reported: The magnitude of deposit changes in some time interval is related to size of bank; small banks by law have maximum loan limits and by location and specialization are likely to appeal to individuals making relatively small transactions. The number of deposit transactions per period is an increasing function of bank size. The combined effect of these two factors is that the coefficient of variation of the level of demand deposits or the maximum monthly percentage deposit loss declines as bank size increases. The elasticity of the coefficient of variation with respect to bank size is on the order of 0.25. These conclusions have been obtained from studying banks in very different banking markets and concern short-term fluctuations in a bank's demand deposits.

A bank's short-term deposit level variability and its deposit level unpredictability are likely to differ because changes in its deposit level in successive periods are likely to be related. For example, suppose a deposit increase in a bank can be traced to expenditures from some new project, like the construction of a new factory. Expenditures on the project will continue for many weeks; positive net deposit inflows from it should be recorded by the bank during these weeks.

As a second example, theories of the demand for cash suggest that individuals or business establishments receiving deposit increments are not likely to hold such balances idle. A bank should expect to see part or all of the increments withdrawn in succeeding weeks. The withdrawn funds will tend to be redeposited in the same or other banks.

These two characterizations imply different specifications of the stochastic process describing the level of a bank's demand deposits. The

10. See, for example, Federal Reserve Bank of Kansas City [1957], Hester [1962], Gramley [1962], Hester [1964], Morrison and Selden [1965], Rangarajan [1966], and Struble and Wilkerson [1967].

first characterization is described by expression (2.4.1) and the second by (2.4.2).

$$(2.4.1) \qquad d_t = \max \begin{cases} d_{t-1} + v_t \\ 0 \end{cases}$$

$$v_t = \alpha p_t + \varepsilon_t, \qquad \infty > \alpha > 0$$

where

d_t is the level of a bank's demand deposits at the end of period t,

p_t is the flow of expenditures from a project during period t, and

ε_t is a serially independent random variable with finite variance and expected value of zero.

$$(2.4.2) \qquad d_t = \max \begin{cases} d_{t-1} + w_t \\ 0 \end{cases}$$

$$w_t = \beta w_{t-1} + \varepsilon_t, \qquad 0 > \beta > -1.$$

In what follows, it is assumed that the nonnegativity constraint is never effective.

Neither alternative can be excluded a priori, but only the latter can be studied with available data resources. Moreover, the first model is seriously incomplete because additional information is required to identify which projects and what associated values of α are to be employed in different situations. Therefore, apart from arguments at the end of this section, it will be assumed that deposit levels are described by an auto-regressive process similar to (2.4.2) with an order that will be determined experimentally. This process is assumed to be stationary and stable and to vary among banks. The processes to be examined empirically for each bank studied are given by (2.4.3).

$$(2.4.3) \qquad \bar{d}_t = \sum_{i=1}^{n} \beta_i \bar{d}_{t-i} + \varepsilon_t$$

where

$$\bar{d}_t = d_t - d_{t-1}.$$

Stability implies that the modulus of the largest root of the polynomial (2.4.4) is strictly less than unity.

$$(2.4.4) \qquad y^n - \beta_1 y^{n-1} - \cdots - \beta_{n-1} y - \beta_n = 0.$$

An additional assumption made about this process, which is intuitively appealing, is that a bank receiving a deposit inflow should eventually have its own deposits permanently increased. This assumption and the stability assumption will be satisfied if the following condition holds:

$$(2.4.5) \qquad\qquad -\infty < \sum_{i=1}^{n} \beta_i < 1.$$

The autoregressive process is likely to vary among banks and depends upon the percentage of a community's financial transactions which a bank participates in. Thus, a monopoly bank might expect to retain 100 percent or more of a stochastic deposit inflow. A bank in a highly competitive market is likely to retain a very small percentage of a deposit inflow. A bank's *retention ratio* is defined as

$$(2.4.6) \qquad\qquad rp = \frac{1}{1 - \sum_{i=1}^{n} \beta_i}.$$

The process is also likely to vary considerably among different types of deposits. Demand deposit shocks are likely to be withdrawn rapidly because, as suggested above, firms and individuals do not want to hold excess idle balances. Therefore, coefficients on recent lagged changes in demand deposits in expression (2.4.3) are likely to be negative and large absolutely; they should decline in absolute value as the subscript increases. A corresponding process for time and savings deposits or for mutual savings bank deposits is not expected to exhibit this pattern; owners of these deposits view them as medium-term investments and do not plan to withdraw them immediately. In the case of many time deposit accounts, they cannot withdraw them until a specified time interval has elapsed.

The recent emergence of negotiable certificates of deposit (CDs) increased the likelihood that no very stable relationship between present and past changes in commercial bank time deposits exists. More important for the present study, emergence of this instrument strongly suggests that banks may have varied interest rates offered on CDs in order to obtain funds for desired short-term portfolio objectives. This in turn suggests that previous assumptions about the independence of a bank's time and demand deposit sequences and the exogeneity of interest rates may be incorrect for banks issuing CDs. During part of the period studied in subsequent empirical chapters, a small number of large banks were issuing CDs. Large banks will be studied separately in chapter 8. As stated above, it is not possible to incorporate the emergence of CDs formally in the models of this monograph.

The process might also be sensitive to a bank's portfolio composition. Introductory economic textbooks state that the banking system "creates money." A dollar injection of "high powered" money produces additional dollars of deposits. Because the system consists of individual banks, it is not unreasonable to suggest that, as time passes, a bank will share in the deposits that it creates. In particular, a bank that lends locally is more likely to benefit from deposits it creates than one that buys bills in the national money market. An assumption of the present study is that a bank's portfolio behavior is not a significant determinant of its deposit fluctuations.

b. Interest and amortization

In addition to deposits, banks receive a large flow of allocable funds from interest and amortization payments on outstanding loans and investments. During most years these flows considerably exceed net deposit inflows for both commercial and mutual savings banks.[11] Loan repayments typically are specified in advance by agreements; these flows and loan renewal requests tend to be highly predictable.[12] Flows from interest and amortization of government securities are also extremely predictable. For the most part, therefore, banks can plan their future portfolios with accurate estimates of repayment flows. It follows that banks can reinvest these funds cheaply by making commitments far in advance of actual repayments. In the next chapter it will be argued that foreseeable fluctuations in repayment flows are not likely to determine bank portfolio composition importantly.

To be sure, some randomness occurs in the time sequence of repayment flows. Borrowers may prepay or they may fail to meet scheduled payments. In principle, such shocks should be studied separately. Because they are not observable in available data files, it is necessary to ignore this random determinant of portfolio composition. From interviews it appears that it is not of great importance.

c. Capital and other minor liabilities

The remaining nonasset balance sheet items are quite heterogeneous for both commercial and mutual savings banks. The largest items are

11. For evidence supporting this assertion for mutual savings banks, see the *National Fact Book* of the National Association of Mutual Savings Banks [1965, p. 23]. Corroborating information about commercial bank flows is less accessible. However, given the fact that commercial bank loans and investments are of shorter maturity than those of mutual savings banks, there can be little quarrel with the assertion in the text.

12. A small number of bankers who were interviewed confirmed that these flows are in fact very predictable.

capital accounts for commercial banks and general reserve accounts for mutual savings banks; they represent net worth. Changes in capital accounts reflect new issues of equities or subordinated debt, net losses and charge-offs, and flows of undistributed net income; the last two items alone determine changes in savings bank general reserves. Because bank income is relatively stable from year to year and loss rates are low, banks can be assumed to forecast these flows with considerable accuracy.

Nondeposit commercial bank liabilities include certified and officers' checks, mortgages and other liens on bank property, rediscounts, acceptances, and other liabilities. These items individually tend to be small. Some clearly are at least partly consciously determined by bank portfolio policies. A simplifying assumption of this monograph is that they can be perfectly foreseen. A similar assumption is made for remaining mutual savings bank liabilities, which include Christmas club, industrial, school savings, and other miscellaneous deposits and other liabilities.

d. Rates of return

Many theories of portfolio choice are based upon uncertainty about rates of return. Contributions by Tobin [1958], Markowitz [1959], and Samuelson [1967] suggest that this uncertainty is an important factor explaining portfolio diversification. The model of the present monograph neither requires nor precludes uncertainty about rates of return as an explanation for bank portfolio diversification. Therefore, this topic will be discussed in some brevity.

A number of considerations led to a deemphasis of rate-of-return uncertainty as a central element of the model. First, interest rates on assets available to banks are very highly correlated. If a bank's objective function is quadratic in rate of return and rates of return are perfectly correlated, usually no unique optimum portfolio exists. In figure 2-1 any point in the interior of the opportunity locus AA' is obtainable from a number of different combinations of assets A, A', and A''.

Second, since assets have many characteristics, it seems artificial and unnecessary to restrict thinking simply to one, the rate of return. Hester [1962] argued that lending interest rates are jointly endogenous with a number of other lending terms in an individual financial transaction. If carried to an extreme, this view suggests that no relationship should be expected between market interest rates and portfolios unless other asset characteristics are held constant.

Third, the distribution of future changes in rates of return for banks and other investors has not been very successfully analyzed. The extensive

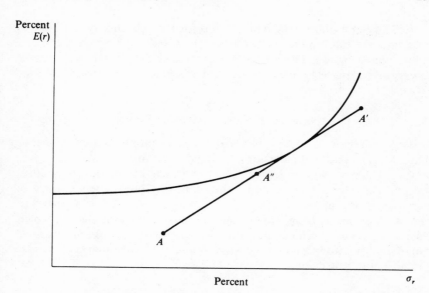

FIGURE 2-1. INVESTOR PORTFOLIO EQUILIBRIUM WHEN ASSET RATES OF RETURN ARE
PERFECTLY CORRELATED

recent literature on the structure of interest rates suggests that a number of quite different theories are consistent with available evidence.[13] These theories tend to be incomplete in that they exclude determinants of the supplies of new debt instruments. They also seem to have quite different implications about how future rates of return should be forecasted.

Fourth, market interest rates, which are available for empirical analysis, are gross rates of return. The relevant rates of return for describing bank portfolio behavior are net of costs of acquiring and servicing assets. It is shown in chapter 10 that assets with relatively high gross returns need not have high net rates of return.

Rather than build on this foundation, an extremely simple stochastic process is assumed to describe bankers' interest rate expectations. Specifically, bankers are assumed to have unitary elasticities of expectations of interest rates for each asset and liability considered.

It is true that significant variations in deposit interest rates and factor costs exist among financial institutions.[14] This variability will require that estimation procedures in subsequent chapters be modified to allow for

13. Cf. Meiselman [1962], Malkiel [1966], and Telser [1967].
14. Cf. *Time Deposits in New England* [Federal Reserve Bank of Boston, 1963] and Hester [1967].

individual bank differences. The reasons for the existence of these interbank interest rate differentials are not clear and are beyond the scope
of the present study. The crucial assumption is that banks are not free
to vary either interest rates or factor-cost schedules in response to deposit
shocks.

e. National economic events and policy

Bank behavior is likely to have other substantial random elements.
Thus, local or national recessions, national economic policy, riots, arson,
wars, balance-of-payments problems, and spurts of inflation may affect
various behavioral relationships studied below quite independently of
variables mentioned in this section. An individual banker is assumed to
view such events as being independent of his own deposit and net worth
fluctuations. Perhaps most important for this study, a banker is assumed
not to modify his deposit forecasts in response to an open-market purchase
or a discount rate change.

5. Institutional Factors and Costs of Adjustment

If economic agents were able to adjust their activities to new conditions
instantaneously and without cost, then forecasting, planning, and dynamic
microeconomic theory would be pointless. Bankers cannot do so for two
reasons. First, it is prohibitively costly for a banker to inform himself about
all conditions in his economic environment. Second, even if all conditions
could be known, banks will experience considerable costs when rapidly
changing their loan portfolios.

To gain insight into dynamic bank behavior, this section attempts to
identify and quantify (very approximately) a bank's important frictional
costs. It assumes that a bank has current information about its creditors,
debtors, and legal environment. The amount of accumulated information,
which clearly differs among banks, depends upon the skill of the bank's
staff, the accessibility of information about its clients, the cohesiveness
and homogeneity of its clients, and the rate of growth of its assets.

a. Information about loan applicants and its assimilation

The evaluation of bank lending opportunities will now be considered
in some detail and interpreted in terms of the costs of making overall
portfolio adjustments. Suppose a commercial bank desires to place
$100,000 in commercial loans. For simplicity, assume that the bank's sole

objective is to maximize its discounted stream of expected future net income and that market loan interest rates exceed rates of return available from securities and other portfolio assets. The bank recognizes that loans have default risks and that these risks can be reduced by extensive and costly reviews of potential borrowers' financial statements, integrity, previous repayment histories, and so on. It also recognizes that different firms have different expected future rates of sales growth and that a relationship with a growing firm is likely to yield the bank future profits both from loans and compensating deposit balances. No doubt, it also recognizes that bargaining strengths of different potential borrowers vary and that bank profits can be augmented by discriminating among potential borrowers. Firms in need of funds can be induced to provide the bank with confidential information about themselves and, rather importantly, about other business firms with which they trade. A lending transaction between the bank and a client is a subtle multidimensional negotiating situation that requires cautious appraisal by skilled personnel.

The bank typically has a number of potential borrowers who are willing to take out loans at, say, the prime interest rate; it must choose carefully among them. If it had foreknowledge of the availability of the $100,000, it would have had an opportunity to study its loan applications and could place its funds efficiently and promptly. If, however, the bank is suddenly and unexpectedly presented with an opportunity to place this money, it might lend it quickly with only a superficial review of potential borrowers. Such behavior would tend to increase the probability of a loan default and/or result in the bank's failure to exploit its opportunity fully.[15] Alternatively, it could delay making a loan until it had exhaustively reviewed all potential applicants; high loan interest rate income would have been foregone and high investigatory costs would have been incurred. Instead, the bank is likely to place unexpectedly received funds in loans only after a lag, which is determined by the structure of interest rates and the length of time and expense necessary for bargaining, reviewing, and formally processing loan requests.

If very substantial amounts of funds (relative to a bank's total assets) are to be placed, this time interval is likely to be quite long. Banks have a

15. The reader may object by saying that any banker worth his salt would have a set of potential borrowers who had already been extensively screened. However, this objection is not easily maintained, for any single borrower is not likely to be able to wait for occasional random loans from a bank. He must have a steady sure source of finance. Consequently, this "unsatisfied fringe" of qualified borrowers is likely to be changing quite frequently. A bank must constantly review these new firms in order to be assured of their soundness. It would have to do this even though, as assumed in the text, it did not expect to be able to lend to them. Maintaining a small excess supply of potential borrowers could be quite expensive!

fixed trained staff of lending officers, and their capacity for reviewing proposals will temporarily be exceeded by large injections of funds. This is particularly true if a bank's objective function is of a form that commends diversification in the loan portfolio. Similarly, if very substantial positive shocks in potential loan funds occur, a bank may wish to advertise that it is willing to expand its loan portfolio. New borrowing prospects may require further time to react efficiently to the advertised availability of funds. Capacity considerations aside, the length of time between receiving funds and lending may be quite long if an advertising campaign is undertaken. These arguments suggest the hypothesis that the observed lag in adjustment is likely to be an increasing function of both the size and the variability of the flow of loanable funds. This hypothesis is tested in chapter 6.

A lagged response to negative changes in loanable funds is also likely for reasons that previously have been suggested by Hodgman [1963]. While banks receive a large continuing predictable flow of loan amortizations, they cannot instantaneously withdraw these funds from their loan portfolio. Good customers of the bank, with their substantial balances, will be offended and possibly seriously hurt if their loan renewal requests are not met. These customers typically have outstanding commitments for purchases of equipment or inventories for which bank financing may be essential. Also, marginal customers of the bank may not be capable of instantaneously liquidating bank credit; inducing borrower bankruptcies does not improve the image of the bank. The lags in response to unexpected positive and negative shocks to loanable funds may differ. However, in subsequent empirical research, it is necessary to assume that these two lags are of similar length. Some evidence in support of this assumption is reported in chapter 6.

b. Digression on searching a random sequence of loan requests

Another characterization of lags in bank lending in response to unexpected fund flows is suggested in this digression.[16] It requires few institutional assumptions, but implies a dynamic bank behavioral pattern similar to that just described. As in the previous subsection, a commercial bank is assumed to maximize the discounted stream of its future net income.

16. A characterization along these lines was informally suggested to us by G. H. Orcutt when a preliminary paper underlying this monograph was presented at a seminar at the University of Wisconsin in November 1966. We are grateful to him for this suggestion, but he is not liable for the development in the text.

Loan requests are assumed to be governed by a stationary stochastic process in which lending opportunities appear at regular intervals but have randomly distributed associated rates of return. A bank is assumed to know the moments of this distribution and to have an external rate of return that it can realize with probability one from some nonloan asset in its portfolio, say, Treasury bills. The bank then establishes a confidential internal threshold interest rate such that all loan requests at or above this threshold rate are automatically accepted. All others are rejected. It is assumed that no investigatory or other costs are associated with reviewing or making loans and that no customer relationships exist. The threshold level will be a function of the bank's external rate of return, the frequency of loan applications, the distribution of loan rates of return, and the existing flows of funds available for lending. The threshold interest rate will always exceed the external rate of return because the bank can always hold bills in lieu of lending. Because the distribution of interest rates is stationary, it is possible to determine the expected time interval between the date when funds become available and the date on which they are lent. Ceteris paribus, this interval will be an increasing function of the external rate, the dispersion of the distribution of loan interest rates, and the frequency of loan applications; it will be a decreasing function of the flows of loanable funds.

This characterization is a convenient expository vehicle, but it is only a caricature. In particular, a bank following this decision program would soon find itself with a portfolio of unsound loans. However, when integrated with the previous version, this characterization helps to provide the foundation for what follows. It is analyzed in more detail in chapter 3.

c. Costs of adjustment for other bank assets

Commercial loans represent a relatively small, albeit important, component of bank portfolios. In table 5-5 it can be seen that the New England commercial banks studied in this monograph had approximately 16 percent of their assets in cash, balances with other banks, and cash items; 24 percent in United States government securities; 16 percent in consumer loans; 15 percent in commercial and industrial loans; 14 percent in real estate (mortgage) loans; 7 percent in state and local securities; and the rest in miscellaneous minor assets. Furthermore, mutual savings banks hold the bulk of their assets in mortgage loans. To describe dynamic bank portfolio responses to unexpected fund flows, it is necessary to describe adjustment costs for each of these other assets briefly.

i. Cash: Apart from required reserves, cash assets can be acquired and released with little cost to a bank.[17] Minor transaction costs are imposed by armored car service firms when currency and negotiable claims are transferred. Some bank officer time is expended in reviewing and executing federal funds transactions. Similarly, officers must review decisions involving a bank's balances kept at correspondent banks. These balances reward correspondents for services rendered and facilitate clearing of checks; they are more valuable to correspondents if they remain idle. A more substantial transaction cost is sometimes associated with decisions to borrow at the Federal Reserve Bank discount window.[18] This subjective cost depends on the sensitivity of a bank's officers to criticism from the administrator of the discount window and on their fear that the flow of discount window funds can be terminated. Nevertheless, it is generally clear that cash balances can be adjusted with the greatest ease of all principal bank assets. A cash asset is nearly perfectly liquid, reversible, predictable, and divisible.

ii. United States government securities: Most publicly held debt obligations of the United States government are broadly traded in a market that is quite efficient relative to those servicing other assets. For a few dollars, an individual can buy or sell a $1,000 long-maturity Treasury bond; bills and other short-term assets can be traded at even smaller brokerage charges. Table 2-1 shows that during the period studied in the subsequent empirical chapters, all existing commercial banks held approximately one-third of this outstanding marketable debt; this sum represented more than 20 percent of the aggregate commercial banking system portfolio. More than 80 percent of these bank investments matured within five years, and more than 35 percent matured within one year. Prices of bills and other short-term assets are more predictable than long-term securities. Both predictability of price and low brokerage fees are important factors in explaining the apparent bank preferences for short-maturity securities.

As suggested in models of the transactions demand for cash, banks will choose to hold government securities rather than idle cash whenever the income from holding securities seems likely to exceed brokerage and the other nuisance costs of acquiring and disposing of securities in the

17. As noted previously, the possibility that banks may endogenously adjust their cash position through varying the interest rate paid on negotiable certificates of deposit is not formally considered. If such transactions were considered, it would eliminate the traditional (and somewhat artificial) distinction made here between substitution among assets and substitution between assets and liabilities. With the exception of borrowing from the Federal Reserve, the only choices available to banks involve switches among assets.

18. Cf. Polakoff [1960].

open market. Banks may also hold government securities in order to be eligible depositories for funds of the United States Treasury and various state and local government treasuries.

TABLE 2-1. PERCENTAGE DISTRIBUTIONS OF OUTSTANDING UNITED STATES GOVERN-
MENT MARKETABLE SECURITIES HELD BY THE PUBLIC, MARCH 31, 1962

	Maturity				
Owner	*within 1 year*	*1–5 years*	*5–10 years*	*10–20 years*	*over 20 years*
Commercial banks	30.2%	53.6%	36.0%	17.3%	3.7%
Mutual savings banks	1.5	3.0	9.3	6.8	10.7
Insurance companies	2.1	4.1	9.0	12.9	22.1
Nonfinancial corporations	12.6	2.8	0.5	0.3	0.1
Savings and loan associations	0.8	1.6	3.8	3.7	3.8
State and local governments	6.6	2.5	4.7	11.8	30.5
All other investors	46.3	32.4	36.6	47.2	29.2
Total	100.0%	100.0%	100.0%	100.0%	100.0%

SOURCE: *Federal Reserve Bulletin* 48 (June 1962), p. 731.

Apart from brokerage fees and predictability differences, banks have other reasons for distinguishing between long- and short-maturity securities. Small banks typically hold longer maturity securities than large banks; this practice apparently reflects the indivisible nuisance costs encountered by very small banks when they frequently make purchases of Treasury bills.

More importantly, during the period studied, tax laws artificially distinguished between capital gains and coupon income flowing from securities. Different tax rates and differences in before-tax rates of return made portfolio switching decisions quite subtle, particularly when a bank was attempting to determine whether a tax year should be one in which it realized losses or gains.[19] The opportunity costs associated with untimely trading of long-term securities can be large. Therefore, we expect to observe commercial banks frequently and predictably making short-term

19. The importance of concentrating realized capital gains and losses in different tax years was a consequence of an irrationality built into the federal income tax statutes. Capital losses could be deducted from ordinary income before computing corporate income taxes, but only after such losses were first offset against realized capital gains, if any. Because the two types of income were taxed at different rates, the law induced firms to have gain and loss years. For details about taxation of income from bank securities, see Parks [1958]. This anomaly was removed with passage of the Tax Reform Act of 1969.

security adjustments. Medium- and especially long-maturity bonds may have very different trading costs for individual banks, and these variations impair empirical descriptions of bank holdings of these assets.

   iii. State and local securities: Coupons, maturities, collateral, and risk ratings of state and local securities differ considerably. Brokerage charges associated with trading these securities are higher than those incurred when trading United States government securities. In most instances they are small when compared to costs realized when acquiring or disposing of loans. Markets for securities of a local government may be quite "thin" because of indivisibilities, imperfect information about the issuer, and the small volume of its outstanding debt. Such securities typically have a long maturity and are not free from default risk.

   Prices of long-maturity bonds tend to fluctuate substantially in response to market interest rate movements. Therefore, banks can calculate only very approximately the opportunity costs of trading these instruments on specific dates in the future. If banks' objective functions are convex functions of discounted future net income, then this feature will decrease the value of these assets as temporary repositories for funds. Like long-maturity United States bonds, capital gains resulting from trading state and local securities were subject to different tax rates than coupon income. This institutional feature will again impair the precision with which subsequent empirical chapters describe bank trading of these securities.

   On the other hand, banks desire to hold state and local securities in their long-run equilibrium portfolios because coupon income from these assets is tax exempt, and nominal interest rates are sufficiently high to make them profitable on an after-tax basis. They are less costly to service than loans because credit reviews tend to be less frequent and because their maturities are longer. Unlike loans, however, a large portfolio of tax-exempt securities does not cement long-term customer relationships. Bank holdings of state and local securities, long-term United States government bonds, and commercial loans in their equilibrium portfolio are a function of the economic characteristics of the area that a bank serves, the bank's objective function, its tax rate, and so on.

   In what follows, state and local securities are viewed as lying between long-term United States government bonds and commercial loans with respect to reversibility, predictability of price, and liquidity. Relative to long-term United States government bonds, state and local securities typically are less liquid and less predictable but have a somewhat higher after-tax rate of return.[20]

   20. For evidence on this point, see table 10-2.

iv. Consumer loans: These assets consist of installment loans to purchase automobiles and other consumer durables, installment loans to repair and modernize property, business installment loans, and single-payment loans for household, family, and other personal expenditures. They are ordinarily of small denomination (divisible) and, with the exception of single-payment loans, have maturities ranging from twelve to sixty months. They have high rates of return and are relatively expensive to service. Furthermore, because of their small denominations they are relatively costly to initiate. All loans require some standard initial credit analysis and documentation; this paperwork can be very costly in relation to the interest income from small loans. No organized secondary market exists for selling or discounting such loans.

Single-payment loans permit a bank to support individuals with a flexible short-term credit instrument. Such credits are convenient tools for establishing relationships between a bank and valuable future clients. Therefore, relatively high opportunity costs may be associated with rejecting a single-payment loan request or requiring rapid repayment of a loan except, of course, where default loss or fraud is imminent.

Installment loans constitute the majority of consumer loans. Borrowers are frequently not depositors of a bank, and there is no strong customer affiliation between them and the bank. Banks usually play a passive role in initiating such loans; contractors and salesmen arrange them while negotiating transactions. A bank can decline new loans only at the peril of terminating a valued customer relationship between it and these individuals. The comparatively long maturity of these loan agreements effectively deters rapid liquidation of installment loans.

v. Mortgage loans: These loans have long nominal maturities; in recent years the average contract maturity has been about twenty-two years for commercial banks and about twenty-five years for mutual savings banks [Federal Home Loan Bank Board, 1968]. These contractual maturities are rarely realized. Because the American population is mobile, the mean realized mortgage maturity is between six and eight years. An important characteristic of mortgage loans is whether or not they are insured by the Federal Housing Administration, the National Housing Administration, or the Veterans Administration.

At the end of 1962 all commercial banks held $23.5 billion of residential mortgages of which $9.2 billion were insured. On the same date mutual savings banks held $29.2 billion of which $19.0 billion were insured [Board of Governors of the Federal Reserve System, 1968]. Insured mortgage loans are traded on an organized secondary market that is supported by the Federal National Mortgage Association. Dealers in this market process orders for future delivery of mortgage loans; typical lead times between order and delivery dates are from three to twelve months.[21] We have little direct evidence on brokerage charges prevailing in this market but are informed from interviews that brokerage charges tend to be a declining function of the lead time. Therefore, insured mortgage loans have more liquidity and reversibility than other loans, particularly conventional mortgage loans, but less than state and local securities.

Mortgage lending by banks is reasonably profitable, if judged by estimates reported in chapter 10. The fact that mortgage loans may be very illiquid does not discourage banks from engaging in this activity, for, as Porter [1961] has noted, the likely "deposit low" in any time period is high enough to permit a bank to place considerable funds in illiquid form. However, mortgage lending is likely to be less profitable over time than other forms of commercial bank lending. Once a mortgage loan is made, a bank does not necessarily have any subsequent personal contact with the borrower. Therefore, a profitable future relationship is less likely to evolve from a mortgage loan than from a comparably long sequence of short-term loan accommodations. Of course, a timely mortgage loan to a rising young corporate treasurer may lead to a profitable future relationship between his firm and the bank.

Mutual savings banks are much more likely to prefer mortgage loans than commercial banks because their lending powers are narrower. Indeed, it is likely that the reason for and the effect of these lending restrictions is to subsidize home ownership. Mutual savings banks apparently prefer insured mortgage loans to conventional mortgage loans because of their greater liquidity and safety even though the latter have higher rates of return. State regulations on mutual savings banks also often require that all nonlocally originated mortgage loans be insured.

The conclusion from this review is that individual assets have very different associated transactions costs and long-run roles to play in bank portfolios. In part, the composition of long-run equilibrium portfolios is determined by servicing costs and observable market rates of return. The review suggests, however, that the principal determinants of these long-run portfolios are likely to be a complicated, interrelated set of transactions and expectations involving a bank and each of its clients. The existence of these continuing relationships strongly suggests that banks will not wish to adjust their portfolios instantaneously in response to externally

21. Dealers package groups of insured mortgage loans with maturities and geographic dispersion acceptable to purchasers. Lead times for delivery in this market may range to eighteen months although such leads are quite rare.

engendered changes in their situation. In addition, the structure of effective brokerage costs associated with contemporary financial markets makes rapid portfolio adjustments of some assets very costly. For both reasons, quite apart from any assumptions about the autoregressive structure of deposit shocks, it is likely that banks will respond to deposit flows slowly. This suggests in turn that econometricians are much more likely to be successful in describing short- and intermediate-run portfolio adjustments to shocks than the drift in long-run equilibrium bank portfolios. Fortunately, the design of stabilization policy also depends on short- and intermediate-term descriptions.

Table 2-2 attempts to summarize schematically the expected patterns of commercial bank portfolio adjustment in response to an unanticipated deposit inflow. The table shows three different time intervals which can be interpreted roughly as the first two weeks after the shock, the next three months, and the subsequent nine to fifteen months. Entries in the table indicate whether a bank is expected to be increasing (+), decreasing (−), or not changing (0) its holdings of an asset during each interval. Doubtful cases are indicated by a question mark. The pattern of portfolio adjustments for a mutual savings bank is expected to be similar for its smaller set of assets.

TABLE 2-2. EXPECTED SIGNS OF TIME DERIVATIVES OF COMMERCIAL BANK ASSETS FOLLOWING A DEPOSIT INFLOW

	Time Derivative Sign		
Asset	*First Period*	*Second Period*	*Third Period*
Cash	−	− ?	0
Short-term government securities	+	?	−
All other government securities	+ ?	?	+
State and local securities	0	+ ?	+
Commercial loans	+ ?	+	+
Consumer loans	0	+ ?	+
Mortgage loans	0	0?	+

6. A SUMMARY OF ASSUMPTIONS TO BE EMPLOYED IN CONSTRUCTING A MODEL OF BANK PORTFOLIO BEHAVIOR

In this section the assumptions discussed in this chapter and frequently invoked in subsequent chapters are collected for ready reference.

a. Objective function

(1) All commercial banks have a common objective function reflecting interests of owners and management. Important arguments in this function include the discounted stream of expected net income, bank size, rate of growth of assets and income, stability of reported net income, number of conspicuous losses, and community appreciation of management.

(2) All mutual savings banks have a common objective function reflecting interests of directors and management. Important arguments in this function include bank size, stability of reported net income, number of conspicuous losses, and community appreciation of management.

b. Activities

(1) Each asset in a bank portfolio is uniquely associated with a flow of borrower services.

(2) Each deposit liability in a bank portfolio is, subject to contractual arrangements, controlled by individuals outside of the bank.

(3) Asset and liability inflows and outflows have symmetric effects on and/or are symmetrically affected by other variables in the system.

(4) Interest rates, cost schedules for acquiring and disposing of assets, advertising and promotional fees, and other schedules of costs and revenues that are incurred while servicing portfolios are determined externally and, hence, are exogenous to a bank.

c. Risk and uncertainty

(1) Demand deposits of individuals, partnerships, and corporations; demand deposits of other banks; and demand deposits of the United States government can be aggregated for an individual commercial bank without loss of information.

(2) Time sequences of demand and time deposits are independent.

(3) Sequences of demand and time deposits are generated by stationary and stable stochastic processes that vary across banks.

(4) A bank experiencing a stochastic shock in demand or time deposits expects to retain permanently some positive fraction of each shock.

(5) Sequences of demand and time deposits are each independent of a bank's asset portfolio composition.

(6) Sequences of interest and repayment flows and changes in the levels of capital and other liabilities are perfectly predictable by a bank.

(7) Banks have unitary elasticities of expectations of interest rates for each asset and liability in their portfolio.

(8) Banks view their deposit sequences as being independent of national economic events and policy.

d. Institutional factors and costs of adjustments

(1) Cash assets are nearly perfectly liquid, reversible, predictable, and divisible.

(2) United States government securities are free from default risks and quite liquid. For various institutional reasons, however, they are more indivisible and less reversible and predictable than cash assets.

(3) State and local securities are not free from default risks. They are less divisible, liquid, reversible, and predictable than United States government securities.

(4) Commercial loans, consumer loans, and uninsured mortgage loans are subject to greater default risks than are state and local securities. They are less divisible, liquid, reversible, and predictable than these securities.

CHAPTER 3

Models of Bank Portfolio Behavior

In this chapter several theoretical descriptions of bank portfolio behavior are constructed. They all derive from a model of a primitive "archetypal" bank which is presented in section 1. Typically, the models can be applied to either commercial or mutual savings banks. The reader may find it helpful to think of sections 1–4 as successively enriching this elementary model. Sections 5 and 6 represent a different approach to describing banks and build directly from the archetypal bank. The last section summarizes the principal findings of the chapter.

Through the first five sections deposits are viewed as exogenous to a bank. Through the first four sections banks are assumed to be price takers in loan markets; they can make any amount of loans they wish without affecting the loan interest rate. For convenience, bank assets will be restricted to cash, loans, and government securities, each of which is perfectly divisible. The liability side of a bank's balance sheet is assumed to consist of two items, capital and deposits. Deposits are withdrawable on demand, and no income taxes exist. These specifications clearly reduce the complexity of the bank portfolio selection problem, but do not compromise its essential features.

Other exogenous factors to be considered include (1) transactions costs, (2) the rate at which bank deposits grow, (3) the predictability of deposits, (4) properties of secondary asset markets, (5) loan demand, (6) the perfection of nonfinancial factor markets, and (7) interest rate uncertainty.

1. THE ARCHETYPAL BANK

In this section a bank exists in a world of (1) perfect certainty, (2) no transactions or variable costs, (3) no long-term deposit growth, and (4) competitive loan markets. The bank is assumed to maximize profits and initially is assumed to be served by secondary markets in both government securities and loans. It is subject to a fractional reserve requirement, ρ, on its deposits. All securities and loans have a maturity of one period and are default free. Loan interest rates always exceed interest rates on securities, and the latter in turn exceed the zero rate of return on cash.

In this trivial case the bank maximizes

(3.1.1)
$$\pi = r_l l + r_s s - \eta$$

subject to

$$l, s \geqq 0$$

$$l + s + c = g + k$$

$$c \geqq \rho g$$

where

π = bank profits in the period,
l = loans of the bank made at interest rate r_l,
s = securities of the bank bearing interest rate r_s,
c = cash,
g = deposits,
k = bank capital,
η = fixed costs of servicing bank deposits and capital, and
ρ = fractional deposit reserve requirement.

The optimal portfolio is

	A		L	
1. cash	ρg	4. deposits	g
2. securities	0	5. capital	k
3. loans	$(1 - \rho)g + k$		

and profits are given by

$$\pi = r_l((1 - \rho)g + k) - \eta.$$

The percentage of a bank's deposits invested in different assets is invariant with respect to the time path of deposits within the period. If, however, a secondary market exists for securities, but not for bank loans, these percentages will depend upon the path of deposits. In this case loan acquisitions and disposals may be executed only at the beginning of the period. With these modifications, the model becomes a caricature of the model of bank portfolio behavior suggested by Richard Porter [1961], which focused on a bank's deposit low. Let g_o be the deposits of the bank at the beginning of the period, and suppose, for example, that the bank knew deposits would follow a path which at one point reached a minimum of $.9g_o$. Then its optimal initial portfolio would be

A	L
1. ρg_o	4. g_o
2. $.1(1 - \rho)g_o$	5. k
3. $.9(1 - \rho)g_o + k$	

and its profits would be diminished. Profits are diminished because the bank must substitute securities for loans in order to meet deposit with-drawals during the period.

Thus, a diversified bank portfolio can be optimal in the absence of uncertainty when not all assets have secondary markets. Alternatively, if costs of converting loans into cash are sufficiently high, banks will hold funds in either cash or securities.[1]

So long as the relation $r_l > r_s > 0$ holds, for a given path of deposits the optimal portfolio is not affected by changes in either of the specified interest rates. A bank's demand for loans is perfectly interest inelastic over wide ranges of interest rates. Within the period the bank's portfolio is very sensitive to the path of deposits, as suggested in figure 3-1. Loans

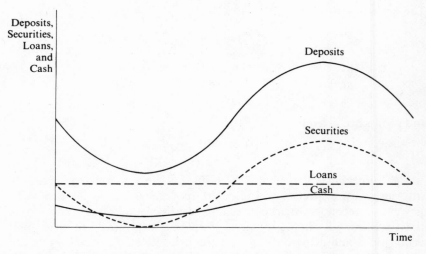

FIGURE 3-1. WITHIN-PERIOD PORTFOLIO ADJUSTMENT: NO SECONDARY MARKET FOR LOANS

1. A similar argument has previously been reported by Morrison [1966].

as a fraction of bank assets reach a maximum when deposits are at a minimum and vice versa. All fluctuating paths have coincident peaks and troughs.

Finally, because all assets mature at the end of each period, the multi-period extension of this model consists of a sequence of single period replays. In this archetypal bank, it is never necessary to consider past or future periods when choosing an optimal portfolio.

2. Deposit Predictability and the Archetypal Bank

In this section a bank exists in a world of uncertain deposit levels, no expected long-term deposit growth, and competitive primary loan markets.[2] Primary loan market transactions occur only at the beginning of a period. As in the preceding section, the bank is subject to a reserve requirement, ρ, on its deposits; all securities and loans have a maturity of one period and are default free; and market interest rates are perfectly predictable and satisfy the relation $r_l > r_s > 0$. The bank is assumed to maximize expected profits and is served by a perfect secondary market in government securities; loans cannot be sold but may be discounted at a penalty rate, h, such that $h > r_l$. Banks are assumed to earn loan interest income when loans are discounted, but bank profits are diminished by the average amount of borrowing multiplied by the discount rate.

Deposits during a period are assumed to be described by a stationary stochastic process. Let $g(t) = g_o(1 + \varepsilon(t))$ where ε is a continuous random variable defined over the domain of one period, and g_o is the value of the bank's deposits at the start of the period. The continuous variable, $\varepsilon(t)$, is assumed to have zero expected value and finite variance. In repeated trials the underlying stochastic process can generate a sample of time sequences of deposits for the representative period. The probability that a sequence will reach an arbitrarily low deposit level is an increasing function of the variance of ε and the length of the period. For a given length of period and generating process, a three-dimensional representation can be constructed which shows the probability of the bank having any level of deposits, g, at any particular time in the period. Figure 3-2 is such a diagram where g_o is the level of deposits at the beginning of the period, and $(g_o - a_o)$ is the maximum deposit loss which the bank can initially withstand without discounting loans.[3]

2. For purposes of this monograph, a primary loan transaction creates a debt instrument; a secondary transaction involves the transfer or exchange of existing debt instruments.

3. $(g_o - a_o) = s/(1 - \rho)$ where $0 < \rho < 1$.

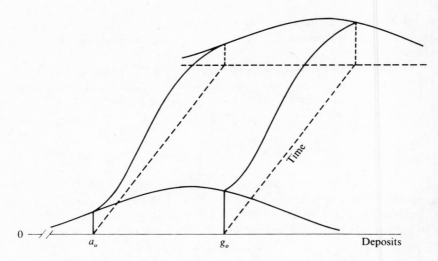

FIGURE 3-2. INTRAPERIOD DENSITY FUNCTION FOR BANK DEPOSITS

The expected value of discount window costs is

$$(3.2.1) \qquad E(C) = \int_0^a \int_0^1 h(1 - \rho)gf(t, g)\, dt\, dg$$

where

(i) $f(t, g)$ is the density function in figure 3-2,

(ii) $a = \dfrac{l - k}{1 - \rho} = \dfrac{l^*}{1 - \rho}$, and

(iii) h is the interest rate at which a bank may discount loans.

The expected value of these costs is a function of a bank's beginning port-folio. Costs will be low when banks have relatively few loans and/or when the ratio of bank capital to assets is high.

Expected bank profits are

$$E(\pi) = r_l l^* + \int_a^\infty \int_0^1 (1 - \rho)r_s gf(t, g)\, dt\, dg - r_s l^* + r_l k - \eta - E(C).$$
(3.2.2)

To avoid bankruptcy inelegancies, it is assumed that discount window costs in any period are less than a bank's initial capital. Expected profits are a function of the exogenous variables r_l, r_s, h, and the distribution of deposits within a period. Because the secondary market for securities is perfect, a bank will never hold cash in excess of required reserves. The bank has one variable to determine when maximizing expected profits, l^*. This maximizing value can be found by defining $f(g) = \int_0^1 f(g, t)\, dt$ and assuming that the constraints $g_0 = \int_0^\infty f(g)\, dg = 1$ and $l^*, s \geq 0$ are satisfied. Then,

$$E(\pi) = r_l l^* + r_s(1 - \rho)\int_a^\infty g f(g)\, dg - r_s l^* + r_l k - \eta$$

(3.2.3)

$$- h(1 - \rho)\int_0^a g f(g)\, dg.$$

Differentiating with respect to l^* yields

(3.2.4)
$$\frac{dE(\pi)}{dl^*} = r_l - r_s - (r_s + h)f\left(\frac{l^*}{1 - \rho}\right)\left(\frac{l^*}{1 - \rho}\right).$$

Letting

$$H\left(\frac{l^*}{1 - \rho}\right) = f\left(\frac{l^*}{1 - \rho}\right)\left(\frac{l^*}{1 - \rho}\right)$$

and setting (3.2.4) equal to zero yields

$$H\left(\frac{l^*}{1 - \rho}\right) = \frac{r_l - r_s}{r_s + h}$$

or, providing the inverse function is well defined,

(3.2.5)
$$l^* = (1 - \rho)H^{-1}\left(\frac{r_l - r_s}{r_s + h}\right).$$

If the frequency function is unimodal, as illustrated in figure 3-2, then H is strictly monotonic in the range from zero to its mode, and the inverse function operator is well defined. The second derivative of (3.2.4) with respect to l^* indicates that if a solution to (3.2.5) exists, then it will be a maximum for values of $l^*/(1 - \rho)$ that are less than the mode. This interior solution implies that loans are an increasing function of r_l and a decreasing function of r_s and h.[4]

If r_l and h were nearly equal and r_s were small, then a corner solution could occur. This corner solution implies that a bank places all its resources, net of required reserves, in loans. As r_l decreases relative to h, corner solutions are less likely to be observed for a given r_s and $f(g)$.

4. This result is quite similar to results obtained previously by Poole [1968] and Aigner and Sprenkle [1969] although neither paper considered the banking model studied in the text.

This model suggests that in the face of deposit uncertainty banks that maximize expected profits will place all of their capital, but only a fraction of their deposits, in loans. Therefore, high capital-deposit ratios should be associated with high loan-asset ratios. Parallel predictions obviously apply if banks are observed to have different mixes of stable time and fluctuating demand deposits. Evidence about this hypothesized pattern of equilibrium portfolios is reported in subsequent empirical chapters.

3. Growth, Capacity, and Factor Market Imperfections

In all important respects the preceding theoretical discussion concerned static models of bank behavior; in the present section the shackles of static analysis are partly dropped. Banks are assumed to maximize profits in a world characterized by perfectly predictable deposits and interest rates. Loans continue to be made at the beginning of each period and, initially, no secondary market for loans exists. Deposits grow continuously; the bank is subject to a reserve requirement, ρ, on its deposits; all securities and loans have a maturity of one period and are default free; and market interest rates satisfy the relation $r_l > r_s > 0$.

A new feature in this section is that the volume of a bank's loans in some period may be restricted because of the time and effort necessary to process loan applications. Loan officers are viewed as factors of production who function with a constant level of efficiency up to some capacity ceiling. A loan officer must be trained by the bank, and it is assumed that a significant fixed cost must be incurred by the bank to train an officer. As before, securities and cash transactions are assumed to require negligible administrative effort.

Banks must make two decisions: (1) What proportion of their assets should be held as loans? and (2) How many loan officers should be retained? A complicating factor in the maximization problem is that officers can only be hired in integer quantities. Formally, the problem is to maximize a discounted future stream of profits

$$(3.3.1) \qquad\qquad \theta = \sum_{t=0}^{\infty} \pi_t \Big/ (1 + i)^t$$

$$\pi_t = r_l l_t + r_s s_t - \eta - w n_t - \lambda \Delta n_t$$

subject to

(i) $l_t, s_t \geqq 0$

(ii) $l_t + s_t + c_t = g_t + k_t$

(iii) $c_t \geqq \rho g_t$

(iv) $l_t \leqq n_t q$

(v) $g_{t+1} > g_t$

where:

(i) $n_t = \sum_{-\infty}^{t} \Delta n_t$

(ii) Δn_t is integer

(iii) $\dfrac{w}{q} < r_l - r_s$

and:

i = the rate at which a bank discounts future net income,
w = salary per period to a loan officer,
λ = training costs of a new loan officer,
n = number of officers employed, and
q = the maximum value of loans which an officer can process in a period

If loan officers can be hired only at the beginning of a period, loans will tend to respond with a lag to continuous changes in deposits. If access to the discount window were permitted, as argued in section 2, the amount of discounted loans would depend upon the relative magnitudes of r_l, r_s, and the discount rate, h. With discounting, banks will tend to adjust the number of their loan officers in response to movements in some average level of deposits rather than the minimum level of deposits in a time period. In this situation a bank's loans will respond to deposits with an erratic lag.

The solution is also sensitive to the rate, i, at which a bank discounts future net income. This sensitivity is a consequence of the training costs, λ, which banks must experience when expanding their staff of loan officers. Lags will be more pronounced if it is assumed that training an officer involves time as well as training expenses. Thus if it requires two years to train an officer, banks which discount future earnings at a high rate will be concerned that the officer is fully occupied when trained.

In summary this section has sketched a model that is capable of exhibiting lagged portfolio adjustments to deposit inflows when no uncertainty is present. Four important elements have been added to the model of section 1: (1) interperiod growth in bank deposits,[5] (2) a nonportfolio factor of production which can be employed only up to a capacity ceiling, (3) market imperfections associated with changing the flow of that factor's services, and (4) the interest rate at which banks discount future net income.

The imperfections are of two types: (a) integer restrictions on using the factor and (b) training costs associated with changing the number of officers employed. With appropriate parameters either kind of imperfection could lead to lagged portfolio responses. They were merged in the discussion because banks are likely to face them simultaneously.

The lags that may be expected are complicated functions of the parameters in (3.3.1), the time path of deposits, the length of the period, and whether or not a bank has access to the discount window. An analytical solution is neither easy to obtain nor likely to be insightful because of the large number of necessary parameter assumptions. In the next section, after examining how deposit uncertainty is likely to affect this picture, an attempt will be made to map these determinants into a time sequence of hypothetical cost parameters. A set of simulation solutions to this substantively simplified problem is then exhibited.

4. DEPOSIT FORECASTING AND COSTS OF PORTFOLIO ADJUSTMENTS

a. Deposit uncertainty and forecasting

Uncertainty about deposits greatly extends the complexity of the maximization problem just considered. The complexity occurs because the solution is functionally dependent on the time path of deposits. The assumptions of the preceding section describe banks here, except that now (1) deposits are random, (2) use of the discount window is permitted, and (3) banks seek to maximize expected profits.

If a bank is uncertain about the time path of its deposits, its realized profits will ordinarily fall short of the profits that it could obtain with perfect foresight. This shortfall occurs because some bank decisions are imperfectly reversible, and over a number of periods random deposit

---

5. In principle an exactly parallel argument can be constructed for a bank suffering a deposit outflow. In that case the coefficient λ must be interpreted as a termination penalty for discharging an officer. In the case of a loan officer who has established close relationships with a number of corporate treasurers, this parameter could be interpreted as a consequent good-will loss to the bank. Obviously there is no theoretical reason for λ to be the same for growing and declining banks. The reader should recall, however, that a symmetrical response was assumed in the preceding chapter in order to exploit available data resources.

sequences will cause some decisions to be wrong ex post. In the present model loan decisions can be modified, but only at some cost within a period. Similarly, loan officer staff changes can be effected only with some expense to the bank; this second type of irreversibility carries across successive time periods. In the case of actual banks, the existence of customer relationships is likely to be a prime source of loan irreversibility.

It follows, of course, that expected bank profits are an increasing function of the predictability of bank deposits. The sensitivity of profits to variations in deposit predictability is not easily judged. The importance of deposit predictability for understanding bank portfolio behavior is investigated empirically in chapters 8 and 9. As reported in the preceding chapter, that investigation is based on very specific, albeit plausible, assumptions about the process that generates deposit fluctuations. The necessity for this very narrow empirical specification discouraged formal analysis of the relation between deposit predictability and expected bank profits. It is not feasible to exhibit solutions to this mixed-integer, dynamic programming problem. The discussion of its rather simple antecedents suggests that solutions are likely to be very sensitive to parameter specifications.

The remainder of this section will summarize the major properties of the model's antecedents and then exhibit some possible solutions. It will be seen in subsequent chapters that this procedure provides a basis for empirical analysis.

From the preceding discussion, it is expected that:

a. Interest rates are an important determinant of bank portfolio composition. At a point in time, when all banks face the same schedule of rates, interbank variations in portfolios cannot be explained by market interest rates. Over time, allowance can be made for changes in interest rates.

b. A bank's liability and capital structure is also an important determinant of its long-run equilibrium portfolio composition. This structure is important because liabilities differ from one another, and particularly from capital, in their predictability. As their liabilities become less predictable, banks will prefer to hold assets served by strong secondary markets.

c. Because many bank assets and factor inputs are traded in imperfect markets, banks will not adjust to equilibrium instantaneously. Therefore, a bank's portfolio on some date, t, is very likely to be a function of prior values of interest rates and its deposits. The length of these lags depends, in part, upon a number of cost parameters, such as those appearing in expression (3.3.1). The values of these parameters are not known and are likely to vary among banks.

As predictability of deposits decreases, the relation between histories of deposits and interest rates and bank portfolio composition becomes obscure and depends essentially upon whether banks believe that past deposit sequences contain information about future deposits. If past deposit changes contain no information about future deposit changes, then the present model becomes a blend of the models discussed in sections 2 and 3 of this chapter. In this case, banks that expect to grow will tend to place large fractions of recent deposit inflows in high-yield irreversible assets like loans. However, if a bank believes its deposits are described by the autoregressive process suggested in expression (2.4.3) and the accompanying text, banks will tend to place only a small fraction of recent deposit inflows in loans.[6]

The reason for this difference in behavior is that with the assumed autoregressive structure a bank expects to retain permanently only a fraction of an initial deposit shock. It recognizes that depositors who receive such inflows will not hold idle balances for long. If the bank had expanded loans as much as possible with the inflow, subsequent deposit withdrawals would have forced it to liquidate loans entailing significant transactions costs.

b. Costs of asset transactions

The most distinctive feature of the model reported in this subsection is the emphasis placed on the cost of rapid adjustments of bank portfolios to deposit inflows. Even though loans nominally bear high interest rates, the net income of a bank can be quite low if it attempts to lend newly received funds too promptly. A bank will tend to maximize expected profits if it first purchases securities and then gradually replaces them with loans.

To illustrate this argument, it is convenient to define a net rate of return on a loan that equals the nominal rate of return minus origination or transactions costs, which are expressed as a percentage of the face value of a loan. These origination costs reflect overtime pay for existing loan officers, advertising and promotional expenses, errors that are made in processing new loans, and so on. They are assumed to be a declining function of the length of time between the period in which the deposit

---

6. To be sure, other stationary stochastic processes exist that could produce very different portfolio adjustment paths. The process underlying (2.4.3) seems to correspond well with actual bank deposit data and therefore is the only one considered in the text.

inflow occurs and the period in which the loan is actually put on the books.[7]

The net rate of return on securities is also assumed to be an increasing function of the length of time between a decision to acquire securities and the actual purchase of them. Because the market for securities is relatively perfect, the value of foreknowledge is less, and the slope of the function is postulated to be less than is the case for loans. In table 3-1 hypothetical

TABLE 3-1. ASSUMED VALUES OF NET RATES OF RETURN

Number of Periods since Deposit Inflow	Loans	Securities
0	5%	6.0%
1	6	6.1
2	7	6.2
3	8	6.3
4	9	6.4
5	10	6.5
6	11	6.6
7	12	6.7
8	13	6.8
9 and thereafter	14	6.9

net rates of return are reported, showing what a bank would realize by ordering a loan or a security at the time of a deposit inflow for delivery t periods later. It is assumed in the table that before transactions costs the nominal market rate of return on loans is 15 percent; the corresponding market rate on securities is 7 percent. The difference between reported net rates and these market rates are (1) assumed transactions costs and (2) assumed servicing costs of 1 percent per period for loans and 0.1 percent for securities. Apart from the fourth and fifth cases to be considered below, no other assumptions about transactions costs are employed in this section.

A second distinctive feature of the model concerns the rate at which profit-maximizing banks discount future net income. If the maximization problem is to be well defined, the interest rate with which net income is discounted must exceed the maximum obtainable portfolio rate of return. In a world of uncertainty, this formulation may require that banks (and investigators) consider an indefinitely long sequence of time

7. See also sections 5 and 6 of chapter 2.

periods when determining an optimal portfolio response to a deposit shock.

It is not convenient to study a very large number of periods in this subsection. Instead, for expositional purposes, banks are assumed to maximize total profits (undiscounted) over ten consecutive periods subsequent to the deposit inflow. They are assumed to discount completely income received beyond this ten-period horizon. While admittedly inelegant, this approach suffices to convey some important characteristics of the model suggested in the preceding and present sections. These characteristics concern variable loan maturity, the relation between loan maturity and interest rates, nonlinear portfolio adjustment costs, and deposit forecasting.[8]

A bank, initially in equilibrium, is assumed to receive a permanent deposit flow, normalized to be of unit value, and it is subject to a 20 percent reserve requirement. No secondary loan market or discount window exists. Formally, the bank maximizes

$$(3.4.1) \qquad \Delta\pi = \sum_{t=1}^{10} (r_{l,t}\Delta l_t + r_{s,t}\Delta s_t)$$

subject to

$$\Delta l_t + \Delta s_t = .8$$

and other conditions which will be made specific in the text, where

$$t \text{ is a time index, and}$$
$$r_{l,t} \text{ and } r_{s,t} \text{ are } net \text{ rates of return.}$$

Case 1: perfect foresight, single-period loan maturity.

The bank is assumed to have foreknowledge of the deposit inflow and has prepared its staff and a number of future borrowers so that when the funds appear the bank can realize the maximum net return on loans, 14 percent. The bank lends at this rate each period and obtains a net profit of 1.12, as indicated in the first column of table 3-2.

If loan maturity had been ten periods instead of just one, column 1b in table 3-2 shows that the bank maximizes net income by lending .8 in period 0 and again earns 1.12. The restriction that banks must lend at long maturities imposes no sacrifice on a bank with perfect foresight and steady or rising deposits. A portfolio of long-term loans can, of course, prove

8. Nonlinear adjustment costs refer to the expenditure that must be incurred to process one unit of loans. The fourth restriction in expression (3.3.1) is too stringent; the capacity of a group of loan officers is not that well defined. In the present section the costs of processing loans are at times assumed to be described by a parabola having arguments l and l^2.

inconvenient for banks that experience deposit outflows, depending upon secondary market arrangements.

Case 2: no foresight, single-period loan maturity.

In this experiment the bank has no foreknowledge of the deposit inflow and is unable to prepare its staff and future borrowers for the increased availability of funds. Therefore, it holds securities for two periods and lends thereafter. For the assumed interest rates the value of foreknowledge is .35; the bank's net income in this instance is .769. For such rate structures deposit forecasting can considerably enhance profits.

Case 3: no foresight, ten-period loan maturity.

In this experiment the requirement that loans have a ten-period maturity induces banks to acquire loans at a much slower rate than in case 2.[9] Bank profits decline to .652 in the ten periods being considered, reflecting the opportunity cost of lending long term when net rates of return are rising.[10] This case suggests that a bank will be willing to make short-maturity loans at lower rates of interest than long-term loans.

Case 4: no foresight, ten-period loan maturity, small adjustment non-linearities.

In this and the subsequent case an attempt is made to refine the previous evaluation of the role of bank lending capacity in describing portfolio behavior. The modified view is that with some given staff of officers, a bank can always process more loans in some time interval, but it may be prohibitively costly for it to do so. The underlying specification is the third case. Consider profits in the tth period. In the third case they were equal to

$$(3.4.2) \qquad \Delta\pi_t = r_{l,t}\Delta l_t + r_{s,t}\Delta s_t$$

In the present case they are

$$(3.4.3) \qquad \Delta\pi_t = r_{l,t}\Delta l_t + r_{s,t}\Delta s_t - \sigma\Delta l_t^2$$

9. Because long-maturity loans cannot be "undone," it pays a bank to wait for the best buy. Short-maturity loans can be committed more promptly because they do not tie up bank resources when future profitable lending opportunities become available. In arranging long-maturity loans, banks will take into account the time path of their net rates and, in effect, discriminate against those who would borrow long in early periods. No actual price discrimination can occur because nominal market interest rates underlying table 3-1 are assumed to be constant across periods.

10. The maximization problem is rather artificial in cases 3, 4, and 5 because of the assumption that profits earned after period 9 are ignored by the bank. Solutions in table 3-2 illustrate qualitatively how a bank's portfolio will respond to the assumed institutional changes. If a longer period were studied, loan acquisitions would occur later, but in case 3 never beyond the point where loan net rates of return leveled off.

where σ equals 10. In table 3-2, the profit-maximizing solution implies that the bank will acquire loans in six consecutive periods commencing with period 3. The largest number of loans is acquired in the sixth period, as was true in the third experiment, but rapidly rising marginal costs of lending have induced the bank to acquire three-fourths of its loans in surrounding periods. Bank profits are .613 or about .039 below those achieved in the third experiment. The bank is fully loaned up at the end of the experiment.

Case 5: no foresight, ten-period loan maturity, large adjustment non-linearities.

The only structural difference between this and the preceding case is that the quadratic cost of adjustment parameter, σ, has been increased by a factor of ten. This increase radically alters bank portfolio behavior. Bank profits barely exceed the return to a no-loan portfolio described in the last column of table 3-2. With rapidly rising marginal lending costs, the bank is unwilling to lend more than .04 in any period; at the end of ten periods, it has lent only 24 percent of its deposit inflow.[11]

TABLE 3-2. BANK LOAN ACQUISITIONS AND PROFITS UNDER SELECTED REGIMES

				Case			
Period	1a	1b	2	3	4	5	No-Loan
0	.8	.8	0	0	0	0	0
1	.8	0	0	0	0	0	0
2	.8	0	.8	0	0	.01	0
3	.8	0	.8	0	.02	.02	0
4	.8	0	.8	.0	.13	.04	0
5	.8	0	.8	0	.19	.04	0
6	.8	0	.8	.8	.20	.04	0
7	.8	0	.8	0	.17	.04	0
8	.8	0	.8	0	.08	.03	0
9	.8	0	.8	0	0	.02	0
Net Profits at End of Ten Periods							
	1.120	1.120	.769	.652	.613	.532	.516

11. If the maximization problem were bounded, such that $i > \max_t r_{l,t}$, and the problem were to be solved for an indefinitely large number of periods, the bank would still not be loaned up at the end of ten periods, although it would be eventually. If loan maturities were one period, the bank would never choose to be fully loaned up because it would have to reprocess all its loans each period.

Together, these cases suggest that lending capacity, loan maturity, and deposit predictability are very important determinants of the time path of a bank's assets in response to a deposit inflow.

5. IMPERFECT LOAN MARKETS

The model to be considered in this section differs markedly from those in the preceding pages. It exploits the random loan search approach introduced in section 5 of chapter 2 and is best viewed as an extension of the archetypal model.

In this section a bank is assumed to receive a permanent deposit flow (normalized to unity) at the beginning of period zero. The reserve requirement is assumed to absorb 20 percent of this flow. Loan demand is stochastic, but otherwise the model is nonrandom. Banks may rediscount loans at a penalty rate; they may not acquire loans in secondary markets.

Uncertainty about loan interest rates is introduced as an important determinant of bank portfolio composition. Loans are assumed to be default free, somewhat indivisible, and of equal size. Rates of return on securities, the interest rate at which banks may discount loans, and deposits are perfectly predictable. A bank is again assumed to have a fixed time span over which it desires to maximize an objective function. For expository purposes it is convenient to think of this function as quadratic in overall portfolio rate of return.

A bank that has just received a deposit inflow is viewed as regularly receiving a stream of loan requests that differ only in the net rate of return that the bank will realize.[12] These requests should be thought of as arriving sequentially with the bank being forced to accept or reject a request before considering the next one in the sequence. The length of time necessary to process this sequence is important for describing the lagged adjustment of the bank's portfolio to a deposit inflow, but for the moment is ignored. All loans mature at the end of the assumed time span.

The problem is to determine a decision rule or strategy that will maximize the bank's objective function. The process generating the sequence of loan requests (loan bids), the number of bids, the number of loans that the bank can accept before approaching the discount window, the interest rate on securities, and the penalty rate at which the bank can discount loans are assumed to be exogenous and known by the bank.

12. Stating the problem in terms of a deposit inflow may lead to some confusion. The reader may prefer to view the bank as having a certain quantity of funds that must be lent or invested in each period. The funds may be loan and investment interest, loan amortization, or new deposits.

Risk exists for two reasons: (1) the rate of return earned from any set of accepted loans is a random variable, and (2) the number of loans that will in fact be accepted is also random.[13] The latter risk increases the variance of portfolio rate of return because net rates of return from loans and securities typically differ.

This timeless model will be analyzed in two stages to show how results are affected by the magnitude of the penalty discount rate. In the first stage the amount of the penalty is assumed to be zero, that is, the discount window merely takes over loans and the income therefrom after the bank becomes fully loaned up.[14] In the second stage a substantial penalty rate is charged for loans that are discounted. The usefulness of this model for describing portfolio adjustment paths is briefly considered at the end of this section.

a. Zero-penalty rate case

Loan interest rate bids are assumed to be described by a finite variance, continuous probability distribution, $f(r_l)$. The expected value of $f(r_l)$ is assumed to equal or exceed the net rate of return from securities, r_s. A bank is assumed to have sufficient free funds to make m loans; it receives n loan requests, where n exceeds m.[15] The bank's strategy consists of establishing a threshold loan acceptance rate, r_a; all bids at or above r_a will be accepted. For given m, n, and $f(r_l)$, as r_a rises the average rate of interest on accepted loans rises and the expected number of accepted loans declines. A sufficiently high r_a will mean with high probability that the bank will have residual funds to invest in securities. The expected rate of return from the bank's portfolio is

$$(3.5.1) \qquad E(\pi) = (.8 - s) \int_{r_a}^{\infty} r_l f(r_l)\, dr_l + s r_s.$$

Its maximum occurs when

$$(3.5.2) \qquad \frac{\partial s}{\partial r_a}(E(r_l)_{\text{accepted}} - r_s) = (.8 - s) r_a f(r_a).$$

Since every term in (3.5.2) is positive, securities are an increasing and loans are a decreasing function of r_s. The variance of a portfolio's rate of

13. The maximizing strategy, once adopted, cannot be altered. This assumption is intended to reflect the high cost of changing operating rules in large organizations where very large numbers of agents (loan officers) are implementing policy on a decentralized basis.

14. This assumption is equivalent to assuming that a perfect secondary loan market exists.

15. The problem is degenerate if $m > n$; a risk-averting bank will accept all bids which exceed r_s.

return is less easy to derive, for it depends upon a number of specialized assumptions about the distribution $f(r_l)$ and its relation to r_s. Instead, a small number of risk-return loci, showing expected value and standard deviation of rates of return, are reported in figures 3-3, 3-4, and 3-5. These loci have been generated using a computer program designed to produce mean and variance estimates by numerically integrating the appropriate compound probability distributions.[16] Each diagram is

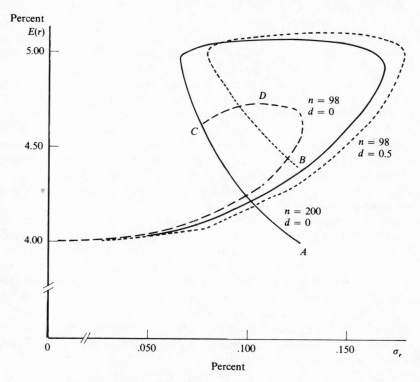

FIGURE 3-3. RISK-RETURN LOCI FOR A BANK PORTFOLIO: NORMALLY DISTRIBUTED LOAN BIDS

16. The probability is compound because it must include both the distribution of rates of return on loans that the bank makes and the probability that a bank will not be fully loaned up. The distribution of loan rates of return is a truncated distribution defined by $f(r_l)$ and the threshold loan rate, r_a. The probability that the bank will be loaned up is obtained by using the area of $f(r_l)$ exceeding the truncation rate, r_a. Assuming that successive loan applications are independent, the number of loans that a bank makes is given by the binomial distribution. The second distribution then describes the probability of a bank making $m - 1$, $m - 2, \ldots, 1$, or 0 loans when n loan applications are processed.

based on a different assumed probability distribution for $f(r_l)$. Thus, figure 3-3 assumes bids are normally distributed, figure 3-4 assumes bids are uniformly distributed, and figure 3-5 assumes that bids are distributed by the chi-square distribution having one degree of freedom. In every curve a bank is assumed to be capable of making forty loans.

Figure 3-3 shows three risk-return loci that differ because of variations in (1) the number of loan requests and (2) the relation between the expected value of r_l and r_s. In all three figures, r_s is arbitrarily assigned a value of 5 percent. The difference between the expected value of r_l and r_s is denoted by d in the figures. For a very high threshold value of r_a, a bank will make no loans. Because r_s is known with probability one, the return from a no-loan portfolio is riskless, and it falls on the ordinate.[17]

As the threshold level falls, the corresponding portfolio values of $E(r)$ and σ_r trace out a locus which in turn depends on the assumed number of loan requests, n, and d. When d is the same for two loci, they converge as at point A in figure 3-3. This occurs because with a sufficiently low threshold value, r_a, the probability that a bank will accept the first m loan requests approaches unity. Since the bids are generated by the same distribution, $f(r_l)$, it follows that corresponding loan portfolios should have its mean; their standard deviation equals the distribution standard deviation divided by the square root of m.

The dashed curve in figure 3-3 originates with a very low threshold at point A. At that threshold the bank essentially accepts all loan requests. As the threshold rises, the bank increasingly rejects low bids, but it continues to make m loans with a probability that is only negligibly less than unity for some time. Rejecting low bids produces dual benefits for the bank; the expected return on loans rises, and the variance of portfolio return declines. This "inefficient" span continues up to point C, where the decline in portfolio variance from discarding extreme low values is exactly offset by the rising risk that with such a high threshold the bank will not be able to count on making m loans.[18]

At point C the bank will almost always be fully loaned. As the bank continues to raise its threshold, the expected return rises until a maximum is reached at point D. At point D the expected number of loans accepted by the bank is slightly less than m. In this efficient range risk is rising because the probability of having to hold a significant volume of low-yielding securities is rising.

17. The portfolio rate of return is 4 percent at this intersection because of the assumed reserve requirement of 20 percent. For simplicity, bank capital and its use are ignored throughout this section.

18. For a discussion of portfolio efficiency in the case of quadratic utility functions, see Markowitz [1959, p. 22].

After point *D* further increases in the threshold rate cause the expected return from the portfolio to decline. The incremental improvement in the interest rate on accepted loans associated with a rising threshold is more than offset by the decline in portfolio income associated with the bank placing a larger percentage of its portfolio in low-yielding securities.

The solid curve in figure 3-3 shows how an increase in the number of loan requests, *n*, from 98 to 200 makes a bank better off. Except for very risk-averse banks, which might prefer to hold a portfolio very heavily invested in securities, the opportunity locus available to a bank with more loan requests dominates the locus of a bank receiving few requests.[19]

The dotted curve in figure 3-3 shows how the opportunity locus is affected by having the expected value of $f(r_l)$ exceed the securities interest rate by .5 percent. Point *B* has the same portfolio variance as point *A*, but its associated portfolio rate of return rises by .4 percent. It is interesting that depending upon their objective functions banks have a preference for having either a lower expected return and larger number of bids or the reverse. This in turn appears to be related to the nature of competition in banking markets, but its implications remain to be explored. With the exception of extremely risk-averse banks it appears that bankers will always prefer higher expected values of $f(r_l)$ and more bids.

Figure 3-4 suggests that a similar locus can be constructed for a bank that has a uniform distribution of loan bids. The numerical values differ primarily because, in this example, the assumed variance of the uniform distribution is much larger than in the preceding diagram. The opportunity locus is quite sensitive to variations in the variance of $f(r_l)$. If the variance of $f(r_l)$ were zero, as might be expected in perfectly competitive markets, the locus would collapse to a point.

Figure 3-5 illustrates how sensitive the locus is to higher moments of the distribution $f(r_l)$. The asymmetry of the chi-square distribution leads to a remarkable opportunity locus in which optimal bank portfolios are almost insensitive to the risk aversion in a bank's objective function. The exception again is for banks that are extremely risk averse.[20]

19. The variance associated with an expected return-maximizing portfolio rises with the number of loan requests because as the number rises the average interest rate on accepted loans rises. The risk associated with being incompletely loaned up is an increasing function of the difference between the expected rate of return on accepted loans and the interest rate earned on securities.

20. This result also illustrates why a direct mathematical analysis of this model would have been extremely tedious. At times numerical integration on high-speed digital computers is a most illuminating research approach, even if it lacks soul!

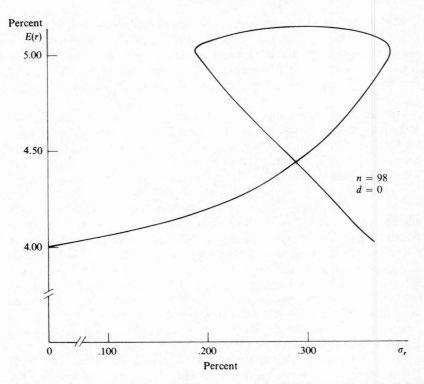

FIGURE 3-4. RISK-RETURN LOCUS FOR A BANK PORTFOLIO: UNIFORMLY DISTRIBUTED
LOAN BIDS

b. Nonzero-penalty rate case

The model here is identical to the preceding one except that banks which adopt a low decision rule value of r_a are likely to have to borrow at an assumed penalty rate of 8 percent at the discount window. Banks are, of course, permitted to retain the interest income from loans that are discounted. Thus, if the expected rate of return on a bank's accepted loans were 6 percent, that bank would pay an effective penalty of 2 percent on the volume of loans in excess of its maximum lending capacity.[21]

21. This discussion suggests why free access to the discount window could be quite inequitable in a world of imperfectly competitive banking markets. For a given $f(r_l)$, a bank with few loan applications would tend to pay a higher effective penalty rate than one with many for exceeding its lending capacity by a given amount. It is also easy to imagine that a hypothetical discount rate would be a penalty rate for one bank and a subsidy rate for another. Rationing credit at the discount window is quite defensible when imperfectly competitive loan markets exist.

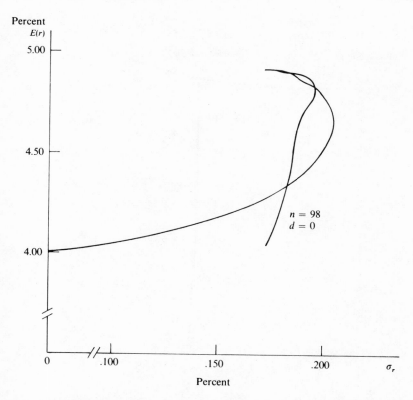

FIGURE 3-5. RISK-RETURN LOCUS FOR A BANK PORTFOLIO: CHI-SQUARE DISTRIBUTED
LOAN BIDS

Figure 3-6 and its detail reproduced in figure 3-7 correspond to figure 3-3 except for the above change. The shape of the locus for $n = 98$ and $d = 0$ is substantially altered by this change for two reasons. First, because banks are assumed to retain interest income from discounted loans, the lower end of the locus has shifted to the left. The horizontal distance between this point and the ordinate has been diminished by a factor of $\sqrt{m/n}$. This reduction in variance of portfolio rate of return is, of course, a consequence of the law of large numbers. Relative to the no-penalty case, the locus in figure 3-6 illustrates that banks will have lower portfolio risk for every value of the threshold, r_a, so long as there exists a possibility that they will have to discount loans. The difference in portfolio risk between the two cases diminishes as the expected number of accepted loans declines toward m.

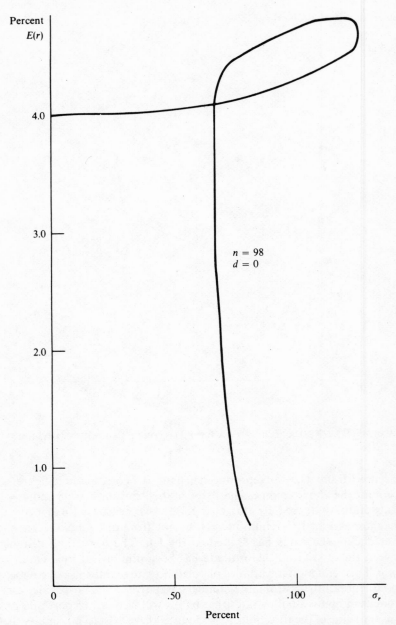

FIGURE 3-6. RISK-RETURN LOCUS FOR A BANK PORTFOLIO WHEN A PENALTY RATE IS
EFFECTIVE: NORMALLY DISTRIBUTED LOAN BIDS

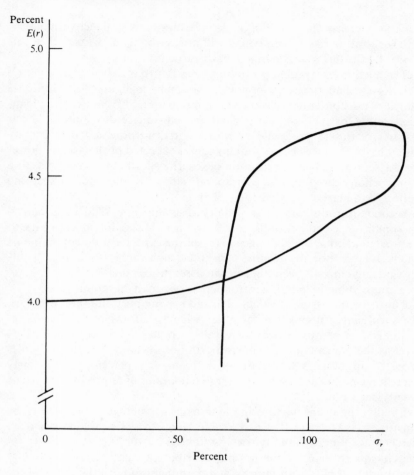

Second, for low values of the threshold rate, the bank's portfolio rate of return is almost zero in this example.[22] The portfolio rate rises monotonically with the threshold because fewer loans are being discounted and because the average rate of return on accepted loans rises. For all but the highest thresholds, a bank's portfolio rate of return is lowered by introducing a penalty rate. The possibility exists with appropriate combinations of $f(r_l)$, r_s, h, n, and m that introduction of a penalty discount rate will

---

22. The minimum rate of return is actually 0.52 percent in this example. For larger values of n it would eventually become negative.

actually increase the value of a risk-averting bank's objective function. Risk-neutral or risk-loving banks will always be made worse off in this model by the introduction of a penalty discount rate.

The maximum expected portfolio rate of return is indicated at point C; it is lower than the corresponding maximum in figure 3-3. Table 3-3 indicates portfolio rates of return for a number of different expected loan-asset ratios for the assumed normal and chi-square distributions. Four features of this table should be noted. First, introduction of a penalty discount rate induces banks that maximize expected profits to seek lower loan-asset ratios. This substitution of securities for loans in response to a rising penalty discount rate corresponds closely to the result concerning perfect loan markets reported in (3.2.5).

Second, introduction of a penalty discount rate reduces a bank's maximum expected portfolio rate of return. The reduction appears to be greater when d, the difference between the expected value of loan bids and r_s, is large. For given values of m and n, high values of d induce profit-maximizing banks to seek higher loan-asset ratios; such banks are, therefore, more vulnerable to the introduction of penalty discount rates.

Third, for the assumed values of m and n, bank portfolio rates of return are surprisingly insensitive to rather wide variations in the loan-asset ratio. This is because the average rate of return on accepted loan bids rises as the percentage of loans in portfolios declines. For the examples reported in table 3-3, variations in loan-asset percentages of thirty percentage points did not affect overall bank rates of return by as much as twenty basis points!

Finally, the profit-maximizing loan-asset percentage is revealed to be sensitive to the form of $f(r_l)$. From table 3-3 it can be seen that maximizing percentages (underscored entries) are about 15 to 20 percent lower for the chi-square than for the normal distribution case.[23] The probability distribution of bids is an important determinant of both the shape of the risk-return locus and the loan-asset ratio that maximizes expected profits.

c. Time consuming inflows of loan requests from imperfect loan markets

Up to this point the time necessary for a bank to invest in earning assets was ignored. The simulations merely describe a bank that has a fixed

---

23. Note that these rather low profit-maximizing loan-asset ratios obtain even when deposits are perfectly predictable.

TABLE 3-3. PORTFOLIO RATES OF RETURN FOR SELECTED LOAN-ASSET RATIOS

Normal Distribution

			Loan-Asset Ratio		
	.83	.75	.68	.61	.54
(a) $n = 98, m = 40, d = 0$					
no penalty	4.717%	4.729%	4.718%	4.691%	4.655%
penalty	4.603	4.691	4.709	4.690	4.655
(b) $n = 98, m = 40, d = 0.5$					
no penalty	5.103	5.096	5.056	4.995	4.925
penalty	5.017	5.067	5.049	4.994	4.925

Chi-Square Distribution

			Loan-Asset Ratio			
	.85	.78	.72	.67	.62	.57
(a) $n = 98, m = 40, d = 0$						
no penalty	4.794%	4.855%	4.891%	4.908%	4.914%	4.913%
penalty	4.653	4.798	4.872	4.903	4.913	4.912
(b) $n = 98, m = 40, d = 0.5$						
no penalty	5.185	5.231	5.246	5.240	5.222	5.198
penalty	5.079	5.189	5.232	5.236	5.221	5.198

NOTE: Underscored figures indicate profit-maximizing percentages.

volume of funds to invest each period in a market with a limited number of loan requests. If the bank has the same volume of funds and loan requests in every period, the solutions are long-run equilibria. However, these timeless solutions are not useful in describing the speed at which banks respond to unanticipated deposit inflows. In this subsection it will be assumed that loan requests arrive at a bank at a regular rate, say two per day, and that bank deposits are random. As before it is convenient to view a bank as maximizing profits over a fixed period; future net income is assumed not to be discounted within this period and totally ignored after it passes. For simplicity loans are assumed to mature after the period passes. In all other respects the regime is the same as that just considered.

There are two cases depending upon whether or not the loan request flow is too sparse relative to a deposit inflow for the bank to expect to reach equilibrium during the planning period. If the flow is sparse, the bank will set its threshold rate equal to the rate it can earn on securities, and, on average, the bank will be observed to acquire loans over the entire period. Such a bank might be observed to attempt to influence the distribution of its incoming bids through advertising and promotion, but this possibility will not be considered further. The bank's actual acquisition path will be random; over a large number of periods it will be observed to acquire loans at roughly a constant rate.

As the flow of bids increases relative to a given deposit inflow, a loan threshold rate that maximizes the rate of return increasingly tends to exceed the rate on securities. For a given threshold rate, a temporary deposit outflow may force the bank into the discount window. If such conditions persist, the bank no doubt would respond by raising its acceptance threshold and/or rationing credit.[24]

Whether or not an adaptive response occurs in the loan threshold acceptance rate, it is clear that bank loans should be observed to respond to deposit shocks with a somewhat irregular lag. Securities should respond to deposit shocks almost instantaneously and should be well explained by a time sequence of deposits. In discussing the model of section 4, there was no reason to think that lagged deposits would describe securities better than loans. The prediction that such a difference may be observed flows from the imperfect loan market model of this section.

---

24. In footnote 13 it was assumed that varying a strategy was prohibitively expensive. This assumption was justified in terms of institutional rigidities associated with coordinating decentralized decision-making organizations. The justification is no less relevant here, but the assumption is relaxed because something must "give" when the environment of a bank changes.

6. Customer Relationships, Endogenous Deposits, Loan Defaults, and Portfolio Adjustment Paths

In the preceding two sections, two distinct and rather intractable models of bank portfolio behavior have been described which suggest how bank portfolios might respond to a deposit injection. Both models suggest that market imperfections are likely to cause bank portfolios to respond to inflows with a pronounced lag. The present section suggests how this pattern is likely to be affected by certain institutional features of contemporary banking markets.

a. The long-term customer relationship

Failure to accept a loan request by a good bank customer may result in a substantial loss of deposits to the bank and, more importantly, a loss of a stream of profitable future loan and service arrangements. A bank or a loan officer must estimate the present value of each loan transaction in the context of this multiperiod relationship. Assuming that such long-term values can be assigned to each loan application, the random loan search approach can be adapted quite directly when long-term customer relationships exist. Instead of maximizing some function of current net income, the bank's objective is to maximize a function of the present value of the bank's relationships. The previously suggested equilibrium and adjustment path properties appear to follow directly from this reformulation. The distribution of the present value of incoming loan offers is admittedly very difficult to imagine; no doubt, the difference between great and mediocre bankers is largely measured by differences in their abilities to place values on relationships and to judge the shape of this distribution.

b. Endogenous deposits

Except for this short digression, it is assumed throughout this monograph that deposits are exogenous to banks. Prior to the emergence of negotiable certificates of deposit, this assumption would have been quite consistent with observable banking practice.[25] The purpose of this

25. This statement is slightly strong, for banks have long had compensating balance arrangements with their customers. However, those balances tend to be idle (nonfluctuating), and as a first approximation it is reasonable to view them as exogenous. Banks expect customers to maintain compensating balances at a certain level over rather long periods of time. Typically a bank does not require borrowers to keep compensating balances precisely at some fraction of a borrower's outstanding loans or line of credit.

digression is to suggest how the models of this chapter are affected when banks bid competitively for deposits.[26]

If funds can be acquired in a competitive market whenever they are required to satisfy needs of nonbank firms and individuals, how will bank portfolio behavior differ from the pattern just described? In a competitive loan market situation, where no customer relationships exist, it is likely that banks will partly adjust to demand deposit inflows (outflows) by selling (acquiring) time funds. Heretofore, all responses to deposit shocks were assumed to occur in securities and loans or at the discount window. Bank assets will tend to be less well described by demand deposit histories as time funds become more endogenous. The decision between liquidating securities and purchasing new time funds will be based to a considerable extent on how individual banks foresee future trends in a large number of interest rates. Interest rate forecasts will probably vary considerably among banks; therefore, it is expected that the ability of economists to describe bank portfolios in the short run will decline as deposits become more endogenous.

In imperfect loan markets profit-maximizing banks will tend to purchase time funds whenever attractive loan bids occur. The relation between time funds and loans should tend to strengthen and be more nearly simultaneous than heretofore.[27] However, it would be very misleading to interpret banks as adjusting loans to deposit inflows; both assets and liabilities will be a function of a large number of unobserved interest rates.

c. Loan defaults

Default risks on loans have been ignored until this point because their relation to portfolio risk is very sensitive to assumptions about the degree of loan indivisibility and the size distribution of loans. Perfect divisibility of loans was assumed in early sections of this chapter. The relation between loan default risk and portfolio risk is not well defined when divisibility is perfect. In the random loan market model, discussion of default risks was postponed in order to facilitate exposition of its basic structure.

26. At the time of the final drafting of this monograph, negotiable certificates of deposit are among the most orthodox vehicles banks have for soliciting new deposits. Recent exotic innovations include repurchase agreements, Eurodollar loans, Virgin Island branch solicitation programs, and one-bank holding company commercial paper sales. In the future exogenous deposit shocks are likely to be increasingly less important determinants of bank portfolios; demand deposits are likely to decline relatively as a source of bank funds.

27. To the extent that time funds are raised through holding companies, which subsequently acquire bank loans, this increasing simultaneity of loan acquisitions and time funds purchases is likely to go unobserved in conventional bank statements. Binding Regulation Q ceilings and other similar nonmarket interferences with bank behavior obscure descriptions of commercial banks as prime financial intermediaries.

Default risks concern the probability of losses of interest and principal owing to borrowers' failure to meet their contractual obligations to a bank and of nonrecoverable costs that the bank must incur when attempting to enforce contractual compliance. The possibility of such losses tends to increase risk in bank portfolios depending upon the fraction of assets held as loans. For illustrative purposes loan defaults will be considered in the context of the imperfect loan market model, in which all loans are assumed to be of equal size.[28] Each loan will be assumed to have an identical probability distribution of losses owing to default. For simplicity, these distributions are assumed to be independent of one another.[29]

Referring to figure 3-3, introduction of loan default risk causes point A to shift southeastward by a distance and direction which depends upon the assumed distribution of default losses. The other end of the locus (which lies on the vertical axis) is not affected by the introduction of loan default risk. Intermediate points like D and C shift less than A; the actual amount of their shift is an increasing function of their associated expected loan volume.

The introduction of loan default risks, then, twists the risk-return locus as suggested in figure 3-8. The portfolio that maximizes a bank's expected rate of return is associated with a lower expected loan-asset ratio when default risks are introduced. Risk-averting banks with quadratic objective functions will hold maximizing portfolios that consist of more securities and fewer loans as loan default risks increase.

7. SUMMARY AND A UNIFORM SET OF NOTATION FOR SUBSEQUENT CHAPTERS

a. Summary

In this chapter a number of distinct models of bank portfolio behavior have been described in an attempt to suggest the relation between bank portfolios and some of their determinants. This piecemeal strategy was adopted because of the considerable complexity of the problem and because the various models do not always build directly upon one another.

Complex or not, all of the models are very pale approximations of the financial institutions studied empirically in later chapters. For example, a

28. The portfolio risks of defaults on large loans are obviously much greater than those on small loans. The amount of credit investigation and other preventives against loan defaults should be observed to rise more than proportionately with the size of the loan.

29. This assumption is in no sense innocuous, a fact familiar to all students of the Great Depression.

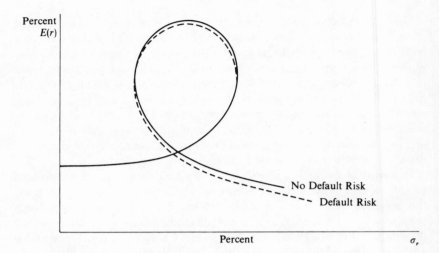

FIGURE 3-8. THE EFFECT OF INTRODUCING LOAN DEFAULT RISK

bank's expectations about nominal market interest rates have been assumed to be stationary. No attempt has been made to model the tax schedules or tax and loan account regulations which are critical for understanding bank security transactions. Bank portfolios were limited to three assets and two liabilities (counting borrowings at the discount window) plus capital. No discussion of branching, merging, holding companies, trust services, and so on appears. The difference between stock and mutually chartered organizations has not been exploited, and implicitly all banks have been viewed to have the same objective function.

On the other hand, collectively the models do incorporate many aspects of contemporary banking that are expected to influence portfolio composition importantly. These include (1) deposit variability and predictability, (2) primary and secondary loan market imperfections, (3) imperfect factor markets, (4) a bank's capital-asset ratio, (5) risk aversion, (6) default risks, (7) bank lending officer capacity, (8) variable loan maturity, (9) discount window policy, and (10) the structure of interest rates. Models have been described that suggest how each of these factors influences bank portfolio behavior. With the exception of the trivial archetypal bank that appears in introductory economics textbooks, all of the models suggest that a bank ordinarily will be observed to hold a diversified portfolio consisting of loans, securities, and cash reserves. The existence of uncertainty is one reason for portfolio diversification, but by no means the only explanation. Imperfect reversibility of assets can lead to a diversified portfolio in a world of perfect certainty.

Considerable emphasis was placed on describing the dynamics of bank portfolio adjustment to an unanticipated change in deposits. This emphasis reflects an underlying belief that market interest rates are not very good estimators of net rates of return that banks actually earn from different assets in the short run. Market interest rates are more likely to be the principal determinants of bank portfolio composition in long-run equilibrium, but few policy decisions will be improved by a knowledge of the very distant future. Bank deposit flows can be strongly influenced by monetary authorities in the short run, and knowledge of the dynamics of bank portfolio adjustments to deposit flows is important for formulating policy.

Market imperfections of various types were considered and in all but pathological cases caused lagged adjustment of portfolios to deposit flows. Because securities were assumed to be traded in more perfect secondary markets than loans, they are expected to respond to deposit flows with shorter lags than loans. Although little mention was made of this, because cash is traded in a more perfect market than securities, it is also likely that securities adjust with a longer lag than cash.

In the present chapter three different arguments were proposed to account for this behavior. First, banks may believe that their deposits are described over time by a high order autoregressive process, in which they ultimately expect to retain only a small fraction of a deposit inflow. Realizing that deposit inflows are largely transitory, they choose to avoid sizable transactions costs by lending only the permanent component of a deposit inflow; other funds are held as cash or securities depending upon the date on which the deposits are expected to be withdrawn.

Second, in a world of imperfect factor markets and of detailed credit analyses that precede loan transactions, banks must consider not only nominal market interest rates, but also their own costs of lending when making portfolio adjustments. Figure 3-9 shows hypothetical net rates of return which a bank realizes from deciding at time zero to order different short-maturity assets for delivery at time t. If a bank unexpectedly receives a deposit inflow, it will maximize profits by holding cash until t_1. At t_1 it will dispose of nonrequired cash and acquire securities; at t_2 it will dispose of securities and acquire loans. Because banks are always responding to shocks, they will be observed to be holding diversified portfolios.

Third, in a world of imperfect loan markets, profit maximizing banks cannot instantaneously place newly received funds in loans at the highest

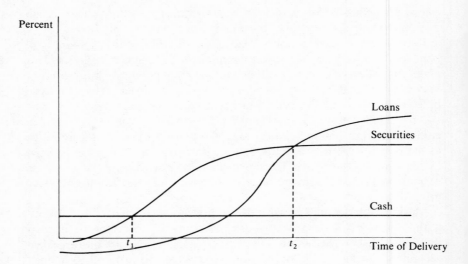

FIGURE 3-9. NET RATES OF RETURN FOR DIFFERENT SHORT-TERM ASSETS

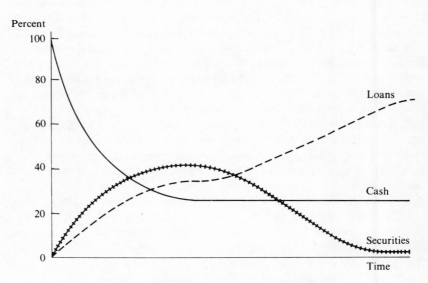

FIGURE 3-10. DYNAMIC PORTFOLIO ADJUSTMENT PATHS

available interest rates. They will hold funds temporarily as securities until they are able to lend to their most valued customers or, alternatively, to place their funds in the most profitable loans.

Each of the three arguments suggests that banks' portfolios will respond to deposit inflows in the manner suggested at the close of chapter 2. Figure 3-10 illustrates the pattern for an assumed deposit injection.

The "cash" curve in figure 3-10 includes both idle free reserves and required reserves. The vertical sum of the three curves in the figure is always unity for the model under discussion because of the balance sheet identity. The pattern of the figure can be approximated algebraically by relating each asset to a time sequence of first differences of a bank's deposits and its capital. This algebraic approximation has the advantage of being able to accommodate an indefinitely large number of assets; it is employed extensively in subsequent chapters.

b. Uniform notation for subsequent chapters

It was not convenient to define a uniform set of notation for the monograph until now. Henceforth, the following symbols have the definitions indicated in table 3-4.

TABLE 3-4. SYMBOL DEFINITIONS

d	the level of a commercial bank's demand deposits on a date or averaged over a specified time interval.
s	the level of a commercial bank's time and savings deposits on a date or averaged over a specified time interval.
m	the level of a mutual savings bank's regular savings deposits on a date.
c	the difference between a bank's total assets and its deposits on a date or that difference averaged over a specified time interval.
a	the level of an asset of a financial institution on a date or averaged over a specified time interval.
z	the total assets of a financial institution on a date or averaged over a specified time interval.
y	the income flow accruing from the portfolio of a bank during some specified time interval.

It is convenient to define some vectors that will be used extensively. Assuming that $\bar{d}_t = d_t - d_{t-1}$, define for the ith bank on the tth date a vector

$$(3.7.1) \qquad \mathbf{D}_{it} = \begin{bmatrix} \dfrac{\bar{d}_{it}}{z_{it}} \\[2ex] \dfrac{\bar{d}_{i,t-1}}{z_{it}} \\[1ex] \vdots \\[1ex] \dfrac{\bar{d}_{i,t-P+2}}{z_{it}} \\[2ex] \dfrac{d_{i,t-P+1}}{z_{it}} \end{bmatrix}.$$

This vector contains $P - 1$ deposit differences and the immediately preceding level of deposits, all divided by a bank's total assets on date t. P is an arbitrary but suitably large number of time periods. The elements in this vector sum to (d_{it}/z_{it}). An exactly corresponding vector exists for a commercial bank's savings and time deposits; it is denoted by $\mathbf{S}_{it}$. An appropriate vector for a mutual savings bank's deposits will be given in chapter 4.

CHAPTER 4

Estimation of the Models: Problems and Techniques

This chapter reports estimation methods used to study the models presented in chapter 3. In section 1 some common problems of macroeconometric estimation are surveyed, with particular reference to recent studies of bank behavior. The discussion suggests that a less aggregative approach might have proven illuminating for those studies. Section 2 considers the effects of aggregation over time and across economic units on the estimated dynamic structure of econometric models. In section 3 a description of statistical procedures for estimating the bank portfolio models is presented. The last section describes a model determining a bank's net income.

1. COMMENTS ON MACROECONOMETRIC STUDIES OF BANK BEHAVIOR

In formulating aggregative theories of bank behavior, economists usually think in terms of decision-making units.[1] Assuming that microtheory is the logical foundation for macro-theory, a method of aggregation is necessary if hypotheses are to be tested at the macro-level. Similarly, if microeconometric studies are to prove useful in macroeconomic applications, a rigorous method of aggregation must be available. Therefore, the choice between using microeconometric estimates or macroeconometric estimates in aggregative studies does not hinge on the feasibility of aggregation.

No doubt the most critical problem with macroeconometric studies is the small number of observations available to investigators. As time passes, moreover, the appropriate specification of a model will change because of varying institutions, technology, regulations, and so on. Therefore, the informational content of available aggregative time series is very limited. Because time-series data are available in such limited quantity, published

1. This section, with minor modifications, is taken from an earlier paper by the authors. Cf. Hester and Pierce [1968].

time series are used repeatedly by the same investigator, and more insidiously by different investigators. Continued experimentation may seriously dissipate the value of data in discriminating among competing models, if researchers respond to "outliers."

The fact that the United States economy has generated values of most economic measures that are highly intercorrelated over time makes the paucity of macroeconomic observations all the more serious. Most macroeconometric equations consist of comparatively few variables. In part this specification follows from the relative simplicity of models. Probably a more important explanation, however, is that estimated standard errors of coefficients are likely to be intolerably large when a number of highly correlated independent variables are included in a regression.

One example of oversimplification in model specification occurs in money supply models. A bank is assumed to be concerned only with the allocation of its assets between excess reserves and total earning assets [Meigs, 1962; Teigen, 1964b]. Borrowing from the Federal Reserve is the principal endogenous liability. In fact, the composition of commercial bank portfolios varies considerably through time. If differences in asset rates of return or liability costs influence bank demand for excess reserves, then parameter estimates of money supply models are suspect.[2]

Another example of the problem is when a number of strongly intercorrelated market interest rates appear in a single equation. How do investigators choose among alternative plausible specifications? A common assumption when building aggregative models is that all assets are gross substitutes. An increase in the expected rate of return on one asset is assumed to induce an investor to hold more of that asset and less of other assets. This assumption is not an obvious conclusion of portfolio theory, but is frequently invoked to judge the acceptability of asset demand equations.

A promising approach to overcoming the effect of multicollinearity in aggregative models is to combine cross-section and time-series estimates of structural parameters.[3] Even if no combination is intended, cross-section studies are especially useful because they permit investigators to identify the relation between cross-section variables like income and cash balances when interest rate and price variables are frozen. The potentially

---

2. For a careful discussion of the microeconomic underpinnings of the aggregate money supply function, see Brunner [1961].

3. An excellent example of the use of cross-section data in an aggregative model to overcome problems of multicollinearity is reported in Tobin [1950].

important effects of bank size, location, and reserve classification on portfolio behavior can best be evaluated with cross-section studies.

An important feature of many recent aggregative models has been the incorporation of dynamic behavior in structural equations. Investigators argue that (1) formation of expectations and/or frictional costs of adjustment are important, and (2) optimal policy implementation must exploit this dynamic structure. Initially, specifications involved lagged endogenous variables and implied that the effects from a shock declined exponentially as time passed [Koyck, 1954]. In recent years more intricate lag operators, which need not incorporate lagged endogenous variables, have attracted many investigators [Almon, 1965; Jorgenson, 1966; Tinsley, 1967].

It is easy to agree that dynamic properties of a model are important for policy formation. However, parameter estimates are biased when lagged endogenous variables are present [Hurwicz, 1950]. Furthermore, conventional statistical tests appear to be very weak in discriminating among different lag operators [Griliches and Wallace, 1965; Griliches, 1967]. Feasible techniques for estimating such operators place a heavier demand on economic theory than presently seems justified.[4]

As indicated in chapter 1, the use of simple distributed lag operators has not produced a clear picture of the lag structure for money supply models. De Leeuw [1965] finds evidence of a long lag between an initial reserve injection and subsequent bank holdings of desired earning assets. His results indicate that banks achieve only 4.6 percent of their total excess reserve adjustment within one quarter and only 27 percent of their total borrowing response within that quarter. On the other hand, Goldfeld [1966, chap. 5] estimated for reserve city banks that there is no lag in adjustment to desired excess reserve positions and that some 40 percent of their total borrowing response is achieved in one quarter. For country banks 60 percent and 30 percent of the total response of excess reserves and borrowing respectively are achieved in the first quarter. De Leeuw and Gramlich [1968] report that banks achieve approximately 30 percent of their total free reserve adjustment in one quarter, much slower than found in another study by Rasche and Shapiro [1968]. Studies by Teigen [1964a, 1964b] and by Rangarajan and Severn [1965], using quarterly and semimonthly data respectively, found no evidence of a lag in the response of the money supply to a permanent change in non-borrowed reserves. Brunner and Meltzer [1964] have not stressed the role of lags in their econometric analyses of the money supply function.

4. Compare Taylor and Wilson [1964], Wallis [1967], and Griliches [1967].

Bryan and Carleton [1967] applied a Koyck distributed lag formulation to models explaining an individual bank's demand for excess reserves and for borrowed reserves. Their estimates, obtained from weekly time series for an individual bank, indicate rapid rates of adjustment by a bank. Bryan [1967] reported the same sort of results for an excess reserve model applied to aggregates of nineteen banks.

Studies of aggregate bank portfolio behavior have generally found long lags in portfolio adjustments. For example, Goldfeld [1966], using a Koyck distributed lag formulation, estimated that banks achieve only 16 percent of their total commercial loan response in the first quarter following a shock. Hendershott [1968] using similar techniques also found slow adjustments of loan portfolios. Bank holdings of United States government securities and municipal securities appear to respond even more slowly than loans [Goldfeld, 1966; de Leeuw, 1965].

This confusing array of results indicates that severe problems are encountered when estimating lag structures from aggregative data. The moral seems clear: "to get better answers to such complicated questions we shall need better data and much larger samples" [Griliches, 1967, p. 45]. This is precisely the reason for utilizing micro-data.

The main check against incorrect inferences in classical statistical theory is the possibility of replicating results from independent evidence. This replication is rarely possible with aggregative data. If theories are capable of being tested with cross-section data, the possibility of establishing a common analytical framework through replication is vastly enhanced.

In chapter 3 the time paths of portfolio adjustments by a bank in response to a deposit shock were predicted to exhibit specific shapes. These relations could be estimated with polynomial approximations developed by Almon [1965], Jorgenson [1966], and Tinsley [1967]. However, in view of the preceding criticisms by Griliches and because available data resources are large, the procedure employed in this monograph is a direct, brute-force estimation of lag structures.

2. TIME AGGREGATION AND THE ESTIMATION OF DYNAMIC SYSTEMS

The previous section dealt with some of the problems that can result from the use of data that are aggregated over economic units. This section discusses problems that can result from the aggregation of data over time—for example, aggregation of monthly data to construct quarterly observations.

Mundlak [1961] and Zellner [1968] have shown that intertemporal aggregation generally will produce misspecification and biased estimates of adjustment coefficients in Koyck distributed lag models. They argue that the average lag in adjustment will typically be overestimated. Bryan [1967] has applied a Koyck lag model to commercial bank micro-data to obtain the kind of results predicted by Mundlak. This application of Koyck's distributed lag model to weekly data summed over nineteen banks produced an estimate of 5.2 weeks as the time required to close 95 percent of the gap between desired and actual excess reserves.[5] For the same group of banks Bryan estimated the lag structure from monthly data and found an interval of 28.7 *months* was required before this gap was similarly closed. These latter results are in accord with some of the macro-estimates discussed in section 1.

Bryan's results must be interpreted with considerable caution for two reasons. First, during the period he studied, city banks had a one-week settlement period with the Federal Reserve, and country banks had a two-week period with no carry-over provisions. His sample of Federal Reserve member banks had to conform with this externally imposed rhythm when making decisions. The reserve period serves to make changes in a bank's excess reserves independent in successive time intervals. When Bryan analyzed monthly changes in excess reserve positions, he was averaging together independent weekly or biweekly observations. This procedure will cause error terms in his regressions to be positively serially correlated, as Working [1960] and Telser [1967a] have argued. If the Koyck distributed lag approach is applied in these circumstances, estimates of lags will be inconsistent and positively biased. The considerable difference in the lags Bryan estimated from weekly and monthly data can be explained at least partially in this manner. The period of observation should correspond to the period of the decision process. Second, it is difficult to draw conclusions for the banking system as a whole from a sample of nineteen banks. Error terms on a particular date for different banks tautologically cannot be independent for all banks in a closed banking system. As one bank adjusts to equilibrium, another bank is automatically shocked into a new disequilibrium. Theoretically a single bank should be able to adjust its cash position quickly in response to deposit inflows, but the banking system may react slowly.[6]

5. The comparable average lag for each bank taken separately was estimated to be 3.2 weeks. Both estimates may be negatively biased, if Bryan's sample banks had a 2-week reserve settlement period. For such banks, a positive reserve position in one week is likely to be matched by a negative position in an adjoining week. This negative serial correlation will produce biased estimates for reasons similar to those discussed in the subsequent paragraph.
6. The complexities of the relationships between individual components and aggregates in a simultaneous dynamic system have been discussed by Allen [1967] and Tucker [1966].

In chapter 12 simulation experiments are described which explicitly allow for the dynamic interaction of banks in a banking system. These experiments indicate that the response pattern of the banking system is not a simple image of the pattern for individual banks. In particular, except under very restrictive assumptions, the banking system adjusts its excess reserves, or any other asset for that matter, much less rapidly than does an individual bank. The dynamic reactions of the banking system do not depend solely upon the portfolio adjustment parameters of individual banks. They also depend upon the saving habits of the non-banking public, the rates at which loans are repaid and securities mature, the magnitude and timing of flows of funds within the system, and the dynamic adjustments of other financial intermediaries in the system. While the simulation results give no evidence that the banking system can adjust its desired excess reserve position within three or four weeks, they do suggest that estimates of lags provided by some macro-studies are much too long.

Macroeconometric studies of bank behavior necessarily describe the behavior of banking systems and not the behavior of an individual bank. While macroeconometric models often do draw on micro-theory to justify equation specifications, micro-theory may not always be a reliable guide. Most microeconomic arguments do not stress that adjustments by one agent will necessarily displace other agents in a closed system.

3. ESTIMATION TECHNIQUES FOR BANK PORTFOLIO MODELS

The models of chapter 3 predict that bank portfolio behavior should be well described by time sequences of a bank's deposits, by interest rates, and by its net worth. Predictability of deposits was also seen to be an important determinant of bank behavior. The approach in this section and in chapters 6 through 9 is to construct two parallel models, an "input-output" model and an "adaptive-expectations" model, which differ depending upon whether banks do or do not attempt to forecast deposits. Both models should have asset adjustment paths similar to those appearing in figure 3-10. Their paths will differ from one another if individual bank deposit forecasting equations are not identical.

In subsections a and b of this section, the input-output models for commercial and mutual savings banks are developed. Subsection c describes a model for predicting deposits. Subsection d outlines the adaptive-expectations model which exploits the forecasting structure of subsection c.

In addition to sequences of deposits, interest rates, and the level of current net worth, the discussion in chapter 2 suggested the existence of bank-specific determinants of portfolio composition. These "bank effects" are assumed to cause additive displacements in asset equations and are attributable to variations in management ability, differences in local loan market conditions, differences in information flows within banks, and differences in the aggressiveness and risk preferences of loan and security officers.[7] In chapter 6 the hypothesis that bank effects do not exist was tested and rejected for the sample of commercial banks. In subsections a and d, which concern commercial bank portfolios, bank effects were removed by measuring all variables about individual bank means. For mutual savings banks, considered in subsection b, all variables have been measured as first differences. This procedure conveniently eliminates additive bank effects.

Throughout the remainder of this chapter, the following subscript conventions will be observed:

Observation characteristic	Subscript	Range
bank	i	$i = 1, \ldots, I$
call report	j	$j = 1, \ldots, J$
asset	k	$k = 1, \ldots, K$
deposit lag	p	$p = 1, \ldots, P$
time	t	$t = 1, \ldots, T$

a. The input-output model for commercial banks

The input-output model for commercial banks can be described using notation defined at the end of the preceding chapter. The share of the ith bank's total assets held as the kth asset on date t is given by a_{ikt}/z_{it}. It is convenient to define an $I \times K$ matrix, $\mathbf{A}_j$, having individual bank asset shares as elements, which exhaustively describes assets in bank portfolios on call report date j. By stacking these matrices, a summary array, $\mathbf{A}$, having $(J \times I) \times K$ elements may be constructed.

Elements in $\mathbf{A}$ are to be explained by time sequences of demand and time deposits and by levels of other liabilities and net worth observed for the I banks on the J call report dates. At the end of chapter 3, two $P \times 1$ deposit vectors, $\mathbf{D}_{it}$ and $\mathbf{S}_{it}$, were defined in order to describe a sequence of first differences and immediately preceding levels of bank i's demand and time deposits, expressed as a fraction of its total assets, as observed on

7. Banks that engage in mergers are also expected to exhibit special behavior; they have been eliminated from the sample. See chapter 5 for details.

date t. It is convenient to construct $P \times I$ arrays, $\mathbf{D}_j$ and $\mathbf{S}_j$, which describe past demand and time deposit sequences for all banks as viewed from call report date j. Horizontally stacking these arrays yields the $P \times (J \times I)$ matrices, $\mathbf{D}$ and $\mathbf{S}$, which are the major components of the commercial bank input-output model.

In order to incorporate other liabilities and net worth in the model, it is convenient to define an $I \times 1$ vector, $\mathbf{C}_t$, with elements, c_{it}/z_{it}. Such vectors for each of J successive call reports can then be collected in a $(J \times I) \times 1$ column vector, $\mathbf{C}$. Note that the row sums of elements in matrix $\mathbf{A}$ must equal unity. Similarly, the sum of corresponding column sums of elements in $\mathbf{D}$ and $\mathbf{S}$ plus the corresponding element in $\mathbf{C}$ must equal unity, because of the balance sheet identity.

Because interest rates and economic conditions vary through time and because bank portfolios are likely to respond to such variations, a set of call report dummy variables is introduced. The hypothesis that individual call report cross sections can be pooled without such an adjustment is rejected in chapter 6. Let $\mathbf{V}$ be a $(J \times I) \times (J - 1)$ matrix as follows:

$$
\mathbf{V} = \begin{bmatrix}
1 & 0 & \cdots & 0 \\
\vdots & \vdots & & \vdots \\
1 & 0 & \cdots & 0 \\
0 & 1 & \cdots & 0 \\
\vdots & \vdots & & \vdots \\
0 & 1 & \cdots & 0 \\
\vdots & \vdots & & \vdots \\
0 & 0 & \cdots & 1 \\
\vdots & \vdots & & \vdots \\
0 & 0 & \cdots & 1 \\
0 & 0 & \cdots & 0 \\
\vdots & \vdots & & \vdots \\
0 & 0 & \cdots & 0
\end{bmatrix}.
$$

One additional array was introduced because it was believed that banks' responses to very substantial deposit shocks might differ from their responses to the modest shocks they usually experience. This modification was introduced when it became apparent that a small number of banks occasionally experienced temporary shocks that caused their demand or time deposits to double or triple within a week. Frequently these shocks were offset within a few weeks by a second shock. It seemed plausible that banks had specific knowledge about such large deposit changes and would, therefore, alter their portfolio allocations to exploit this information. Quite arbitrarily it was assumed that weekly percentage declines in deposits that were more than 20 percent or increases greater than 25 percent were "special."

To account for the unusual character of these large deposit changes in the model, two "overflow" variables, $_df_{it}$ and $_sf_{it}$, were defined for large demand or time deposit changes respectively in the history of the ith bank as viewed from date t. If a bank had experienced no special change in the $P - 1$ weeks preceding a call report, these variables had a value of zero. If the bank experienced a special shock, then a "normal" value, divided by total assets on date t, was assigned to the appropriate element of the $\mathbf{D}_{it}$ or $\mathbf{S}_{it}$ vector, and the remainder of the change, divided by total assets, was assigned to two intermediate "counter" variables.[8] The counter variables continued to be nonzero so long as the observed level of demand or time deposits remained more than 25 percent above or more than 20 percent below the generated normal series. No observations were accepted if either counter variable remained nonzero for more than eight consecutive weeks.[9] If the counter variables were nonzero at the time of a call report, their values were shifted to the corresponding overflow variables. The sum of the two overflow variables was added to the ith bank's value of c_{it}/z_{it} as well, in order to preserve conventional balance sheet identities.

The two overflow variables can be viewed as a 1×2 vector, $\mathbf{F}_{it}$. On any call report the overflow status of all banks can be depicted by an $I \times 2$ matrix, $\mathbf{F}_j$. By stacking these matrices, a summary $(J \times I) \times 2$ matrix, $\mathbf{F}$, is constructed which shows the overflow status of all banks on all call reports.

The input-output model can now be written as

(4.3.1) $$\mathbf{A} = \mathbf{D}'\boldsymbol{\alpha} + \mathbf{S}'\boldsymbol{\beta} + \mathbf{C}\boldsymbol{\gamma} + \mathbf{V}\boldsymbol{\delta} + \mathbf{F}\boldsymbol{\zeta} + \boldsymbol{\varepsilon}$$

where $\boldsymbol{\alpha}, \boldsymbol{\beta}, \boldsymbol{\gamma}, \boldsymbol{\delta}$, and $\boldsymbol{\zeta}$ are $P \times K, P \times K, 1 \times K, (J - 1) \times K$, and

8. The normal series of deposits was generated by taking the level of deposits immediately prior to the shock and adding the average weekly deposit change of the same bank, which was observed during a different period (calendar 1960), to form a new level in each succeeding week.

9. Details of this editing procedure are reported in chapter 5.

$2 \times K$ matrices of coefficients respectively, and ε is a $(J \times I) \times K$ matrix of error terms.

The matrix of error terms is assumed to satisfy the following:

(4.3.2)   (i) $E(\varepsilon_{ij,k}) = 0$ for all i, j, k,

(ii) $E(\varepsilon_{ij,k} \cdot \varepsilon_{\widehat{ij},k}) = 0$ if $ij \neq \widehat{ij}$,

$= \sigma_k^2$ if $ij = \widehat{ij}$, and

(iii) ε is independent of $\mathbf{D}'$, $\mathbf{S}'$, $\mathbf{C}$, $\mathbf{V}$, and $\mathbf{F}$.

The first part of (4.3.2) is required for (4.3.1) not to be misspecified. The second assumption implies that error terms are homoskedastic for each asset studied and that bank call report observations are independent. The latter in turn implies that banks serving a given market do not interact while competing for assets and that they are subjected to independent random shocks.

The third assumption implies that the elements of ε and $\mathbf{D}'$, $\mathbf{S}'$, $\mathbf{C}$, $\mathbf{V}$, and $\mathbf{F}$ are contemporaneously uncorrelated. Subsequent empirical results are likely to be distorted if this assumption is seriously violated; therefore, a rather extended discussion of it is now presented.

Consider one asset, commercial and industrial loans. The covariance of the most recent elements of the $\mathbf{D}'$ matrix with the commercial and industrial loan disturbances could be nonzero for the following reasons:

1. A borrower simultaneously takes out a loan and withdraws funds from a demand deposit account.
2. A bank makes a loan by augmenting a borrower's demand deposit balance.
3. As a consequence of an increase in interest rates, borrowers simultaneously reduce their deposit balances and repay a loan.
4. Interest rates vary across banks so that for some banks interest rates are rising with the outcome of case 3 obtaining, and for other banks interest rates are falling with the negative of case 3 obtaining.

The covariance of the elements of the S′ matrix with the commercial and industrial loan disturbance term could be nonzero if:

5. A bank actively solicited a time deposit in order to make a loan.

The covariance of $\mathbf{C}$ with the commercial and industrial loan disturbance could be nonzero if:

6. Doubtful loans were written off and simultaneously deducted from a bank's reported capital account.

Assumptions stated at the end of chapter 2 are sufficient to exclude cases 4 and 5 from further consideration. All conclusions from any statistical model are of course conditional on the underlying assumptions being satisfied. Case 3 is irrelevant if call report dummy variables are included; then, effectively, all banks face the same interest rates.

Cases 1 and 2 cannot be excluded a priori. If they occur, then the coefficients of very recent deposit inflows in loan regressions are likely to have positive biases. There are good reasons for thinking that the source of bias mentioned in case 2 will be weak. First, the great majority of loans have not been made in recent weeks. Second, when making loans, banks would be foolish to create a deposit for a loan prior to the expected takedown date unless a borrower immediately begins to pay interest on this unused loan. Banks immediately incur a reserve requirement for such deposits. Borrowers, on the other hand, will prefer to pay no interest until they need to use the loan. Together banks and borrowers have established a line-of-credit arrangement that permits the simultaneous creation of loans and takedown of loan balances. For such arrangements there will be no correlation between observed recent deposit changes and bank portfolio composition.[10]

Similarly, to the extent that borrowers must keep compensating balances in proportion to existing lines of credit, there is reason to believe that case 1 also will be a relatively infrequent event. On the other hand, if compensating balances are tied to the use of the credit line, case 1 can be serious. Evidence about compensating balances is not available to evaluate these arguments.

Case 6, which concerns the simultaneous writing off of bad loans and capital, remains to be considered. If this case occurs frequently, then the regression coefficients for capital should be high for assets that are subject to such accounting adjustments. On the other hand, banks holding such assets are likely to have higher than ordinary capital-deposit ratios to protect against possible losses. Therefore, a large regression coefficient on capital for a risky asset is not necessarily evidence that the estimates are biased. Given the anomalies of accounting, it seems safest to assume that any biases attributable to case 6 are relatively unimportant.

To facilitate empirical analysis, "capital" has been defined to include all nondeposit liabilities of a bank as well as the usual accounting measures of net worth. These nondeposit liabilities include certified and officers'

---

10. To interpret a line of credit in terms of the analysis of chapter 3, it is necessary to express a bank's willingness to extend lines of credit as a function of recent deposit inflows. Thus, after a deposit inflow a bank processes new applications for lines of credit and after an economically efficient time span accepts an appropriate amount of new credit lines.

checks, bank mortgages and other liens, rediscounts, acceptances, and other liabilities. To the extent that banks are able simultaneously to adjust those liabilities when determining their asset portfolio, an additional potential source of bias exists. For most banks such liabilities are very minor items in balance sheets with small variances over time. It is assumed that they can be regarded as exogenous.

The validity of this assumption is questionable when banks borrow at the Federal Reserve or in the Federal funds market. Tobin [1959], Polakoff [1960], Meigs [1962], Teigen [1964a, 1964b], and Goldfeld [1966], for example, have argued that banks are likely to run greater risks of visiting the discount window when money market interest rates are high relative to the discount rate. Their argument does not seem to be important in the present study, since call report dummy variables are included. Also, the administration of the discount window by the Federal Reserve effectively precludes banks from actively using discounts as a source of funds. For the banking system as a whole, discounts rarely exceed 0.2 percent of total assets. Federal funds transactions are an insignificant source of funds for all but a few large banks in the sample studied.

The estimated coefficients in chapter 6 will be reviewed critically to see if the suspected biases are present. While this review cannot disprove the presence of biases, it will be seen that the estimates are not inconsistent with a hypothesis that no biases exist.

The preceding discussion has emphasized the relation between loan equation disturbances and independent variables. With less justification, similar questions might be raised about other assets in bank portfolios as well. The empirical analysis is based on the assumption that such questions are of no consequence.

Apart from assumptions about the error terms, four further features about the specification in (4.3.1) should be noticed. The first is a consequence of the balance sheet identity and was discussed in the preceding chapter. The sum of coefficients in rows of α, β, and γ are identically unity. Consequently the row sums of the δ, ζ, and ε matrices are zero.

Second, since the sum of elements in each row of $\mathbf{D'}$, $\mathbf{S'}$, and $\mathbf{C}$ is unity, it is not possible to have an intercept in (4.3.1). In addition, since all variables are measured as deviations from individual bank means, caution must be used when interpreting the magnitudes of individual coefficients. Coefficients in the model are indeterminant if all variables have zero means. To avoid this indeterminancy, all balance sheet variables were augmented by the sample mean during estimation. This procedure serves to normalize the fitted least-squares regressions so that they describe the mean sample bank as it would have been observed on the last call report.

The third feature concerns the choice of the time interval over which elements of D' and S' are to be defined. Deposit data were available in sufficient detail to permit analysis of weekly averages of a bank's close-of-day position. However, a preliminary study suggested that the period of adjustment for a financial institution might be quite long, perhaps a year or more.[11] An empirical specification that kept the degree of "resolution" of the D' and S' arrays at week intervals, therefore, seemed excessive, for it would require that regressions have approximately one hundred variables.

A high degree of resolution is desirable when individual assets are expected to be very sensitive to week-to-week fluctuations in deposits. From figure 3-10 it is apparent that deposit inflows are likely to be held as cash for only a brief interval. Therefore, it will be necessary to get frequent measurements of the most recent deposit changes in order to describe cash holdings with any accuracy. Earlier deposit inflows are likely to affect portfolio composition over a longer time interval and thus can be averaged together without greatly sacrificing efficiency. Therefore, rather arbitrarily, the first three columns of the D' and S' arrays were measured as differences in weekly averages of a bank's daily deposits, the next column was measured as the difference between the fourth preceding week's average deposits and the mean of the fifth through eighth preceding weeks' deposits, and the remaining first-difference terms measure successive earlier changes in a bank's four-week averages of deposits. The final term is the average level of a bank's deposits during the earliest four-week period considered. This convention led to some awkwardness in executing simulation experiments reported in chapter 12, but otherwise proved very practicable in empirical work.[12]

The final feature of expression (4.3.1) requiring elaboration concerns the length of the deposit history that is to be imposed in regressions. As noted in chapter 3, the length of this time period will be a function of a

11. The preliminary study concerned mutual savings banks and appears in a revised form as chapter 7 of the present monograph. See Hester [1965].

12. A minor problem was encountered when merging data files described in the next chapter. Bank portfolio information was collected from call reports, which measure bank assets and liabilities at the close of a particular day. Data on demand and time deposits consisted of weekly averages of daily deposit figures. To synchronize the two files it was necessary to use the averaged demand and time deposit measures for the week enclosing the call report instead of the demand and time deposits appearing on the call report itself. Capital was then defined as total assets on the call report minus the sum of the *averaged* demand and time deposits. All banks studied in chapters 6 and 9 had small discrepancies between call report and averaged deposit measures.

large number of unobserved costs. Because assumptions about the length of the time period cannot be independently tested, a cautious pragmatic approach was adopted. Three time spans—forty-four, forty-eight, and fifty-two weeks—were selected for consideration. An analysis of covariance was then employed to test whether the coefficients on the demand and time deposit levels differed significantly from the corresponding earliest first differences for each of ten major bank asset variables. With the exception of mortgage loans, no coefficients were significantly different from the stock coefficients at the 5 percent level in a two-tailed test for either of the two longer spans. Therefore, it was concluded that a fifty-two week history was adequate for analyzing the input-output model.

It was assumed that the same time span was appropriate for both the time and demand deposit sequences. In chapter 6 it will be seen that the model experiences significant losses of explanatory power for deposit sequences appreciably shorter than forty-four weeks and that these losses will occur in both the demand and time deposit sequences. It will also be seen that mortgage loan coefficients of the earliest first differences do not differ appreciably from the deposit level coefficients.

b. The input-output model for mutual savings banks

When studying mutual savings banks, a modified form of the preceding statistical model was employed in order to test the theory of chapter 3. A different model is desirable because of the nature of available data re-sources and because the observed aggregative savings bank portfolio will be seen not to correspond with predictions flowing from the commercial bank model.

First, data concerning mutual savings bank assets were recorded at monthly intervals, about three times as frequently as those for commercial banks. These relatively frequent measurements permit first differences of assets to be studied as functions of first differences of regular savings bank deposits.[13] This emphasis on flows corresponds more closely to the spirit of the theory than the statistical approach that was dictated by commercial bank data resources. Neither additive bank effects nor ancient portfolio positions can obscure statistical tests of the hypothesis when first differences are studied.

Second, inspection of savings bank balance sheets in table 5-8 suggests that these institutions were substantially out of long-run equilibrium during the sample period. Thus, between January 1959 and December 1963

---

13. Regular savings deposits are the principal liability of mutual savings banks and are briefly discussed in the next chapter.

sample banks placed approximately 100 percent of their change in total assets in mortgage loans, but on the latter date only about 75 percent of their assets were mortgage loans. Therefore, it is not possible to estimate the length of the adjustment process by comparing coefficients for early deposit flows and immediately preceding stocks. However, if it is assumed that the evident disequilibrium was independent of deposit flows, behavioral structures comparable to those of commercial banks may yet be identified.

In specifying the input-output model for savings banks, the notation defined at the end of chapter 3 will again be used. The dollar amount of asset k held by savings bank i at the end of month t is denoted by a_{ikt}.[14] The change in this asset during month t, $a_{ikt} - a_{ik,t-1}$, is $\bar{a}_{ikt}$. An exhaustive description of changes in the portfolio of the ith bank in month t is given by the $1 \times K$ vector, $\bar{\mathbf{A}}_{it}$. Changes in asset portfolios of all savings banks during month t are shown by the $I \times K$ matrix, $\bar{\mathbf{A}}_t$. Finally, stacking such matrices together for a total of T months gives the $(I \times T) \times K$ matrix, $\bar{\mathbf{A}}$, which is to be explained by deposit changes and by changes in savings banks' surplus and miscellaneous other liabilities.

The dollar amount of regular savings deposits held by a bank at the end of month t is m_{it}, and the change in these deposits during the month is $\bar{m}_{it}$. It is postulated that changes in assets are described in part by a sequence of P current and previous monthly changes in regular savings deposits. Let $\bar{\mathbf{M}}_{it}$ be a $1 \times P$ vector of current and past changes in regular savings bank deposits as viewed at the end of month t. Current and past changes in savings deposits at all savings banks on date t are represented by an $I \times P$ matrix, $\bar{\mathbf{M}}_t$; and stacking such arrays together for T periods permits the construction of the $(I \times T) \times P$ array, $\bar{\mathbf{M}}$.

Because changes in the sum of a savings bank's surplus and other minor liabilities are assumed to be accurately forecasted, lagged changes in this sum should not influence the current change in the bank's assets. To represent the contemporaneous value of this sum, recall that total assets of the ith bank at the end of month t is given by z_{it}, and that the change during the tth month is represented by $\bar{z}_{it}$. Then from the balance sheet identity, the change in this sum, $\bar{c}_{it}$, is equal to $\bar{z}_{it} - \bar{m}_{it}$.[15] For all banks, the change in this sum on date t is given by the $I \times 1$ vector $\bar{\mathbf{C}}_t$; and stacking such vectors over T months yields the $(I \times T) \times 1$ vector $\bar{\mathbf{C}}$.

14. The subscript conventions are the same as in the preceding subsection; the limits of subscripted arrays have the same symbol, but their numerical equivalents differ in commercial and savings bank specifications.

15. In empirical work $\bar{c}_{it}$ was compiled independently from savings bank balance sheets in order that the balance sheet identity could be used to verify that data were accurately recorded.

The input-output model as applied to mutual savings banks can now be specified formally as

(4.3.3) $$\overline{A} = \alpha + \overline{M}\beta + \overline{C}\gamma + \varepsilon$$

where α, β, and γ are, respectively, $1 \times K$, $P \times K$, and $1 \times K$ matrices of coefficients, and ε is a $(T \times I) \times K$ matrix of error terms. (It is understood that α is premultiplied by a $(T \times I) \times 1$ vector of ones.)

The balance sheet identity constrains the sum of coefficients in the first row of β and the column sum of elements in γ each to equal unity. The same identity constrains the remaining row sums of β and the column sum of elements in α to equal zero. Row sums of ε also equal zero.

The elements of β and γ matrices have interpretations that correspond closely to their counterparts in the preceding subsection. If savings banks can accurately forecast changes in capital and nonregular savings deposit liabilities P periods in advance, then elements of γ have identical interpretations in the commercial and mutual savings bank models. Elements of the β matrix for mutual savings banks correspond to first differences of successive column elements in the β matrix for commercial banks.

The elements of α should be interpreted as measuring the average within-month change in the typical savings bank's equilibrium portfolio. The inclusion of this disequilibrium intercept variable represents a crude attempt to allow for the aforementioned nonstationarity in mutual savings bank portfolios during the period studied. It permits this non-stationarity to occur independently of deposit changes; the coefficients have no meaning outside the period for which they have been estimated.

The matrix of error terms is assumed to exhibit the same properties that were stated in (4.3.2). Perhaps the weakest assumption in the case of savings banks concerns homoskedasticity of error terms in a least-squares regression for an asset. If banks were arrayed in order of increasing total assets, error terms would tend to exhibit heteroskedasticity. Nevertheless, variables were not deflated by total assets because (1) available samples are very large, (2) there is reason to believe that the standard deviation of error terms is not proportional to a bank's total assets, and (3) improper deflation can impair the quality of estimates [Meyer and Kuh, Appendix C, 1957].

Measurement of mutual savings bank dependent variables is less satisfactory for studying the input-output model than was the case for commercial banks. Measurement errors in dependent variables which stem from reporting errors and from accounting conventions that value assets at cost rather than at market are quite insidious. The market values of long-term government securities and insured mortgage loans may bear a weak relation to their recorded book values. Because regular savings deposits are measured quite accurately, the balance sheet identity transfers these dependent variable inaccuracies directly to the **C** vector. Therefore, all estimated coefficients should be interpreted cautiously. A similar error may occur in the case of commercial banks, but it is likely to be much less serious owing to the short maturity of most commercial bank assets.

Aggregation losses are more serious for the mutual savings bank sample than for commercial banks because savings bank data are not available in great detail. For example, data about all United States government securities are reported in a single entry; no doubt, maturities and yields differ considerably across banks. Similarly, mortgage loans include federally guaranteed loans purchased in the national market as well as locally originated conventional loans; these two components are likely to differ considerably in risk and expected return. Consequently, the interpretation of coefficient estimates is somewhat impaired.

Three other differences should be noted when comparing commercial and savings bank results for the input-output model. First, no time dummy variables, corresponding to call report dummy variables, were introduced to allow for intertemporal variations in market interest rates. This tack was followed because otherwise it would have been necessary to estimate some forty additional coefficients in each regression. Interpretation of those additional coefficients would have represented a formidable undertaking. Instead, a series of plots of summed residuals for each of a number of subsamples of banks against time were produced; they suggested that no very regular or easily interpretable pattern existed. Some of these plots are reproduced in chapter 7. In principle, both seasonal fluctuations and shifts in desired portfolio composition attributable to interest rate movements should have been evident. Because these patterns were not apparent, the adopted procedure seemed relatively costless.

Second, because no large shocks were evident in time series of deposits at individual savings banks, no smoothing was necessary. Therefore, no overflow variables appear in (4.3.3).

Third, mutual savings banks are state-chartered institutions, and regulations for these banks differ markedly among states. In addition, savings banks operating in New York City are very large relative to those serving other areas of New York State. To avoid interbank variations attributable to differing regulation standards and scale, at the outset it was decided that the structure should be separately estimated for four subsamples of savings banks which were defined by bank location. The basis for this decision is further explained at the end of chapter 5. This procedure tends to insure that banks in any sample studied are relatively homogeneous and faced similar market conditions.

c. Deposit forecasting models

The discussion in chapters 2 and 3 suggested that forecasting of future deposits by banks was likely to be observed if relatively inexpensive techniques could be developed. It was hypothesized that simple auto-regressive models would describe sequences of an individual bank's demand and time or savings deposits with some accuracy. Parameter estimates for these models are reported in chapter 8; the underlying statistical model is described here. Forecasting equations will be estimated for each commercial and mutual savings bank studied in chapters 6 and 7.

The principal reasons for studying autoregressive deposit structures are the hypotheses (1) that such structures vary among banks and (2) that individual bank portfolio behavior can be better described by exploiting this fact. The first hypothesis is not formally tested because it would have entailed an extremely expensive series of computer runs. However, both visual inspection of summary results reported in chapter 8 and the accompanying text should convince readers that substantial differences exist among sample banks. The second hypothesis is the subject of chapter 9. If differences did not exist, the adaptive-expectations model would not be interesting, because it would not be distinguishable from the input-output formulation just considered.

After time series of deposits at a bank were smoothed to eliminate the aforementioned large shocks, each commercial bank was assumed to view first differences in weekly averages of its demand and time deposits, $\bar{d}_{it}$ and $\bar{s}_{it}$, as being generated by a stationary process.[16] Similarly, a mutual savings bank was assumed to view monthly changes in its regular savings deposits, $\bar{m}_{it}$, as being generated by a stationary process. How should such processes be modeled? In the absence of reliable information about the autoregressive deposit structure at individual banks, the following procedures were adopted. First, each of the three categories of bank deposits was assumed to be described by a different process. Second, to avoid prohibitive computing costs, the specification of lags in the auto-

---

16. Because large shocks are likely to distort estimates of the autoregressive structures severely and because banks are very unlikely to view such shocks in the same way as smaller shocks, it seemed best to smooth deposit series before estimating the autoregressive structure. A detailed discussion of the smoothing procedure appears in the first section of chapter 8.

regressive process for a given category of deposits was assumed to be the same at all banks. Third, in addition to various lagged deposit changes, each process was assumed to have a trend (intercept) and a seasonal component. The latter was estimated by including in the specification the change in a bank's deposits in a week or month exactly one year previous to the deposit change being described—that is, $\bar{d}_{t-52}, \bar{s}_{t-52}$, or $\bar{m}_{t-12}$. Fourth, the remainder of the specification of lags was determined experimentally using small pilot samples of commercial and mutual savings banks. The experiments are described in chapter 8.

The models which were adopted are summarized as follows:

$$\bar{d}_t = \theta_0 + \sum_{\tau=1}^{T} \theta_\tau \bar{d}_{t-\tau} + \theta_{52} \bar{d}_{t-52} + \varepsilon_t, \qquad \tau \neq 52,$$

(4.3.4)
$$\bar{s}_t = \varphi_0 + \sum_{\tau=1}^{W} \varphi_\tau \bar{s}_{t-\tau} + \varphi_{52} \bar{s}_{t-52} + v_t, \qquad \tau \neq 52,$$

and

$$\bar{m}_t = \psi_0 + \sum_{\tau=1}^{U} \psi_\tau \bar{m}_{t-\tau} + \psi_{12} \bar{m}_{t-12} + \mu_t, \qquad \tau \neq 12,$$

where the i subscript has been suppressed for ease of reading, the ~ underscore indicates that the variable may have been smoothed, and ε_t, v_t, and μ_t are generated by independent white noise processes.

The discussion in section 4 of chapter 2 suggests that, with the exception of θ_0 and θ_{52}, coefficients in the demand deposit equation should be predominantly negative. This expectation is based on the premise that depositors will seek to avoid incurring opportunity costs of holding idle balances; therefore, a deposit inflow will be associated with a succeeding sequence of deposit outflows. Coefficients on the most recent lagged deposit changes are expected to be the largest in absolute value, because a depositor's opportunity cost is an increasing function of the period over which funds are held idle. Some positive coefficients, relating to more distant deposit changes, may be observed for individual banks; they are likely to correspond to regular credit rhythms at monthly and quarterly periodicities and are analogous to seasonals. No corresponding a priori predictions exist for comparable parameters in time and savings deposit equations.

The seasonal coefficients, θ_{52}, φ_{52}, and ψ_{12}, are probably the least satisfactory elements of the autoregressive equations. To conserve the number of parameters reported (but not degrees of freedom) they were chosen in preference to a series of dummy variables. The very short length of the time series for each bank would have made dummy variable coefficients very unreliable and made the application of spectral techniques unpromising. The year-ago weekly change variables were adjusted to reflect the movements of dates relative to weeks between successive calendar years, but no effort was made to adjust for irregular calendar variations such as the date of Easter.[17] Therefore, as in most econometric investigations, seasonal factors are removed quite imperfectly.

d. Adaptive-expectations portfolio models

i. Commercial banks: The adaptive-expectations model of bank portfolio behavior exploits the deposit forecasting structure just described and uses resulting vectors of deposit forecasts in place of observed deposits in a variation on the earlier described input-output model. To describe the approach, let $\overline{d}_{it}^{t-1}$ be the forecast of the change in the ith bank's demand deposits in week t as constructed at the end of week $t - 1$. The recursiveness of the autoregressive forecasting equations permits forecasts of the deposit change in week t to be made from a number of earlier dates as well. For example,

$$(4.3.5) \qquad \overline{d}_{it}^{t-2} = \theta_0 + \theta_1 \overline{d}_{i,t-1}^{t-2} + \sum_{\tau=2}^{T} \theta_\tau \overline{d}_{i,t-\tau} + \theta_{52} \overline{d}_{i,t-52}.$$

A forecast change in the ith bank's demand deposits during some period can be converted to a forecast level at the end of that period in an obvious fashion. Now, define a $1 \times P$ vector, $_f\mathbf{D}_{it}$, which is analogous to the vector $\mathbf{D}_{it}$ introduced at the close of chapter 3. Specifically, $_f\mathbf{D}_{it}$ describes the forecast of the ith bank's demand deposit level at the end of period t which was made at the end of period $t - P + 1$ and successive revisions of that forecast, all deflated by the total assets of the bank at the end of period t, z_{it}. In symbols,

$$(4.3.6) \qquad {}_f\mathbf{D}_{it}' = \begin{bmatrix} (d_{it} - d_{it}^{t-1})/z_{it} \\ (d_{it}^{t-1} - d_{it}^{t-2})/z_{it} \\ \vdots \\ (d_{it}^{t-P+2} - d_{it}^{t-P+1})/z_{it} \\ d_{it}^{t-P+1}/z_{it} \end{bmatrix}.$$

17. Specifically, if the week of April 5–11, 1962, were being studied, then a synthetic seasonal weekly change was constructed from the two observed weekly changes in 1961 containing these same dates; each change was weighted by the percentage of dates that overlapped the dates in the 1962 week.

An exactly analogous $P \times 1$ vector, $_fS_{it}$, can be defined for a commercial bank's time and savings deposits. As in the case of the input-output presentation, these vectors can be horizontally stacked to produce $P \times I$ matrices, $_fD_t$ and $_fS_t$, which summarize all forecasts of banks' deposits at the end of period t; and further horizontally stacked across call reports to obtain the $P \times (J \times I)$ matrices, $_fD$ and $_fS$.

The sum of a bank's capital and nondeposit liabilities, expressed as a fraction of the bank's total assets, $_fc_{ij}/z_{ij}$, is obtained by taking the sum of column sums of $_fD_{ij}$ and $_fS_{ij}$ and subtracting this fraction from unity. If no deposit smoothing occurs, $_fc_{ij}$ exactly equals c_{ij}, which appears in the input-output formulation. As in that model, the value of $_fc_{ij}/z_{ij}$ for all banks on the jth call report can be depicted in an $I \times 1$ vector, $_fC_j$, and stacking such vectors for different call reports yields the $(I \times J) \times 1$ vector $_fC$.

Using the previously defined $(J \times I) \times (J - 1)$ matrix of call report dummy variables, V, it is now possible to state the adaptive-expectations model formally as

(4.3.7) $$A = {_f}D'\alpha + {_f}S'\beta + {_f}C\gamma + V\delta + \varepsilon$$

where α, β, γ, and δ are respectively $P \times K, P \times K, 1 \times K$ and $(J - 1) \times K$ matrices of coefficients, and ε is a $(J \times I) \times K$ matrix of error terms.

A difference between the input-output model and the adaptive-expectations version is that in the latter all variations in a bank's total deposits, apart from smoothed demand and time deposits, are assumed to be foreseen. Therefore, no overflow variables appear in (4.3.7). This restriction was imposed because the model is intended to describe the behavior of actual banks, and there was no interview evidence that banks had any model to predict such quantities recursively. No doubt, bankers had some independent information about large shocks, but this information was not available to outside investigators. Omitting special overflow variables tends to handicap the adaptive-expectations version in comparisons with the input-output model.[18]

Again, the matrix of error terms is assumed to exhibit properties that were stated in (4.3.2). This assumption appears to be stronger than was the case for the input-output model, and correspondingly less likely to be satisfied, because of the probable presence of "measurement" errors in the forecasted variables. Forecasts that a bank generates for its own internal use are likely to differ from those flowing from the autoregressive-forecasting equations used in this study. The severity of the problem cannot be

18. The handicap is probably of little consequence. Coefficients and the total fit of the input-output model were only slightly affected when overflow variables were suppressed.

evaluated in the absence of information about the magnitude of measurement errors and about the correlations between measurement errors and
disturbance terms.

This unfortunate state of affairs does not imply that the adaptive-
expectations model should be rejected out of hand, for two reasons. First,
the econometric literature contains many studies that exploit simple
expectations models. Often these models have less complete theoretical
justifications than that reported for the model in the preceding subsection,
and frequently they are estimated with many fewer observations. Analysis
of the adaptive-expectations model may convey some feeling for how much
confidence should be placed in those studies.

Second, if banks do forecast future deposits and if forecasting equations
differ among banks, then the adaptive-expectations formulation may yet
produce better descriptions of bank portfolio behavior than the naïve
(and in this case misspecified) input-output model. The compounding
of structural hypotheses produces many slips between cup and lip, but
more water may be consumed than through a leaky straw!

ii. Mutual savings banks: A sequence of deposit forecasts, analogous to
that suggested in (4.3.4) and (4.3.5), is produced for each mutual savings
bank. Because no smoothing was necessary for savings bank deposits,
the same capital and residual liabilities variable as was used in (4.3.3) is
employed in the adaptive-expectations model.

For an individual savings bank, let

$$(4.3.8) \qquad {}_f\overline{\mathbf{M}}'_{it} = \begin{bmatrix} \overline{m}_{it}^{t-1} \\ \overline{m}_{it}^{t-2} \\ \vdots \\ \overline{m}_{it}^{t-P+1} \end{bmatrix}.$$

Then by exact analogy to the earlier input-output version, (4.3.3), the
adaptive-expectations model for a number of mutual savings banks is

$$(4.3.9) \qquad \overline{\mathbf{A}} = \alpha + {}_f\overline{\mathbf{M}}\beta + \overline{\mathbf{C}}\gamma + \varepsilon$$

where α, β, and γ are $1 \times K$, $P \times K$, and $1 \times K$ matrices of coefficients,
respectively, and ε is an $(I \times T) \times K$ matrix of error terms.

The qualifications for the mutual savings bank adaptive-expectations
model are the same as for the commercial bank model and will not be
repeated. It is important to recall that there is less reason to expect that
the autoregressive forecasting structure will be very informative for

mutual savings banks. Therefore, the adaptive-expectations model is less likely to be successful for mutual savings banks than for commercial banks.

4. EMPIRICAL MODELS TO DETERMINE BANK INCOME FLOWS

In chapter 2 a bank's net income was assumed to be a prime argument in its objective function. In chapter 10 four measures of commercial bank income are studied empirically in considerable detail. The statistical model underlying this empirical analysis is developed in the present section.

The four measures are (1) gross operating income, (2) net current operating income, (3) net income before corporate income taxes, and (4) net income after corporate income taxes. All measures refer to one calendar year. Explanatory variables are weighted averages of balance sheet variables constructed from a bank's call reports in the year of the income statement.

Gross operating income is the sum of interest and discount, dividends, service charges, and miscellaneous residual operating income that the bank receives in a year. This variable approximately measures the value of the services a bank sells in a year. *Net current operating income* is the difference between gross operating income and operating costs. Principal operating costs include wages, salaries, employee benefits, interest paid on deposits, costs of goods and services purchased by the bank, and occupancy expenses.

Net income before taxes differs from net operating income because the sum of charge-offs and recoveries from bad investments and capital losses and gains in trading assets is typically nonzero. Decisions to realize losses, modify loss reserves, or charge off bad debts are somewhat arbitrary depending upon individual bank accounting conventions and management decisions to reveal losses or gains.

Because of progressivity in the corporate tax rate structure, because of specific source-oriented taxation of capital gains income and exemption of interest income from state and local government securities, and because of the possibility of tax carry-forwards and carry-backs, the relation between net income before and after taxes is likely to be loose in the sample to be studied. *Net income after taxes* is the income measure most likely to appear in a bank's objective function, for it corresponds to the return to owners of the bank.

The statistical model for explaining interbank variations in these income measures is best characterized as least-squares cost accounting. It has been successfully applied previously in the transportation industry [Meyer and

Kraft, 1961] and to commercial bank samples from India [Hester, 1964] and the United States [Hester and Zoellner, 1966].

The fundamental hypothesis underlying this section is that (1) rates of return for assets are positive and vary across assets and (2) rates of return for liabilities are negative (usually) and vary across liabilities. If this hypothesis is correct and if individual banks have balance sheets that are not merely scalar multiples of each other, then variations in bank portfolios should explain variations in bank earnings. An important by-product of this exercise will be estimates of unobservable rates of return that banks realize from the assets and liabilities studied.

It is convenient to define a 1×4 vector, $\mathbf{Y}_{it}$, which measures the ith bank's annual gross operating income, net operating income, net income before taxes, and net income after taxes as a fraction of year-end total assets in year t. The corresponding income measures for a sample of I banks can be described by stacking these vectors to form an $I \times 4$ matrix, $\mathbf{Y}_t$. Similarly, these income measures can be represented for the I banks in T different years by an $(I \times T) \times 4$ matrix, $\mathbf{Y}$.

During year t, the ith bank can be viewed as having K_1 assets, exclusive of till cash, cash items in process of collection, and Federal Reserve Bank deposits; the average value of each during the year is represented by a_{itk}. The ith bank is also viewed as having K_2 liabilities, exclusive of its capital account during year t; the average value of each during the year is given by l_{itk}. It is convenient to define a $1 \times (K_1 + K_2)$ vector, $\mathbf{L}_{it}$, as follows:

$$(4.4.1) \qquad \mathbf{L}_{it} = [a_{it,1}/z_{it}, \ldots, a_{it,K_1}/z_{it}, l_{it,1}/z_{it} \ldots l_{it,K_2}/z_{it}],$$

where z_{it} is the total assets of bank i at the end of year t.

Stacking these vectors for a sample of I banks existing in year t produces an $I \times (K_1 + K_2)$ matrix $\mathbf{L}_t$; and stacking observations for T different years together yields the $(I \times T) \times (K_1 + K_2)$ matrix, $\mathbf{L}$.

Finally, to allow for the possibility of economies of scale in banking, the reciprocal of the ith bank's total assets at the end of year t, z_{it}^{-1}, was introduced. To avoid inelegant notation, this variable has been renamed r_{it}. The values of this variable at the end of year t for a sample of I banks can be described by an $I \times 1$ vector $\mathbf{R}_t$. Stacking these for T years allows the $(I \times T) \times 1$ vector $\mathbf{R}$ to be constructed.

The model of bank income can now be formally represented as

$$(4.4.2) \qquad\qquad \mathbf{Y} = \mathbf{L}\xi + \mathbf{R}\omega + \varepsilon,$$

where ξ and ω are, respectively, $(K_1 + K_2) \times 4$ and 1×4 matrices of coefficients, and ε is an $(I \times T) \times 4$ matrix of disturbances.

Elements in the ε matrix are assumed to have expected values of zero. The covariance between different elements in any column of ε is assumed to be zero, while the covariance between elements in any row of ε is likely to be positive. For any measure of income, error terms are assumed to be homoskedastic and independent of balance sheet variables.

The ω vector corresponds to intercepts in the undeflated version of (4.4.2). It measures income flows to banks that are unrelated to balance sheet items. The value of its first element, which is from the gross operating income regression, is expected to be positive. The existence of bank income from trust departments, underwriting, safe deposit facilities, traveler's checks, and so on is the basis for this expectation. Because overhead expenses and operating expenses for electricity, advertising, and officers' salaries, which cannot be uniquely associated with asset or liability variables, may offset these inflows, other coefficients of ω may be either positive or negative. These latter coefficients are important for evaluating whether banks have economies of scale.[19]

Coefficients of the ξ matrix are expected to be positive for bank asset variables in all four regressions. Almost tautologically, an asset is a stock that produces a positive expected rate of return; therefore, asset coefficients should be positive. In the gross operating income regression, asset coefficients should approximately equal market rates of return. For net operating income, the coefficients are estimates of the net rate of return that banks realize from holding an asset, after deducting directly associated operating expenses. Because such costs are believed to be quantitatively important, it is expected that net rates of return from an asset will be less than observed market rates. The difference between the two estimated rates is, of course, a measure of the operating costs associated with servicing that particular asset.

An asset's net income before-tax coefficient and its net operating income coefficient should differ because of losses, recoveries, and changes in loss reserves associated with the asset; the difference may be positive or negative in a year, depending upon the magnitudes of these adjustments. Examination of this difference in a number of different years should roughly suggest loss experiences of sample banks for each asset; this interpretation is rough because loss and loss reserve adjustments are little more than arbitrary decisions by accountants and bank management.

Finally, after-tax asset coefficients should be smaller absolutely than coefficients associated with the other three income measures. The interpretation of after-tax coefficients is somewhat ambiguous because they depend

19. For a discussion of the relation between these coefficients and scale economies, see Hester and Zoellner [1966, pp. 378–83] and Hester [1967b].

upon the proportion of sample banks choosing to realize capital gains and losses in different years. The coefficient on tax exempt securities should be quite similar in before- and after-tax regressions.

Coefficients of liability variables should also be positive, but small, in the gross operating income regression. Banks typically impose small service charges on demand deposit accounts and various nondeposit liabilities. In the case of time deposits, the gross operating income coefficient is not expected to differ significantly from zero.

In regression equations for other income variables, liabilities are expected to have negative coefficients. Banks incur substantial accounting, public relations, transactions, and interest costs when compensating creditors for the use of their funds. Little difference is expected in a liability's coefficient in the net operating income and net income before-tax regressions because the accounting adjustments that distinguish these income measures are oriented toward assets, not liabilities. After-tax regression coefficients for liabilities should be smaller than corresponding net income coefficients by a factor that reflects the mean bank corporate income tax rate.

Elements of the ξ matrix are to be interpreted as marginal rates of return (cost) that banks experience.[20] They are interesting only (1) if all a bank's liabilities and noncash assets appear in numerators on the right-hand side of expression (4.4.2) and (2) if banks experience no direct income or costs from omitted asset variables and capital accounts. The estimated marginal rates are likely to differ from those obtained from more conventional accounting procedures because the criteria for allocating costs and revenues differ.[21] Intertemporal variations in elements of the ξ matrix may suggest the role of interest rates in transmitting monetary policy. In chapter 10 an analysis of covariance is employed to test the hypothesis that realized interest rates were constant during the sample years, 1960–1963.

Gross and net operating income measures are expected to be more closely related to portfolio composition than other income measures because they are free from arbitrary charge-off and transfer-to-reserve decisions. However, there are reasons to expect that even in these re-

20. Readers should be cautious in attempting to interpret these rates as shadow prices. It is possible that no bank could acquire or dispose of an asset bearing the rate of return estimated in chapter 10. Moreover, asset-liability combinations may not be attainable if they are very different from the set of observed portfolios. Finally, swapping assets may cause a bank to have associated changes in its liability structure through compensating balance arrangements and, more importantly, may produce indirect changes in the bank's total assets.

21. See, for example, the functional cost analyses published by the Boston Federal Reserve Bank [Federal Reserve Bank of Boston, 1960–62].

gressions the stochastic terms will be quite large for some banks. First, some categories of assets, for example, commercial and industrial loans, will not be homogeneous across banks. Second, some long-term assets, for example, mortgage loans, may have been acquired many years previously when interest rates were distinctly lower than in the sample period. Third, some assets such as United States government bonds are recorded at par rather than at market values. Others are likely to have been recorded at cost rather than market. In principle, the procedure requires that all assets be recorded at market values. Finally, the arguments of the preceding two chapters suggest that bank costs should be quite sensitive to the rate of change of bank assets, not just asset proportions. This and other questions about bank income flows are studied intensively in chapters 10 and 11, in part by examining estimated residuals of (4.4.2).

No intercept is included in (4.4.2); an intercept would imply the existence of income that is linearly related to bank size, but not related to portfolio composition. In principle, such income can flow from unobserved subsidiary bank activities such as underwriting and trust fund management. However, inclusion of an intercept makes the interpretation of estimated interest rates somewhat ambiguous. On balance, it was decided that the loss of information from suppressing intercepts was less serious than the loss resulting from the ambiguity associated with their inclusion. Intercepts were estimated for all regressions reported in chapter 10; when significant, the relations are often reported both with and without intercepts.

This discussion of the specification is incomplete in two important respects. First, to what extent should balance sheet measures be disaggregated when estimating coefficients of (4.4.2)? This question will be answered empirically by applying analysis of covariance techniques. Demand deposits, loans, and United States government securities are studied at different levels of aggregation in chapter 10.

Second, why should various income measures be linearly related to bank assets and liabilities? Linearity should be expected if (1) a bank does not influence the interest rates at which it borrows or lends by varying its own portfolio mix and (2) the percentage of a bank's resources held as any asset is not related to variations in interest rates across banking markets. The random loan search argument of chapters 2 and 3 appears to be inconsistent with the first of these conditions. A bank that insists upon a fairly high loan threshold interest rate is likely to have a relatively low percentage of its portfolio in loans. In a cross section of banks that face similar markets with different threshold interest rates, an inverse relation should be observed between the loan rate of interest and the percentage of a bank's portfolio in loans. In these circumstances the statistical cost accounting model will produce estimated loan interest rates that are negatively biased.

On the other hand, most discussions of portfolio selection suggest that the second of these two conditions will be violated; banks are crudely viewed as desiring to place high percentages of their portfolios in high net return assets. If they are correct, then the statistical cost accounting procedure would tend to produce estimated loan interest rates that are positively biased. If assets are not gross substitutes, this bias need not be positive.

Neither bias is likely to be very pronounced because competition, albeit imperfect, will tend to prevent interest rate differentials from being very important for long periods of time. Variations in bank portfolios are more likely to reflect differences in portfolio preferences by individual banks than variations in asset markets. It is believed that nonlinearities are of negligible importance in chapter 10.[22]

22. We are indebted to William Brainard for comments about these nonlinearities.

CHAPTER 5

Data Resources, Sample Selection, and the Profile of a Typical Observation

Empirical evaluation of the relationships hypothesized in preceding chapters will be performed by studying large rectangular arrays of data from individual bank balance sheets and income statements. To study the effects of interest rates and other time-varying influences on portfolio composition, it is necessary to have a large number of observations of individual banks at each of a number of points in time.

Commercial and mutual savings bank data have been exhaustively verified and cross checked for use in this monograph. The first section of this chapter describes (a) available commercial bank data, (b) the criteria and details of sample selection, and (c) the profile of a typical commercial bank. The second section reports similar information about the mutual savings bank sample.

1. COMMERCIAL BANKS

Large volumes of data about commercial banks are regularly tabulated by the Board of Governors of the Federal Reserve System, individual Federal Reserve Banks, the Comptroller of the Currency, the Federal Deposit Insurance Corporation, the Securities and Exchange Commission, and state banking commissioners in each of the states and territories that charter banks. Apart from annual reports to stockholders and required disclosure of some parts of call reports, these data are confidential and not ordinarily available to investigators.

Of these agencies, the Board of Governors of the Federal Reserve System and individual Federal Reserve Banks have the greatest interest in collecting information necessary for studying the models specified in earlier chapters. In 1964 the present writers, then at Yale University, applied to the Board of Governors for permission to study confidential individual bank data which are collected in (1) call reports, (2) year-end income and dividends reports, and (3) Federal Reserve Bank daily reports of deposits and currency and coin. The first two of these reports are available to supervisory agencies, while the last is used by Federal Reserve Banks to determine a commercial bank's required reserves.

The Board favorably responded to this request subject to the conditions that (*a*) the data be used for no other purpose than the present study, (*b*) no attempt be made to violate the confidentiality of these data, and (*c*) the data be accepted in an intricately coded form designed to preserve their confidentiality. Because of the large volume of data requested, it was agreed that only data from the First Federal Reserve District (Boston) would be made available. By the end of 1965 all data studied in this monograph were in hand.

Coding of data created a large number of problems which were costly in terms of research time and in loss of data. Considerable computer time was required to convert coded data so that they might be used to study the models described in chapter 4. For the reader to appreciate details of the subsequent sample selection procedures, it is necessary to describe this coding. All numbers, names, and locations that would identify an individual bank were replaced by a single three-digit bank identification number. A bank's number was assigned to all records pertaining to it. All call report variables of a bank were deflated by the bank's total assets as shown on the call report. All income statement variables were deflated by a bank's total assets at year end. Finally, weekly averages of daily deposit report variables were produced. These weekly deposit data were then normalized so that all items took on a value of unity for the week ending January 6, 1960. In all subsequent weeks only weekly percentage changes for each item were provided.

At a later date Pierce joined the staff of the Federal Reserve Board, and he was able to use undisguised data. Unfortunately, by that date a small number of banks had been discarded because the coding procedure caused some information losses. Eventually, all calculations were performed with uncoded data by Pierce.

a. Data resources

Subject to these conditions and conventions, all data concerning an individual bank reported on the indicated reporting forms and available on magnetic tape or cards for the period January 1960 through July 1964 were made available for this study. Thus, if a bank had been in existence from January 6, 1960, through July 1, 1964, the data file contained information from its

1. 16 call reports,[1]

1. The sixteen call report dates were March 15, 1960; June 15, 1960; October 3, 1960; December 31, 1960; April 12, 1961; June 30, 1961; September 27, 1961; December 30, 1961; March 26, 1962; June 30, 1962; September 28, 1962; December 28, 1962; March 18, 1963; June 29, 1963; December 20, 1963; and June 30, 1964.

2. 235 weekly deposit reports, and
3. 4 year-end income and dividends reports.

Tables 5-1, 5-2, and 5-3, respectively, indicate variables on these reports which are available. Some redundant accounting identity items have been deleted, but no information about a bank's current operations has been lost in going from the basic data sources to the set of variables described in the tables. Apart from minor changes noted in footnotes, all three report forms were unchanged during the period studied. The three tables refer to report forms as they actually appeared in the years 1962–64.

TABLE 5-1. CALL REPORT INFORMATION

1. Cash, balances with other banks, and cash items
2. United States government obligations, direct and guaranteed
3. Obligations of states and political subdivisions
4. Other bonds, notes, and debentures
5. Corporate stocks

6. Loans and discounts (net of reserves and other charge-offs)
7. Bank premises owned
8. Real estate owned other than bank premises
9. Investments and other assets
10. Customers' liability on acceptances outstanding

11. Other assets
12. Total assets
13. Demand deposits of individuals, partnerships, and corporations
14. Time and savings deposits of individuals, partnerships, and corporations
15. Deposits of United States government

16. Deposits of states and political subdivisions
17. Deposits of banks
18. Certified and officers' checks, etc.
19. Mortgages or other liens
20. Rediscounts and other liabilities

21. Acceptances
22. Other liabilities
23. Total liabilities
24. Total capital accounts
25. Assets pledged or assigned
26. Securities not secured by United States government[a]

Elaboration of Loan Portfolio
27. Real estate loans secured by farm land
28. Real estate loans secured by residential properties and insured by FHA or VA

Table 5-1 (continued)

29. Real estate loans secured by residential properties (conventional)
30. Real estate loans secured by nonfarm, nonresidential properties
31. Loans to domestic commercial and foreign banks
32. Loans to other financial institutions
33. Loans to brokers and dealers and other loans to financial agents
34. Farm loans guaranteed by CCC
35. Other loans to farmers

36. Commercial and industrial loans[b]
37. Consumer loans to purchase automobiles on installment
38. Consumer loans to purchase other retail consumer goods on installment
39. Consumer installment loans to repair and modernize residential property
40. Other installment consumer loans

41. Single-payment consumer loans
42. All other loans (including overdrafts)[b]
43. Loss reserve for bad debts, unallocated charge-offs, and other valuation reserves

Elaboration of Security Portfolio
44. Treasury bills
45. Treasury certificates of indebtedness
46. Treasury notes maturing within 1 year[c]
47. Treasury notes maturing after 1 year[d]
48. United States government nonmarketable bonds

49. Other United States government bonds maturing within 1 year[e]
50. Other United States government bonds maturing after 1 but within 5 years[f]
51. Other United States government bonds maturing after 5 but within 10 years[g]
52. Other United States government bonds maturing after 10 years[h]
53. Securities guaranteed by United States government[i]

Elaboration of Cash Portfolio
54. Cash items in process of collection
55. Demand balances with banks in the United States
56. Other balances with banks in the United States
57. Balances with banks in foreign countries
58. Currency and coin
59. Reserves with Federal Reserve Bank

Elaboration of Demand Deposits
60. Deposits of individuals, partnerships, and corporations
61. Deposits of foreign governments and official institutions
62. Deposits of United States government
63. Deposits of states and political subdivisions
64. Deposits of banks in United States
65. Deposits of banks in foreign countries

Table 5-1 (continued)

Elaboration of Time and Savings Deposits
66. Savings deposits
67. Deposits accumulated for payment of personal loans
68. Other time deposits of individuals, partnerships, and corporations
69. Deposits of foreign governments and official institutions
70. Deposits of United States government, states and political subdivisions, banks in the United States, and banks in foreign countries

NOTE: All data were collected from call reports submitted by First Federal Reserve District member banks.

[a] Not shown on 1960 call reports.

[b] 1960 data not strictly comparable with other years.

[c] On 1960 call reports, shown as total Treasury notes (no breakdown available and not strictly comparable with other years).

[d] (a) On 1960 call reports, not shown. (b) On April–September 1961 call reports, shown as total Treasury notes (not strictly comparable with other dates).

[e] On 1960 call reports, shown as other United States government bonds maturing within 5 years (no breakdown available and not strictly comparable with later dates).

[f] On 1960 call reports, shown as other United States government bonds maturing within 5–10 years.

[g] On 1960 call reports, shown as other United States government bonds maturing within 10–20 years (not strictly comparable with later dates).

[h] On 1960 call reports, shown as other United States government bonds maturing after 20 years (not strictly comparable with later dates).

[i] On 1960 call reports, shown as FHA debentures (not strictly comparable with later dates).

TABLE 5-2. WEEKLY DEPOSIT INFORMATION

1. Demand deposits due to banks
2. United States government demand deposits
3. Other demand deposits
4. Cash items in process of collection
5. Demand balances due from banks
6. Net demand deposits $(1 + 2 + 3 - 4 - 5)$
7. Time and savings deposits
8. Currency and coin

NOTE: All data were collected from reports of deposits and currency and coin submitted by First Federal Reserve District member banks.

TABLE 5-3. INCOME STATEMENT INFORMATION

Operating Income and Expenses
1. Interest and dividends on United States government obligations
2. Interest and dividends on other securities
3. Interest and discount on loans
4. Service charges and other fees on bank loans
5. Service charges on deposit accounts

6. Other service charges, commissions, fees, and collection and exchange charges
7. Trust department and other current operating revenue
8. Total current operating revenue
9. Officers' salaries; employees' salaries and wages; pension, hospitalization, social security taxes, group insurance payments, and other employee benefits; fees paid to directors and members of executive, discount, and other committees[a]
10. Interest on time and savings deposits

11. Interest and discount on borrowed money
12. Net occupancy expense of bank premises[b]
13. Miscellaneous other operating expenses
14. Net current operating earnings

Recoveries, Transfers from Valuation Reserves, and Profits
15. Profits on securities sold or redeemed
16. Recoveries (securities)[c]
17. Transfers from valuation reserves (securities)[d]
18. Recoveries (loans)[c]
19. Transfers from valuation reserves (loans)[d]
20. Total recoveries, transfers from valuation reserves, and profits

Losses, Charge-offs, and Transfers to Valuation Reserves
21. Losses on securities sold[e]
22. Charge-offs on securities not sold[d]
23. Transfers to valuation reserves (securities)[d]
24. Charge-offs (loans)[e]
25. Transfers to valuation reserves (loans)[d]
26. Total losses, charge-offs, and transfers to valuation reserves

Profits, Dividends, and Net Income
27. Net income before related taxes[f]
28. Taxes on net income
29. Net income after taxes
30. Total dividends declared
31. Net income after dividends

NOTE: All data were collected from income statements submitted by First Federal Reserve District member banks.

Table 5-3 (continued)

[a] Officer and employee benefits not included in the 1960 total (not comparable with later dates).

[b] On 1960 report, shown as taxes on other than net income plus recurring depreciation (not comparable with later dates).

[c] On 1960 report, shown as recoveries plus transfers from valuation reserves (not comparable with later dates).

[d] On 1960 report, not reported separately.

[e] On 1960 report, shown as total losses and charge-offs (not comparable with later dates).

[f] On 1960 report, shown as profits before tax.

b. Sample selection

In selecting the sample of banks to be studied, an overriding consideration was economy in merging the vast volume of data available for an individual bank. This consideration led to deletion of banks from the study whenever they failed to satisfy certain important criteria. Thus, if a bank was involved in a merger in 1961, it was excluded even though its 1962 call reports and income statements were complete and capable of being studied in the rate-of-return analysis of chapter 10. If a merger occurred in 1962 or 1963, the bank was not eliminated from the sample until the date of the merger.

Because of the convention in coding deposit report data, it was not possible to admit banks to the sample which were not in existence on January 6, 1960. Consequently, 25 banks that joined the Federal Reserve System or acquired new names or FDIC identification numbers because of mergers during the sample period were excluded from consideration. Of the remaining 271 banks, 70 were excluded from the analysis because they failed one or more of the following important tests:

i. Deposit criterion: Twenty-four banks were excluded because during the first one hundred weeks of the period they reported that they either had no demand deposits on some date or that they, at one point, lost all of their time deposits and then subsequently received some. If a bank had no demand deposits, it lacked essential characteristics assumed in earlier chapters and was excluded for this reason. A bank was rejected for the time deposit failure because, given the form of deposit report data, it was impossible to reconstruct its deposit history.

ii. Merger criterion: Twenty-eight banks were excluded because during the first one hundred weeks of the period they were involved in a merger or conversion. Of these, seventeen were absorbed into other banks and thus vanished. One bank left the Federal Reserve System and therefore no longer reported deposit information. The remaining ten banks were deleted because it was impossible to reconstruct their deposit history from available data, and their behavior would have been atypical in terms of the models previously specified.

iii. Lost-bank criterion: Five banks were lost through tape errors or format errors on basic data cards which were not detected until they were irretrievable. Errors were encountered while processing in excess of 60,000 deposit report punch cards. Because of the confidentiality conditions and associated incomplete documentation, it is possible that a few more banks were lost. As nearly as can be reconstructed, however, only five banks were lost.

iv. Continuity criterion: Thirteen banks were rejected because of their extremely erratic demand deposit patterns which suggested the possibility of an overlooked merger. Banks that experienced a demand deposit change of 25 percent or more in one week, which was not offset at least once in the subsequent thirteen weeks, were interpreted to be described by a process different from that suggested in chapters 2 through 4.[2] Of the thirteen banks, five were eventually found to be involved in mergers. Deposit reports for banks disappearing in mergers rather peculiarly continued to be tabulated for a number of weeks after the merger took place. Because it was not possible to identify individual banks, the reasons for the aberrant behavior of the other eight banks could not be ascertained.

The remaining 201 banks were studied through part or all of the four-and-a-half-year span in chapters 8 and 10. A bank was studied through all of the period or until a date when it failed either the deposit or merger criterion.

In chapters 6, 9, and 11 a reduced sample of 184 banks was studied. The additional 17 banks were deleted for three reasons. First, 13 banks were excluded because of a disturbing logical discrepancy encountered when merging call report and deposit report files. These banks reported positive time, United States government, or other bank deposits on a call report, but zero corresponding deposits when their daily deposit reports were

2. Specifically, if a bank's average weekly demand deposits changed by more than 25 percent between two consecutive weeks, it was flagged. For flagged banks, a pseudo-deposit series was generated by taking the level of deposits immediately prior to the shock and adding the average weekly deposit change of the same bank observed during 1960 in each successive week until the difference between the actual and pseudo series was less than 25 percent. Flagged banks were discarded if such pseudo series were longer than twelve weeks.

averaged for the week in which the call report was made. This logical inconsistency raised a serious question about the reliability of deposit reports from these banks, and it seemed prudent to exclude them from portfolio composition studies.[3]

Second, three banks were excluded from portfolio composition studies because of a more stringent application of the "continuity criterion" than had been previously employed.[4] Specifically, the continuity criterion was extended to time deposits, and the maximum allowable time period of an aberrant deposit history (week-to-week change of 25 percent or more in time or demand deposits) was shortened to eight weeks.[5] The three omitted banks frequently experienced very sizable shocks in their deposits and were rejected on the grounds that such patterns were too extreme for the models under study. Twelve other banks had a small number of instances in which their deposit histories failed this more stringent application of the continuity criterion. Some, but not all, of their observations were deleted from the analysis of chapters 6, 9, and 11 for the same reason. A total of fifty call report bank observations of these twelve banks were excluded. Finally, one bank had to be dropped because of a computer hardware error that would have been prohibitively expensive to recoup.

Sample banks have balance sheet and income statements that satisfy principal accounting identities to a tolerance of 0.05 percent of a bank's total assets and gross income, respectively.

c. Profile of a typical commercial bank

The median size of a commercial bank in the United States in 1960 and in the sample studied is exceedingly small, certainly less than $10 million in total deposits (see table 5-4). Banks in the sample vary in size from less than $2 million to over $1 billion in total deposits. In the First Federal Reserve District branch banking is common, and large banks have extensive systems.

---

3. The fact that other banks did not fail this logical test does not, of course, imply that their deposit reports are free from error. In the absence of conflicting evidence, it is assumed that information used to compute required reserves is free from error.

4. Results analogous to those in chapter 6 without this second adjustment have been reported elsewhere. See Hester and Pierce [1968].

5. The application of the continuity criterion differed slightly from the previous application in one further respect. Previously a bank's deposit history was examined, in toto, from January 6, 1960, through July 1, 1964. In the second application a bank's deposit history was assumed to commence one year before each call report studied and run until that call report. This change in origin is unlikely to have affected the results meaningfully.

TABLE 5-4. SIZE DISTRIBUTIONS OF SAMPLES OF BANKS

	Sample		
Bank Size[a]	*Total*	*Basic*	*Reduced*
	(number of banks)		
0–2	32	15	12
2–5	77	61	55
5–10	70	58	55
10–25	46	38	35
25–50	19	15	13
50–100	11	6	6
100–300	6	4	4
over 300	6	4	4
Total	267[b]	201	184

[a] Bank size refers to the amount of deposits (in millions of dollars) that a bank held on January 6, 1960.

[b] Of the 5 banks discarded because of the lost-bank criterion, it was not possible to determine size classifications for 4 banks, therefore, only 267 banks appear in the total sample.

Portfolios and earning ratios were reasonably stationary over the period studied. To provide some perspective about the banks studied, table 5-5 shows mean values of selected balance sheet variables pooled over the years 1961–63. The table has been obtained from call report data; all variables are divided by a bank's total assets. Numbers at the right indicate how these variables were constructed from the report described in table 5-1.

Percentages in table 5-5 do not differ markedly from corresponding figures for all member banks computed from aggregative data [*Federal Reserve Bulletin*, June 1962, pp. 715–19]. For example, for all member banks cash assets were 18.76 percent of total assets at the end of June 1961. Similar averages for commercial and industrial loans, real estate loans, consumer loans (loans to individuals), and state and local securities were 18.24 percent, 10.84 percent, 10.52 percent, and 7.14 percent, respectively. Demand deposits were 52.24 percent of total assets, and time deposits were 30.30 percent for member banks on the same date.

TABLE 5-5. PROFILE OF THE MEAN BANK PORTFOLIO IN THE REDUCED SAMPLE

Portfolio Item	Percentage of Total Assets	Item Number(s) in Table 5-1
Assets		
Cash, balances with other banks, and cash items	16.44	1
Obligations of states and political subdivisions	6.77	3
Real estate loans (mortgage loans)	13.97	27, 28, 29, 30
Financial loans	1.45	31, 32
Commercial and industrial loans	14.91	36
Consumer loans	16.47	37, 38, 39, 40, 41
United States government obligations (1-year maturity or less)	8.26	44, 45, 46, 49
United States government obligations (1–5-year maturities)	9.92	47, 50
United States government obligations (more than 5-year maturities)	5.42	51, 52
All other assets	6.39	residual
Total	100.00	
Liabilities and capital		
Demand deposits	58.14	60, 61, 62, 63, 64, 65
Time and savings deposits	28.07	66, 67, 68, 69, 70
All other liabilities plus capital accounts	13.79	residual
Total	100.00	

Earnings measured as a percentage of year-end total assets for sample banks were also very similar to corresponding national aggregates. Mean percentages of net operating income and profits before and after taxes to total assets were 1.30 percent, 1.17 percent, and 0.74 percent, respectively, for the basic sample over the years 1960–63. All member banks in 1961 had aggregative net operating income and profits before and after taxes as a percentage of year-end aggregative total assets equal to 1.34 percent, 1.26 percent, and 0.73 percent [*Federal Reserve Bulletin*, May 1962, pp. 523, 597].

2. Mutual Saving Banks

a. Data resources

In the fall of 1964 the authors obtained permission from the National Association of Mutual Savings Banks to study monthly balance sheet and related variables of individual mutual savings banks over the years 1959–63. As in the case of the commercial bank sample, these data were made available on the condition that they be treated as confidential and used only for this and closely related studies by the authors. Information about banks was keypunched directly from worksheets in the files of the Association. Table 5-6 reports a list of variables that were made available.

TABLE 5-6. BALANCE SHEET INFORMATION: MUTUAL SAVINGS BANKS

---

1. Cash and bank deposits
2. United States government securities
3. State and local securities
4. Other securities
5. Mortgage loans
6. Other loans
7. Other assets
8. Total assets
9. Regular savings deposits
10. Industrial and club deposits
11. School savings and other deposits
12. Other liabilities
13. Surplus and undistributed net income
14. Number of regular savings deposit accounts
15. Number of industrial and club deposit accounts
16. Number of school savings and other accounts
17. Regular savings deposits received during month (including dividends paid)
18. Regular savings deposits withdrawn during month

NOTE: All information was collected monthly from individual mutual savings banks and refers to end-of-month condition.

Mutual savings bank balance sheets were tabulated much more frequently than were those for commercial banks, but they are much less detailed. The highly aggregative nature of the measures of mortgage loans and the various types of securities in savings bank portfolios is particularly unfortunate for the purposes of the present study. Insured and conventional mortgage loans are not distinguished, yet they differ in two very important respects. First, the former, but not the latter, were serviced by a secondary market and consequently had relatively low transactions costs. Second, state regulations differ significantly in the freedom that they allow savings banks in acquiring conventional and insured mortgage loans. Aggregative data on security holdings are likely to conceal many of the trade-offs which were predicted by the theory described earlier.

Although savings bank balance sheets are more frequently tabulated, no weekly series on deposits comparable to commercial bank deposit reports is available. Consequently, hypotheses about the relation between deposit shocks and very reversible assets such as cash and United States government securities can be tested only with low precision; the tests will have low power. Nevertheless, the data studied below appeared to be the best information available on a noncommercial bank intermediary. They represent a rich resource for studying the models of this monograph.

b. Sample selection

Over three hundred savings banks (out of a population of slightly more than five hundred) regularly reported their balance sheets to the National Association. Large banks apparently are more likely to report to the National Association than are small banks and, therefore, are over-represented in the sample. No attempt was made to compensate for this distortion.

As noted in chapter 2, savings banks are regulated primarily by state banking commissioners. Banks in different states must operate under quite different sets of restrictions. To avoid the misspecification and inefficient estimation mentioned in chapter 4, separate structures were estimated for savings banks in different states. During the sampling period, savings bank charters were available in eighteen states; however, only Massachusetts, New York, and Connecticut had populations of fifty or more savings banks. Therefore, sampling was confined to banks in these three states.

On June 30, 1963, there were 181 savings banks in Massachusetts, 127 in New York, and 71 in Connecticut. The files of the National Association contained information about 251 of these banks during the period studied; 115 were in Massachusetts, 98 were in New York, and 38 were in Connecticut. Of the 98 New York State banks, 45 were located in New York City. Because of their location, because of the method of estimation used in chapter 7, and because banks in New York City were very much larger than other savings banks, it seemed advisable to study New York City and other New York State banks separately.

From this group of banks a sample of 201 savings banks was selected. The reasons for dropping banks were (1) irregular reporting or disappearance of bank data owing to mergers sometime in the sixty-month period, (2) irreconcilable errors in the underlying worksheets, (3) coding or data processing errors that were deemed too expensive to correct when detected, and (4) excessive shocks due to a bank's being a continuing bank after a merger.[6] Table 5-7 reports a summary of the editing results for each of the subsamples of mutual savings banks.

TABLE 5-7. SUMMARY OF RESULTS FROM EDITING MUTUAL SAVINGS
BANK SUBSAMPLES

	Connecticut	Massachusetts	New York City	New York State
Sampling universe of 251 banks	38	115	46	52
Banks removed because of				
1. irregular or incomplete records	4	15	5	5
2. irreconcilable errors on worksheets	2	4	1	4
3. too expensive to correct	0	4	0	2
4. continuing bank after merger	0	3	1	0
Sample of 201 banks	32	89	39	41

Data from all banks remaining in the sample have passed relatively stringent consistency checks that derive from balance sheet identities. Thus, in no month does any bank have an absolute deviation between total assets and the sum of the seven reported individual assets that exceeds 0.25 percent of total assets. Considerably less than 1 percent of bank month observations have discrepancies between these two

6. Of the banks that were dropped because of errors too expensive to correct, four banks on the Massachusetts worksheets had various items in their balance sheets interchanged among the banks. To correct this error would have required about ten major computer reruns, and it was decided that both time and financial resources could be better expended on other aspects of the study. Also, very late in the project a computer programming error was detected which caused two New York State banks at the end of a tape to be skipped. To correct for this error would have required that almost all computer runs for this sample be redone.

measures of total assets that exceed rounding error tolerances when all data are measured in thousands of dollars. No bank has liabilities plus surplus exceeding total assets by an amount larger than can be accounted for by rounding errors. The data for all remaining banks have passed a visual scanning test for evidence of unreported mergers.

c. Profiles of typical mutual savings banks

Savings banks in the states from which the sample was drawn had approximately 80 percent of the assets of the mutual savings bank industry. Therefore, apart from the likely oversampling of large banks mentioned previously, the portfolio of a sample bank is likely to resemble the mean savings bank portfolio in the United States closely.

TABLE 5-8. PROFILES OF MEAN MUTUAL SAVINGS BANKS IN SUBSAMPLES
ON JANUARY 31, 1959, AND DECEMBER 31, 1963
(in thousands of dollars)

Balance Sheet Item	Conn.	Mass.	N.Y.C.	N.Y.S.
January 1959				
Cash and bank deposits	1,130	693	7,641	2,216
United States government securities	13,214	13,001	62,120	14,435
State and local securities	723	430	7,163	2,452
Other securities	9,432	4,575	43,829	7,387
Mortgage loans	32,337	23,549	260,320	56,615
Other loans	516	400	986	367
Other assets	667	396	5,561	1,366
Total assets	58,019	43,045	387,621	84,838
December 1963				
Cash and bank deposits	1,395	807	8,332	2,510
United States government securities	7,945	13,730	42,359	10,382
State and local securities	360	252	3,497	1,377
Other securities	11,780	3,760	44,677	8,749
Mortgage loans	56,593	38,146	373,001	86,414
Other loans	1,303	888	5,072	1,068
Other assets	754	651	8,648	2,098
Total assets	80,130	58,234	485,586	112,598

Mutual savings bank liabilities and capital accounts exhibit comparatively little relative variation over time and across banks: as a first approximation, a savings bank has regular savings deposits equal to

90 percent, miscellaneous other deposits and liabilities equal to 2 percent, and reserves and surplus equal to 8 percent of total assets [National Association of Mutual Savings Banks, *National Fact Book*, 1965, p. 15]. During the period studied, surplus and reserves were about 11 percent of deposits in Massachusetts, about 10 percent in Connecticut, and about 9.5 percent in New York.

Table 5-8 shows mean subsample savings bank holdings of different assets at the beginning and end of the period studied in this monograph. Perhaps the most remarkable features of this table are the relatively rapid growth of the mean savings banks and the shifts within savings bank portfolios, with the exception of Massachusetts banks, away from United States government securities and into mortgage loans. It is odd that savings banks are observed to hold tax-exempt state and local securities because for the most part the banks were not subject to income taxes during the period studied.

There appear to be sizable differences in mean portfolios among the subsamples; Massachusetts banks differ considerably from banks in the remaining groups. Also, in 1962 about 56 percent of the value of mortgages held by Connecticut and Masschusetts savings banks were conventional and thus lacking a secondary market. Only 36 percent of New York banks' mortgages were conventional [National Association of Mutual Savings Banks, *Facts and Figures*, 1963, p. 19]. Thus, partitioning of the data file into subsamples seems desirable.

CHAPTER 6

Estimates for the Input-Output Model from a Sample of Commercial Banks

This chapter reports least-squares estimates of the parameters of the input-output model for commercial banks. The underlying statistical model was described in chapter 4, and the sample of 184 banks was described in chapter 5. The first section presents estimates of the model's structure for a set of aggregated bank asset measures.[1] Section 2 reports some further results for this model and section 3 contains an analysis of bank assets at more disaggregated levels. Section 4 provides an analysis of the residuals of the model and studies its ability to predict beyond the sample period. The final section summarizes the principal conclusions from this chapter.

1. PRELIMINARY TESTS AND AN INPUT-OUTPUT MODEL FOR ASSET AGGREGATES

The discussion in preceding chapters suggests three basic questions to be asked of the input-output formulation: (1) Do estimates of the lag structure describing the relationship between deposit histories and current portfolio composition agree with theoretical predictions? (2) Are the lag structures and steady-state asset proportions for demand deposits and savings and time deposits different? (3) Are the lag structures intertemporally stationary?

The estimates of the structure of the input-output model presented below were obtained from 1,843 bank call report observations available for the 1961–63 period. The call report data for June 1964 have been excluded in order to permit a test of the predictive ability of the model.

As indicated in chapter 4, all variables are measured about individual bank means. When bank effects were not removed, the model yielded plausible results, which are reported in the appendix to this chapter. An analysis of variance revealed that bank means differed significantly in all regressions.

The results from the regression analysis of bank asset aggregates are reported in tables 6-1, 6-2, and 6-3. Columns of these tables must be read

---

1. Parts of section 1 are taken from an earlier paper by the authors, cf. Hester and Pierce [1968].

together because coefficients in each column come from the same regression; each asset is regressed on the same set of forty-five independent variables. As explained in chapter 4, in tables 6-1 and 6-2 the first three coefficients refer to recent weekly deposit changes, the next one to a two-week change, the next eleven to four-week changes, and the last coefficient concerns deposit levels at the mean bank about fifty weeks prior to a call report.[2] The notation of chapter 4 has been changed somewhat to facilitate reading of the tables.

Standard errors are reported below each coefficient. No standard errors or *F* values are reported for "other assets" because these coefficients were obtained from an identity or, equivalently, by summing a number of regression coefficients of some minor bank assets.[3] For convenience of exposition, any loan secured by real estate is called a mortgage loan.

It is convenient to discuss these results in terms of the three questions posed at the beginning of the section. First, the lag structure in general does conform to a priori expectations. Deposit flows initially are allocated to liquid assets and gradually are reallocated to less liquid, higher earning forms.

Second, the pattern of coefficients for time deposit flows is different from the pattern for demand deposit flows. An analysis of covariance indicates that when demand and time deposits are summed to form a deposit history for total deposits, the lag structure for demand deposits is significantly different at the 5 percent level from the lag structure for time deposits in the regressions for cash assets, consumer loans, and mortgage loans.[4] Further, the long-run coefficient on the level of demand deposits, d_{m-13}, is different from the coefficient on time deposits for several assets; in general these differences are in the expected direction. At the 5 percent level of significance, the long-run demand deposit coefficient is larger than the time deposit coefficient for cash assets and for consumer loans. The two coefficients are not significantly different from each other in the regressions for state and local securities, commercial and industrial loans, and short- and intermediate-term government securities. The time deposit coefficient is significantly larger than the demand deposit coefficient

2. An informal test of the hypothesis that four consecutive weeks of deposit changes have a common slope was performed by estimating additional weekly change coefficients. The results confirmed the expectation that only the most recent periods need be studied as weekly changes.

3. Separate coefficients were estimated for loans to financial institutions, for government securities maturing in more than five years and for the residual, all other assets. In general, estimating separate coefficients for these components did not provide interesting results so the coefficients were pooled to give the "other asset" coefficients described in the text.

4. See section 2 for details of tests of the lag structure.

	Cash	State and Local	Mort- gage	Comm. and Indust.	Con- sumer	Shorts	1–5s	Other
d_w	.507*	.032	.035*	.048*	.047*	.263*	−.053	.121
	(.028)	(.020)	(.012)	(.022)	(.020)	(.043)	(.035)	
d_{w-1}	.305*	.012	.033*	.112*	.072*	.315*	.095*	.056
	(.039)	(.021)	(.014)	(.025)	(.022)	(.048)	(.039)	
d_{w-2}	.302*	.007	.039*	.106*	.057*	.263*	.122*	.104
	(.032)	(.022)	(.014)	(.026)	(.023)	(.050)	(.040)	
d_{sm}	.378*	.022	.027*	.085*	.064*	.288*	.089*	.047
	(.027)	(.019)	(.012)	(.022)	(.019)	(.043)	(.034)	
d_{m-2}	.287*	.034*	.017	.125*	.076*	.345*	.029	.087
	(.024)	(.017)	(.011)	(.020)	(.017)	(.038)	(.031)	
d_{m-3}	.237*	.004	.044*	.094*	.080*	.343*	.072*	.126
	(.026)	(.018)	(.011)	(.020)	(.018)	(.040)	(.032)	
d_{m-4}	.202*	.039*	.034*	.151*	.076*	.342*	.137*	.019
	(.027)	(.019)	(.012)	(.021)	(.019)	(.041)	(.034)	
d_{m-5}	.245*	−.003	.029*	.097*	.097*	.348*	.078*	.109
	(.025)	(.018)	(.011)	(.020)	(.018)	(.039)	(.032)	
d_{m-6}	.225*	−.001	.061*	.125*	.123*	.308*	.056	.103
	(.025)	(.017)	(.011)	(.020)	(.017)	(.038)	(.031)	
d_{m-7}	.247*	.057*	.049*	.150*	.118*	.177*	.177*	.025
	(.028)	(.019)	(.012)	(.022)	(.019)	(.043)	(.034)	
d_{m-8}	.257*	.024	.051*	.137*	.125*	.150*	.102*	.154
	(.028)	(.019)	(.012)	(.022)	(.020)	(.043)	(.035)	
d_{m-9}	.265*	.042*	.060*	.129*	.140*	.237*	.032	.095
	(.026)	(.018)	(.012)	(.021)	(.018)	(.041)	(.033)	
d_{m-10}	.259*	.004	.078*	.129*	.157*	.105*	.131*	.137
	(.028)	(.019)	(.012)	(.022)	(.019)	(.043)	(.035)	
d_{m-11}	.290*	.099*	.055*	.134*	.185*	−.004	.136*	.105
	(.029)	(.020)	(.013)	(.023)	(.020)	(.045)	(.036)	
d_{m-12}	.298*	.091*	.069*	.141*	.179*	.003	.127*	.092
	(.029)	(.020)	(.013)	(.023)	(.020)	(.044)	(.036)	
d_{m-13}	.267*	.067*	.087*	.149*	.201*	.048*	.104*	.077
	(.014)	(.009)	(.006)	(.011)	(.010)	(.021)	(.017)	

NOTE: See last row in table 6-3 for sources of dependent variables. In this and subsequent tables in this chapter, an asterisk indicates that a coefficient differs significantly from zero at the 5 percent level in a two-tailed test.

	Cash	State and Local	Mort-gage	Comm. and Indust.	Con-sumer	Shorts	1–5s	Other
$\bar{s}_w$	.219	.200*	.062	.123	−.048	.447*	−.093	.090
	(.134)	(.093)	(.059)	(.107)	(.094)	(.207)	(.168)	
$\bar{s}_{w-1}$	.082	.212*	−.029	.124	.119	.427*	.052	.013
	(.129)	(.089)	(.056)	(.103)	(.090)	(.199)	(.161)	
$\bar{s}_{w-2}$	.103	−.078	.095	.140	.217*	.271	.062	.190
	(.129)	(.090)	(.057)	(.104)	(.091)	(.200)	(.162)	
$\bar{s}_{sm}$	.279*	−.070	.055	.142	.126	.287	.092	.089
	(.117)	(.081)	(.051)	(.093)	(.082)	(.180)	(.146)	
$\bar{s}_{m-2}$	.041	.085	.113*	.120	.127	.246	.038	.230
	(.097)	(.068)	(.043)	(.078)	(.068)	(.151)	(.122)	
$\bar{s}_{m-3}$	−.066	.188*	.037	.282*	−.025	.073	.317*	.194
	(.114)	(.079)	(.050)	(.091)	(.080)	(.177)	(.143)	
$\bar{s}_{m-4}$	−.122	.086	.120*	.152	.149	.732*	−.183	.066
	(.114)	(.079)	(.050)	(.091)	(.080)	(.176)	(.143)	
$\bar{s}_{m-5}$	.053	.136*	.148*	.113	.104	.302*	−.032	.176
	(.096)	(.067)	(.042)	(.077)	(.068)	(.149)	(.121)	
$\bar{s}_{m-6}$	−.044	.021	.162*	.210*	.124	.110	.183	.234
	(.099)	(.069)	(.044)	(.079)	(.070)	(.154)	(.124)	
$\bar{s}_{m-7}$	.103	.014	.157*	.245*	−.033	.067	.199	.248
	(.122)	(.085)	(.054)	(.098)	(.086)	(.190)	(.153)	
$\bar{s}_{m-8}$	.009	.097	.253*	.231*	.063	.245	−.011	.113
	(.104)	(.073)	(.046)	(.084)	(.074)	(.162)	(.131)	
$\bar{s}_{m-9}$	−.072	.133	.151*	−.021	.190*	.151	.062	.406
	(.115)	(.080)	(.051)	(.092)	(.081)	(.178)	(.144)	
$\bar{s}_{m-10}$	−.070	.117	.282*	.230*	.201*	.104	.099	.037
	(.120)	(.083)	(.053)	(.096)	(.084)	(.185)	(.150)	
$\bar{s}_{m-11}$	−.010	.111	.254*	.105	−.065	.159	.057	.389
	(.110)	(.076)	(.048)	(.088)	(.077)	(.170)	(.137)	
$\bar{s}_{m-12}$	−.221*	.094	.271*	.145*	.196*	.125	.031	.359
	(.088)	(.061)	(.039)	(.071)	(.062)	(.136)	(.110)	
s_{m-13}	−.134*	.071*	.291*	.140*	.102*	.117*	.080*	.333
	(.028)	(.020)	(.012)	(.023)	(.020)	(.044)	(.035)	

	Cash	State and Local	Mort-gage	Comm. and Indust.	Con-sumer	Shorts	1–5s	Other
				Call Report Dummy Variables				
4-12-61	.014*	−.005*	−.009*	−.004*	−.017*	.020*	.007	.006
	(.003)	(.002)	(.001)	(.003)	(.002)	(.005)	(.004)	
6-30-61	.009*	.001	−.008*	.001	−.011*	.013*	.006	−.011
	(.003)	(.002)	(.001)	(.003)	(.002)	(.005)	(.004)	
9-27-61	.014*	.003	−.008*	−.003	−.014*	.014*	.006	−.012
	(.003)	(.002)	(.001)	(.003)	(.002)	(.005)	(.004)	
12-30-61	.032*	−.009*	−.006*	−.003	−.016*	.007	.016*	−.021
	(.003)	(.002)	(.001)	(.002)	(.002)	(.004)	(.003)	
3-26-62	.014*	−.003	−.007*	.002	−.013*	.017*	.006	−.016
	(.003)	(.002)	(.001)	(.002)	(.002)	(.005)	(.004)	
6-30-62	.010*	.003	−.006*	.004	−.007*	.013*	−.000	−.017
	(.003)	(.002)	(.001)	(.003)	(.002)	(.005)	(.004)	
9-28-62	.010*	.005*	−.006*	−.001	−.010*	.015*	−.006	−.007
	(.003)	(.002)	(.001)	(.003)	(.002)	(.005)	(.004)	
12-28-62	.023*	−.008*	−.005*	−.004	−.012*	.005	.002	−.001
	(.003)	(.002)	(.001)	(.002)	(.002)	(.004)	(.004)	
3-18-63	.021*	−.003	−.006*	.001	−.013*	.005	−.002	−.003
	(.003)	(.002)	(.001)	(.003)	(.002)	(.005)	(.004)	
6-29-63	.007*	.004	−.004*	.004	−.005*	−.002	.002	−.006
	(.003)	(.002)	(.001)	(.002)	(.002)	(.005)	(.004)	
				Overflow				
De-mand	−.008	−.006	.002	−.001	−.003	.027*	−.006	−.005
	(.007)	(.005)	(.003)	(.006)	(005)	(.011)	(.009)	
Time	−.006	−.005	.027*	−.009	.012	.028	−.014	−.033
	(.010)	(.007)	(.004)	(.008)	(.007)	(.015)	(.012)	
				Capital				
c_t	.228*	.078*	.114*	.169*	.229*	.058	.086*	.038
	(.031)	(.021)	(.013)	(.024)	(.021)	(.047)	(.038)	

Table 6-3 (continued)

	Cash	State and Local	Mort-gage	Comm. and Indust.	Con-sumer	Shorts	1–5s	Other
				Summary Statistics				
R^2	.254	.146	.255	.050	.182	.191	.149	N.A.
S_ε	.023	.016	.010	.018	.016	.035	.029	N.A.
F	13.770*	6.898*	13.793*	2.143*	9.015*	9.509*	7.065*	N.A.
Mean	.164	.068	.140	.149	.165	.083	.099	.132
Item Num-ber(s) in Table 5-1	1	3	27, 28, 29, 30	36	37, 38, 39, 40, 41	44, 45, 46, 49	47, 50	Residual

NOTE: The number of observations in each regression is 1,843.

for mortgage loans. These results suggest that the composition and history of deposits are important determinants of portfolio structure. Both dynamic adjustments and long-run responses to demand and time deposit inflows are different for several assets.[5]

Third, the lag structures are intertemporally stationary. An analysis of covariance indicated that, with the exception of mortgage loans, the structures of regressions estimated for each call report did not differ significantly from one another at the 5 percent level. On a call report by call report basis, the structures of the mortgage loan equation did not differ significantly at the 1 percent level. Thus, the effects of variations in interest rates and other excluded variables were approximated by a shifting intercept in the pooled regressions; these intercepts will be discussed later.

A more detailed analysis of the results follows:

(1) The percentage of demand deposits reaching the mean bank at different dates held as cash assets exhibits the expected pattern. Estimated marginal cash asset "reserves" against demand deposits are about 27 percent in the long run. The percentage of time deposits reaching this bank on different dates held as cash assets is erratic, as expected, but in the long run appears quite unexpectedly to be negative. The estimated marginal negative reserves of cash assets held against time deposits are

5. See chapter 8 for evidence on deposit predictability.

13.4 percent.[6] A surprising feature of these results is the wide difference of 40 percentage points between the long-run coefficients for demand and time deposits.

Part of this difference in long-run cash asset holdings for demand and time deposits results from the inclusion of cash items in process of collection and balances due from domestic banks in the definition of cash assets. Section 3 reports results where these items are subtracted from cash assets to form the legal reserve figures of balances at reserve banks plus vault cash. The estimated long-run coefficients for legal reserves for gross demand and time deposits are .106 and −.053 respectively.[7] As reported in the appendix to this chapter, when bank effects are not removed, the estimated legal requirement for gross demand deposits is .091 and that for time deposits is .034.[8] There are two promising interpretations for the low estimated marginal and average reserve holdings against time deposits. These involve the existence of a size aggregation effect and/or a liquidity effect. The size aggregation effect is a consequence of two factors: (*a*) Small banks have distinctly less predictable demand deposits than large banks.[9] In an important way demand deposits at small banks are different kinds of liabilities than demand deposits at large banks; to treat them as the same kind of liability for banks of all sizes introduces an error in variable. (*b*) Small banks in the sample have larger percentages of their deposits as time deposits than do large banks. Because of the coincidence of high demand deposit instability and the high percentage of time deposits at small banks, time deposits "proxy" for this error in the variable, and coefficients are biased in the observed direction. If correct, this interpretation may partly account for the inability of Goldfeld [1966] and investigators working on the FRB-MIT aggregative model [de Leeuw and Gramlich, 1968] to explain the distribution of deposits and assets among reserve city banks, country banks, and nonmember banks.

6. The use of the term marginal should be stressed. As indicated in the appendix to this chapter, when bank effects were not removed, cash asset holdings against time deposits were in excess of 4 percent.

7. Due to differing deposit bases, the "desired reserve requirement" for demand deposits estimated in this study is not strictly comparable with the Federal Reserve's required reserve ratio. The Federal Reserve's net demand deposit measure is obtained by deducting cash items in process of collection and balances due from domestic banks from the gross demand deposit measure used in this study. The time deposit measure is the same as the one used by the Federal Reserve to calculate required reserves against time deposits. Holdings of legal reserves for reserve requirement purposes were computed by the Federal Reserve on a weekly average basis for reserve city banks and a biweekly average basis for country banks.

8. The legal requirement on time deposits was 5 percent until November 1, 1962, when it changed to 4 percent. The estimated time deposit coefficient is not significantly different from 4 percent.

9. This result is reported in chapter 8.

The second interpretation rests on the fact that bank assets, whether financed by demand or time deposits, yield a sizable, predictable cash flow. It is quite possible that the cash flow from assets financed by new time deposits is sufficient to permit a bank to reduce its marginal cash holdings without increasing its "liquidity risk" exposure. If correct, this interpretation suggests that excess reserves are an inadequate measure of bank liquidity protection; gross cash flow variables must be incorporated in models of bank behavior. Further research on this result is clearly important.

(2) The percentage of a bank's assets invested in state and local securities, intermediate-maturity securities (1–5-year United States government obligations), and other residual assets was not very regularly related to either demand or time deposits flowing into the mean bank on different dates. After between eight and eleven months, however, a bank's share of these assets was not particularly affected by deposit flows. Apparently banks purchase these assets when the market seems "right" but typically within about eleven months.

(3) Among loan variables, mortgage loans were only slightly related to demand deposit flows. Specifically, in table 6-1 a significant but minor relationship exists between mortgage loans and deposit flows for approximately three months, and then a gradual, somewhat erratic increase in these loans occurs until the tenth month, when near-equilibrium conditions are met. Time deposit flows begin to affect mortgage loans after about two months, with a gradual and fairly erratic increase in these assets until between nine and eleven months, when mortgage loans have reached near-equilibrium levels. A very similar mortgage-loan adjustment pattern is reported for mutual savings banks in chapter 7.

(4) Flows of demand and time deposits affect commercial and industrial loans quite rapidly with near-equilibrium percentages being obtained in about five months. Demand deposits flow increasingly into consumer loans with equilibrium levels being reached only after about twelve months. Time deposits flow into consumer loans both earlier and much less regularly than demand deposits.

(5) Demand deposits flow into short-term government securities increasingly until about the sixth month. After this interval the percentage of demand deposit flows appearing in these securities declines to a long-run equilibrium of about 5 percent. Time deposits are again less regularly related to short-term security holdings with peaks occurring in the first two weeks and around the fifth month.

(6) Table 6-3 shows the values of coefficients of the dummy time variables referred to in the discussion of intertemporal stability. Each

coefficient should be read as measuring the difference between a bank's portfolio on the call report of the indicated date and the call report of December 20, 1963. These coefficients are interpreted as measuring the collective effects of interest rates and other relevant excluded variables on portfolio composition. Apart from some conspicuous seasonal variations, the interesting and statistically significant changes in this period appear to be: (a) a shift into mortgage loans, (b) a shift out of short-term securities, (c) a shift out of intermediate-term securities, and (d) a shift into other assets. During the same period, interest rates, with the important exception of mortgage rates, were steady or rising; short- and intermediate-term rates rose relative to long-term rates. It is remarkable that in every case the sample banks were moving against interest rates; that is, they were shifting into assets when rates paid on these assets were falling. Superficially, it appears that bank portfolios were better characterized as determining rather than determined by interest rates.[10] If this interpretation is accepted, then the specification of bank portfolio equations in some aggregative models is defective, for such equations are characterized as demand equations in which rates of return are assumed to be externally determined for a bank [Goldfeld, 1966; and de Leeuw and Gramlich, 1968].

(7) The overflow variables performed as expected. Overflows of demand deposits had a significant impact on short-term government securities, and time deposit overflows had a significant impact on mortgage loan holdings. Otherwise, the deposit overflows were diffused over the remaining assets.

(8) Interbank variations in capital and other liabilities also significantly explain differences in bank portfolio compositions. Consumer loans, cash assets, commercial and industrial loans, and mortgage loans were allocated a relatively large proportion of such funds. With the exception of the large capital coefficient for cash assets, these results conform with a priori expectations. The aberrant cash coefficient may reflect the fact that capital was constructed residually when pooling data files.

2. SOME FURTHER RESULTS

This section examines several further characteristics of demand and time deposit lag structures for the eight asset aggregates. First, deposit

---

10. The statement is superficial because, as Brainard and Tobin [1963] have persuasively argued, in theory one must be very cautious in predicting how movements in interest rates affect portfolio composition. Furthermore, the mapping of dummy variable coefficient values with interest rate movements is surely not isomorphic.

histories do account for differences in bank portfolio composition. When the asset variables were regressed on contemporaneous stocks of demand and time deposits along with the overflow and other nondeposit variables in the regressions of section 1, an analysis of covariance indicated that a considerable loss of descriptive power was sustained (significant at the 5 percent level). Thus, costs of asset adjustment appear to be an important determinant of portfolio composition. Second, as reported in section 1, for cash assets, consumer loans, and mortgage loans, the lag structure for demand deposits was significantly different from the structure for time deposits.

Third, there is no reason a priori why the lags on demand deposits and time deposits should be of the same length. To examine this question the number of demand deposit variables was reduced so that the adjustment period was shortened by four months, while the time deposit lag structure was as reported in table 6-2. The hypothesis that the final four months of demand deposits had no influence on the holdings of the eight assets was rejected at the 5 percent level for all except cash assets and commercial and industrial loans. However, a similar hypothesis that reducing the number of time deposit lags by four months had no effect on portfolio description could not be rejected, with the single exception of state and local securities. An implication of this finding is that information about lag structures is lost if bank deposits are not disaggregated into demand and time deposit components.

Several additional hypotheses were tested with the data. At one point the hypothesis that banks react differently to reductions than to increases in their deposits was tested. An analysis of covariance indicated that there was no significant difference in the lag structures for demand and time deposits when separate coefficients were estimated for positive and negative deposit changes. Banks apparently found it as easy to acquire new assets as to dispose of them.

In a similar vein, tests were conducted to determine whether banks react differently to large deposit variations, irrespective of sign, than they do to relatively small changes.[11] The hypothesis that banks respond in the same way to deposit changes in excess of 5 percent in absolute value as they do to smaller changes could not be rejected for demand and time deposits at the 5 percent level.

Tests were also conducted for size effects. The sample was divided into two subsamples depending upon whether or not a bank had more than

11. As reported in chapter 4, deposits were smoothed to prevent increases in excess of 25 percent or decreases in excess of 20 percent.

$25 million in deposits on January 6, 1960. Only the equation for state and local securities was significant at the 5 percent level.[12]

Finally, the impact of deposit predictability on portfolio composition was examined. Banks with unpredictable deposits should have relatively large holdings of liquid assets. Two measures of deposit predictability were available: (1) the standard errors of estimate of the demand and time deposit prediction equations described in chapter 4 and (2) the actual weekly standard deviations of deposit changes over the estimation period.[13] Table 6-4 reports correlations for 184 banks between the average share of some asset in a bank's portfolio and the standard error of estimate in its demand deposit forecasting equation.

TABLE 6-4. SIMPLE CORRELATIONS BETWEEN ASSET SHARES
AND THE STANDARD ERROR OF ESTIMATE OF BANK
DEMAND DEPOSITS

Asset	Correlation
Cash assets	.561*
State and local securities	−.026
Mortgage loans	−.524*
Commercial and industrial loans	.143*
Consumer loans	.240*
Short-term government securities	.236*
1–5-year government securities	−.038

NOTE: An asterisk indicates significance at the 5 percent level.

In general these results are consistent with a priori expectations: banks with unpredictable demand deposits have relatively large holdings of cash assets and short-term government securities and relatively small holdings of state and local securities, mortgage loans, and one- to five-year government securities. The result for consumer loans is a little surprising. Apparently the cash flow from installment loans is sufficiently large that such loans provide a cushion for banks with unpredictable demand deposits. However, table 6-4 is deceptive. Neither the standard error of estimate nor the standard deviation of weekly demand or time deposit changes was statistically significant when added to the input-output model reported in the appendix, where bank effects were not removed

12. Additional tests of size effects are reported in chapters 10 and 11.

13. The standard error of estimate and the standard deviation of weekly changes for both demand and time deposits were obtained for smoothed deposit data. See chapter 8 for details.

(which is the appropriate form of the model for this test). The conclusion is, therefore, that deposit predictability is loosely related to variations in mean bank portfolios, but that once allowance is made for deposit histories, knowledge of predictability does not improve the explanation of variations in bank portfolio composition.

3. Asset Disaggregations

In this section estimates of the structure of the input-output model for disaggregated measures of cash assets, government securities, consumer loans, and mortgage loans are discussed.

a. Cash assets

The estimated coefficients for major cash assets are presented in tables 6-5 and 6-6.[14] Each of these assets responds to deposit shocks in roughly the same manner as total cash assets reported in section 1. Loans to banks, which were included in other assets above, are also reported; loans to banks are very liquid and should be close substitutes for cash assets.

Deposits due from other banks are an important cash asset. Nearly half of the total first week's allocation of demand balances to cash assets is in the form of "due-from" balances. The proportion of demand deposits in due-from balances declines to a steady-state value, which is 40 percent of its initial value. The proportion of time deposits allocated to due-froms is erratic with a negative coefficient in the long run.

The proportion of demand deposits allocated to reserves has a similar pattern. In the long run the proportion of demand balances allocated to reserves is about 45 percent of the initial allocation. Time deposits decline erratically to the long-run negative value discussed in section 1.

Loans to banks receive a significant positive impulse from demand deposit shocks in the current week but decline to zero in the long run. Such loans are apparently only a temporary abode for demand deposit inflows.

b. Government securities

Attempts to break down short-term government securities further into bills, certificates, notes maturing in under one year, and other government

14. In the interest of brevity, estimated coefficients for call report dummy variables are not shown in these tables. As in earlier tables, regressions go through the means of the average bank's variables on December 20, 1963.

TABLE 6-5. INTERBANK CLAIMS: DEMAND DEPOSIT COEFFICIENTS

	Deposits Due from Banks	Total Reserves	Loans to Banks
d_w	.232*	.237*	.090*
	(.020)	(.022)	(.015)
d_{w-1}	.135*	.122*	.053*
	(.022)	(.024)	(.016)
d_{w-2}	.154*	.157*	.071*
	(.023)	(.025)	(.017)
d_{sm}	.183*	.164*	.050*
	(.020)	(.021)	(.014)
d_{m-2}	.145*	.129*	.029*
	(.018)	(.019)	(.013)
d_{m-3}	.076*	.137*	.030*
	(.019)	(.020)	(.013)
d_{m-4}	.099*	.079*	.040*
	(.019)	(.021)	(.014)
d_{m-5}	.098*	.113*	.027*
	(.018)	(.020)	(.013)
d_{m-6}	.104*	.117*	.016
	(.018)	(.019)	(.013)
d_{m-7}	.075*	.138*	.035*
	(.020)	(.021)	(.014)
d_{m-8}	.119*	.124*	.050*
	(.020)	(.022)	(.015)
d_{m-9}	.106*	.125*	.022
	(.019)	(.020)	(.014)
d_{m-10}	.123*	.096*	.048*
	(.020)	(.021)	(.014)
d_{m-11}	.096*	.151*	.027
	(.021)	(.022)	(.015)
d_{m-12}	.128*	.144*	.025
	(.021)	(.022)	(.015)
d_{m-13}	.096*	.106*	.007
	(.010)	(.011)	(.007)

NOTE: See last row in table 6-6 for sources of dependent variables.

TABLE 6-6. INTERBANK CLAIMS: TIME DEPOSIT AND OTHER COEFFICIENTS

	Deposits Due from Banks	Total Reserves	Loans to Banks
$\bar{s}_w$	.217*	−.005	.076
	(.097)	(.104)	(.070)
$\bar{s}_{w-1}$	.039	.024	.080
	(.093)	(.100)	(.067)
$\bar{s}_{w-2}$	−.031	.107	.015
	(.094)	(.100)	(.067)
$\bar{s}_{sm}$	.054	.160	.012
	(.084)	(.090)	(.061)
$\bar{s}_{m-2}$	.035	−.025	−.027
	(.071)	(.076)	(.051)
$\bar{s}_{m-3}$	−.000	−.083	.047
	(.083)	(.089)	(.059)
$\bar{s}_{m-4}$	−.124	.018	.013
	(.082)	(.088)	(.059)
$\bar{s}_{m-5}$	.081	−.127	.003
	(.070)	(.075)	(.050)
$\bar{s}_{m-6}$	−.033	.040	.011
	(.072)	(.077)	(.052)
$\bar{s}_{m-7}$	.111	.090	−.066
	(.089)	(.095)	(.064)
$\bar{s}_{m-8}$	−.001	−.013	−.006
	(.076)	(.081)	(.054)
$\bar{s}_{m-9}$	.029	−.040	.020
	(.083)	(.089)	(.060)
$\bar{s}_{m-10}$	−.011	−.168	−.041
	(.087)	(.093)	(.062)
$\bar{s}_{m-11}$	−.106	.064	−.049
	(.079)	(.085)	(.057)
$\bar{s}_{m-12}$	−.061	−.148*	.036
	(.064)	(.068)	(.046)
s_{m-13}	−.060*	−.053*	.014
	(.020)	(.022)	(.015)
		Overflow	
Demand	−.005	.011*	.008*
	(.005)	(.005)	(.004)
Time	.003	−.004	−.002
	(.007)	(.008)	(.005)

Table 6-6 (continued)

	Deposits Due from Banks	Total Reserves	Loans to Banks
		Capital	
c_t	.007	.206*	.014
	(.022)	(.024)	(.016)
		Summary Statistics	
R^2	.136	.157	.092
S_ε	.017	.018	.012
F	8.021*	9.935*	4.724*
Mean	.045	.081	.003
Item Number(s) in Table 5-1	55	58, 59	31

securities maturing in under one year were not interesting. While the joint influence of the exogenous variables on the value of each security category was significant at the 5 percent level, the estimated coefficients displayed an erratic pattern. One interpretation is that the components of short-term government securities are sufficiently close substitutes that specific market conditions, and not the pattern of deposit flows, dictate when a particular asset is purchased.[15]

c. Consumer loans

The estimated coefficients for different types of consumer loans are reported in tables 6-7 and 6-8. There is a gradual and fairly steady flow of demand deposits into automobile loans; the long-run coefficient is more than twice the coefficient for the first "month." While the long-run coefficient for time deposits is not significantly different from the corresponding coefficient for demand deposits, the time path for a time deposit shock is much more erratic.

---

15. It is interesting that a similar erratic pattern was not obtained for the components of cash assets; apparently cash assets have some "fixed proportions" that need to be explained.

TABLE 6-7. CONSUMER LOANS: DEMAND DEPOSIT COEFFICIENTS

	Automobile	Other Consumer Installment	Repair and Modernization	Single Payment
$\bar{d}_w$	.020	.005	.005	.009
	(.011)	(.005)	(.002)	(.013)
$\bar{d}_{w-1}$	.035*	−.003	.005	.024
	(.012)	(.006)	(.003)	(.015)
$\bar{d}_{w-2}$	.026*	.000	.007*	.014
	(.012)	(.006)	(.003)	(.015)
$\bar{d}_{sm}$	.036*	−.000	.010*	.014
	(.010)	(.005)	(.002)	(.013)
$\bar{d}_{m-2}$	.035*	.002	.006*	.024*
	(.009)	(.005)	(.002)	(.012)
$\bar{d}_{m-3}$	.016	.005	.005*	.038*
	(.010)	(.005)	(.002)	(.012)
$\bar{d}_{m-4}$	.046*	.003	.008*	.010
	(.010)	(.005)	(.002)	(.013)
$\bar{d}_{m-5}$	.037*	.007	.005*	.027*
	(.010)	(.005)	(.002)	(.012)
$\bar{d}_{m-6}$	.044*	.009	.008*	.034*
	(.009)	(.005)	(.002)	(.012)
$\bar{d}_{m-7}$	.032*	.006	.011*	.048*
	(.010)	(.005)	(.002)	(.013)
$\bar{d}_{m-8}$	.043*	.004	.006*	.045*
	(.011)	(.005)	(.002)	(.013)
$\bar{d}_{m-9}$	.021*	.011*	.008*	.059*
	(.010)	(.005)	(.002)	(.013)
$\bar{d}_{m-10}$	.045*	.013*	.011*	.053*
	(.010)	(.005)	(.002)	(.013)
$\bar{d}_{m-11}$	.057*	.002	.009*	.080*
	(.011)	(.006)	(.002)	(.014)
$\bar{d}_{m-12}$	.035*	.014*	.008*	.085*
	(.011)	(.005)	(.002)	(.014)
d_{m-13}	.062*	.012*	.008*	.079*
	(.005)	(.003)	(.001)	(.007)

NOTE: See last row in table 6-8 for sources of dependent variables.

TABLE 6-8. CONSUMER LOANS: TIME DEPOSIT AND OTHER COEFFICIENTS

	Automobile	Other Consumer Installment	Repair and Modernization	Single Payment
$\bar{s}_w$	−.002	.002	.008	−.048
	(.051)	(.026)	(.011)	(.064)
$\bar{s}_{w-1}$	.051	.033	.010	.007
	(.049)	(.025)	(.011)	(.062)
$\bar{s}_{w-2}$	.082	.010	−.002	.021
	(.049)	(.025)	(.011)	(.062)
$\bar{s}_{sm}$	.064	.017	.010	−.058
	(.044)	(.022)	(.010)	(.056)
$\bar{s}_{m-2}$	.008	.011	−.003	.058
	(.037)	(.019)	(.008)	(.047)
$\bar{s}_{m-3}$	.062	.003	.014	−.083
	(.043)	(.022)	(.010)	(.055)
$\bar{s}_{m-4}$	.064	.033	.005	−.028
	(.043)	(.022)	(.010)	(.055)
$\bar{s}_{m-5}$	.041	.017	.001	−.015
	(.036)	(.018)	(.008)	(.046)
$\bar{s}_{m-6}$	.092*	−.024	.009	.040
	(.037)	(.019)	(.008)	(.048)
$\bar{s}_{m-7}$	.060	−.038	.008	−.114
	(.046)	(.023)	(.010)	(.059)
$\bar{s}_{m-8}$	.093*	.041*	.001	−.122*
	(.039)	(.020)	(.009)	(.050)
$\bar{s}_{m-9}$	.061	−.020	.002	.078
	(.044)	(.022)	(.010)	(.055)
$\bar{s}_{m-10}$	.085	.015	.001	.077
	(.045)	(.023)	(.010)	(.057)
$\bar{s}_{m-11}$	.051	−.010	.011	−.168*
	(.041)	(.021)	(.009)	(.053)
$\bar{s}_{m-12}$	.070*	.019	−.003	.018
	(.033)	(.017)	(.007)	(.042)
s_{m-13}	.047*	.013*	.009*	.005
	(.011)	(.005)	(.002)	(.014)
		Overflow		
Demand	−.005*	.002	.002*	.000
	(.003)	(.001)	(.001)	(.003)
Time	−.004	.005*	.002*	.003
	(.004)	(.002)	(.001)	(.005)

Table 6-8 (continued)

	Automobile	Other Consumer Installment	Repair and Modernization	Single Payment
		Capital		
c_t	.071*	.024*	.009*	.082*
	(.012)	(.006)	(.003)	(.015)
		Summary Statistics		
R^2	.112	.047	.032	.090
S_ε	.009	.004	.002	.011
F	6.108*	2.141*	1.403*	4.655*
Mean	.054	.014	.008	.054
Item Number in Table 5-1	37	38	39	41

Both repair loans and single payment loans increase steadily in the periods following a demand deposit inflow. Other consumer loans exhibit a more erratic pattern but are allocated a statistically significant share of demand deposit balances in the long run.

All categories of consumer loans respond erratically to time deposit changes. By the end of a year following a deposit shock, however, with the exception of single payment loans there was no significant difference in the proportions of demand and time deposits allocated to a specific consumer loan category.

d. Mortgage loans

Individual components of the mortgage loan portfolio also respond interestingly to deposit inflows. The deposit coefficients for insured residential, uninsured residential, and nonfarm, nonresidential mortgage loans are reported in tables 6-9 and 6-10.

The flows into insured mortgage loans are very erratic and relatively minor from both demand and time deposit shocks. The existence of an active secondary market for insured mortgage loans apparently makes it possible for banks to buy and sell these assets without concern for precise timing. It does appear, however, that equilibrium values are

TABLE 6-9. MORTGAGE LOANS: DEMAND DEPOSIT COEFFICIENTS

	Insured	Conventional	Nonfarm Nonresidential
$\bar{d}_w$	.007	.011	.011
	(.006)	(.010)	(.007)
$\bar{d}_{w-1}$	.011	.010	.008
	(.006)	(.011)	(.008)
$\bar{d}_{w-2}$	.008	.020	.005
	(.007)	(.012)	(.008)
$\bar{d}_{sm}$	.004	.009	.009
	(.006)	(.010)	(.007)
$\bar{d}_{m-2}$	.008	−.009	.008
	(.005)	(.009)	(.006)
$\bar{d}_{m-3}$	.008	.015	.018*
	(.005)	(.009)	(.007)
$\bar{d}_{m-4}$	.001	.012	.012
	(.006)	(.010)	(.007)
$\bar{d}_{m-5}$	.008	.008	.008
	(.005)	(.009)	(.006)
$\bar{d}_{m-6}$	.012*	.017*	.028*
	(.005)	(.009)	(.006)
$\bar{d}_{m-7}$	.006	.021*	.011
	(.006)	(.010)	(.007)
$\bar{d}_{m-8}$	−.000	.025*	.020*
	(.006)	(.010)	(.007)
$\bar{d}_{m-9}$	.011	.016	.024*
	(.005)	(.009)	(.007)
$\bar{d}_{m-10}$	−.003	.049*	.026*
	(.006)	(.010)	(.007)
$\bar{d}_{m-11}$	−.001	.030*	.018*
	(.006)	(.010)	(.007)
$\bar{d}_{m-12}$	.012	.023*	.026*
	(.006)	(.010)	(.007)
d_{m-13}	.013*	.040*	.028*
	(.003)	(.005)	(.003)

NOTE: See last row in table 6-10 for sources of dependent variables.

TABLE 6-10. MORTGAGE LOANS: TIME DEPOSIT AND OTHER
COEFFICIENTS

	Insured	Conventional	Nonfarm Nonresidential
$\bar{s}_w$	.032	.041	−.008
	(.028)	(.048)	(.034)
$\bar{s}_{w-1}$	.022	.032	−.040
	(.027)	(.046)	(.033)
$\bar{s}_{w-2}$	−.034	.083	.031
	(.027)	(.047)	(.033)
$\bar{s}_{sm}$	−.026	.044	.015
	(.024)	(.042)	(.030)
$\bar{s}_{m-2}$	.024	.070*	.030
	(.020)	(.035)	(.025)
$\bar{s}_{m-3}$	−.003	.086*	−.023
	(.024)	(.041)	(.029)
$\bar{s}_{m-4}$	.068*	.054	−.010
	(.024)	(.041)	(.029)
$\bar{s}_{m-5}$	−.027	.124*	.045
	(.020)	(.035)	(.025)
$\bar{s}_{m-6}$	−.019	.131*	.054*
	(.021)	(.036)	(.025)
$\bar{s}_{m-7}$	.025	.103*	.016
	(.026)	(.044)	(.031)
$\bar{s}_{m-8}$	.037	.132*	.082*
	(.022)	(.038)	(.027)
$\bar{s}_{m-9}$	−.006	.183*	−.014
	(.024)	(.042)	(.029)
$\bar{s}_{m-10}$	.040	.142*	.097*
	(.025)	(.043)	(.030)
$\bar{s}_{m-11}$	.020	.152*	.086*
	(.023)	(.040)	(.028)
$\bar{s}_{m-12}$	.024	.195*	.041
	(.018)	(.032)	(.022)
s_{m-13}	.025*	.185*	.073*
	(.006)	(.010)	(.007)
	Overflow		
Demand	.002	.002	−.002
	(.001)	(.003)	(.002)
Time	.000	.012*	.007*
	(.002)	(.004)	(.003)

Table 6-10 (continued)

	Insured	Conventional	Nonfarm Nonresidential
		Capital	
c_t	.020*	.058*	.034*
	(.006)	(.011)	(.008)
		Summary Statistics	
R^2	.101	.208	.113
S_ε	.005	.008	.006
F	5.368*	16.133*	6.224*
Mean	.020	.075	.038
Item Number in Table 5-1	28	29	30

reached within a year. A somewhat larger proportion of time deposits than demand deposits is allocated to insured mortgage loans in the long run.

The flows into conventional mortgage loans are both more sizable and more steady than is the case for insured loans. While the flow of demand deposits into conventional loans is considerably smaller than is the case for time deposits; it is relatively steady with equilibrium probably being achieved within a year. The allocation of time deposits to conventional loans rises steadily following a deposit shock and reaches an equilibrium value within a year.

Nonfarm, nonresidential real estate loans have an erratic pattern of time deposit coefficients. Time deposits apparently are placed in these loans as credit requests arise; the loans approach their equilibrium share by the eleventh month. The proportion of demand deposits allocated to these loans rises relatively steadily to a value more than twice the initial allocation. Again, however, the long-run share of time deposits allocated to nonfarm, nonresidential loans is greater than that of demand deposits.

4. RESIDUALS AND PREDICTIONS

This section is in two parts. First, the residuals from the regressions of section 1 are analyzed. Second, some measures of the predictive ability of the model outside the sample period are reported.

a. Residuals

The balance sheet identity forces each asset variable's residual to be perfectly negatively correlated with the sum of all other asset residuals. With this fact in mind, it is none the less interesting to examine the pattern of residual correlations in order to see which assets appear to be strong "substitutes."[16] These correlations are shown in table 6-11. The largest negative correlation by a wide margin is between short- and intermediate-term government securities. An interpretation of this finding is that bank investment officers are quite sensitive to interest rate differentials on these two assets. The next two strongest correlations are between short-term securities and cash and short-term securities and commercial and industrial loans. This pattern tends to confirm the widely accepted view that Treasury bills and other short-term government securities provide the interest rate linkage within bank portfolios. Finally, there is some evidence that commercial and industrial loans and consumer loans are weak substitutes.

TABLE 6-11. CORRELATIONS OF RESIDUALS FROM INPUT-OUTPUT MODEL
FOR ASSET AGGREGATES

	Cash	State and Local	Mort-gage	Comm. and Indust.	Con-sumer	Shorts	1–5s
Cash	1.000	−.082	−.076	−.107	−.167	−.251	−.083
State and local	—	1.000	−.063	−.041	−.097	−.153	−.067
Mortgage	—	—	1.000	−.016	.080	−.080	−.017
Comm. and Indust.	—	—	—	1.000	−.180	−.238	−.034
Consumer	—	—	—	—	1.000	−.139	−.007
Shorts	—	—	—	—	—	1.000	−.416
1–5s	—	—	—	—	—	—	1.000

b. Predictions

The June 1964 call report was left out of the sample to provide a basis for measuring the ability of the model to predict outside the sample period. Some results of this experiment are reported here.

16. The term *substitutes* is somewhat misleading. It is not possible to identify substitutes in the sense of consumer demand theory without making further restrictive assumptions.

All variables were taken as deviations from means computed over the full April 1961 through June 1964 period. The estimated coefficients for the eight asset variables of section 1 were used with these data to obtain June 1964 predictions. Selected measures of the predictive ability of the model for the assets of section 1 are reported in table 6-12. The mean error—actual less predicted—and the root mean squared error were computed and the standard error of forecast was evaluated at the mean values of the exogenous variables for June 1964.

TABLE 6-12. PORTFOLIO SHARE PREDICTIONS FOR THE MEAN SAMPLE BANK

		June 1964			
	Average Actual Value			*Root Mean*	*Standard*
		Actual	*Forecast*	*Squared*	*Error of*
Asset	*1961–64*	*Value*	*Error*[a]	*Error*	*Forecast*
Cash	.157	.158	.011	.030	.023
State and local	.082	.082	.017	.027	.016
Mortgage	.149	.148	.005	.022	.010
Comm. and indust.	.158	.160	.007	.028	.018
Consumer	.183	.185	.008	.032	.016
Shorts	.052	.052	−.027	.048	.036
1–5s	.094	.093	−.007	.039	.029
All other assets	.125	.122	−.014	N.A.	N.A.
Total assets	1.000	1.000	0.000		

[a] Actual less predicted.

As the table indicates, the model predicts the mean bank's assets relatively well. With the exception of short-term government securities and state and local securities, the mean errors are moderate. The mean error for every asset except state and local securities was less than its corresponding standard error of forecast. The mean error, of course, partly reflects interest rate movements that have not been allowed for in this forecasting experiment. The model overpredicted mean holdings of government securities and of residual other assets, while it underpredicted cash, state and local securities, and the three loan categories. These results are not surprising given the strong loan demands experienced during the period.

5. Summary and Conclusions

The results of this chapter clearly indicate that it is possible to obtain reasonable estimates of lag structures for a variety of assets from individual bank data. These lag structures accord with a priori expectations, and they are stationary over the sample period. The results indicate that individual banks respond faster to deposit shocks than is often inferred from studies of aggregate data.

The estimated long-run shares of deposits going into different assets largely accord with a priori expectations. In the long run demand deposits primarily flow into cash assets, commercial and industrial loans, and consumer loans; mortgage loans, United States government and state and local securities absorb relatively little of this flow. An increase in time deposits, on the other hand, has its greatest impact on mortgage loans. Capital funds and nondeposit liabilities primarily go into various types of loans and, rather unexpectedly, into cash assets.

In general, the theory is more successful in predicting the lag structure for demand deposits than it is for time deposits. The estimated lag patterns for time deposits are erratic; the negative long-run time deposit coefficients in the cash asset equations are particularly bothersome. Possible explanations for these results are size aggregation effects, liquidity effects, and evidence that the time deposit autoregressive process was not stationary over the sample period.[17] There is a clear need for further research on the nature of stochastic processes generating deposit series and on the predictability and magnitude of the cash flow from existing assets. Very little is known about either of these topics.

The description of bank portfolio management is far from completed. It remains to be seen whether the input-output model can be successfully applied to mutual savings banks. Further, the model is apt to be misspecified if banks actively anticipate future deposit flows; the adaptive-expectations model remains to be tested. Finally, the lag structures estimated in this chapter apply only to individual banks. It is still necessary to determine how the dynamics of individual bank portfolio adjustments are related to the adjustments of the entire banking system. These and related subjects are treated in subsequent chapters.

17. See chapter 8 for details on deposit processes.

Parameter Estimates for the Model
When Bank Effects Are Not Removed

This appendix reports estimates of the parameters of the input-output model when bank means are not removed from the data. The results from a regression analysis of the asset aggregates of section 1 are reported in tables 6A-1, 6A-2, and 6A-3. Results for the legal reserve measure are reported in table 6A-4.

The pattern of deposit coefficients is more erratic for each asset category when bank means are retained; time deposit coefficients are particularly affected. The argument of chapters 2 and 3 suggests that, as special relationships are likely to exist between individual banks and their loan customers, bank effects are more important for loans than for holdings of securities and cash. The results confirm this expectation. The relationships between deposit flows and holdings of commercial and industrial loans, mortgage loans, and consumer loans are particularly erratic when bank means are retained. Retention of bank means has a much smaller impact on the pattern of coefficients for cash assets and securities. The coefficients for cash assets and legal reserves are particularly stable, and both of these asset categories have a positive long-run time deposit coefficient. Holdings of state and local securities, one- to five-year government securities, and other assets are not regularly related to deposit flows, whether bank means are removed or not. Attitudes toward the allocation of capital among assets apparently differ greatly among individual banks, as witnessed by the erratic pattern of coefficients on capital.

TABLE 6A-1. INPUT-OUTPUT MODEL WHEN NO BANK EFFECTS ARE REMOVED:
DEMAND DEPOSIT COEFFICIENTS

	Cash	State and Local	Mort-gage	Comm. and Indust.	Con-sumer	Shorts	1–5s	Other
$\bar{a}_w$	.438*	.121*	−.054	.184*	−.032	.187*	−.071	.227
	(.040)	(.061)	(.064)	(.075)	(.081)	(.061)	(.063)	
$\bar{a}_{w-1}$	.277*	−.072	.021	.421*	−.007	.225*	.143*	−.008
	(.043)	(.065)	(.069)	(.080)	(.087)	(.065)	(.067)	
$\bar{a}_{w-2}$	.370*	−.070	−.065	−.004	.136	.308*	.059	.266
	(.045)	(.068)	(.072)	(.084)	(.091)	(.068)	(.070)	
$\bar{a}_{sm}$	.384*	.149*	.042	−.101	.078	.362*	−.004	.090
	(.037)	(.057)	(.060)	(.070)	(.076)	(.057)	(.059)	
$\bar{a}_{m-2}$	.243*	.016	−.059	.112	.195*	.343*	.046	.104
	(.034)	(.052)	(.055)	(.064)	(.069)	(.052)	(.054)	
$\bar{a}_{m-3}$	.180*	−.042	−.018	.214*	.181*	.294*	.101	.090
	(.035)	(.053)	(.056)	(.065)	(.071)	(.054)	(.055)	
$\bar{a}_{m-4}$	.192*	.089	.029	.044	.083	.414*	.057	.092
	(.036)	(.055)	(.058)	(.068)	(.073)	(.055)	(.057)	
$\bar{a}_{m-5}$	.211*	−.031	−.031	.123	.240*	.296*	.072	.120
	(.034)	(.052)	(.055)	(.064)	(.069)	(.052)	(.054)	
$\bar{a}_{m-6}$	.161*	.011	.013	.111	.287*	.303*	.103*	.011
	(.032)	(.048)	(.051)	(.059)	(.064)	(.048)	(.050)	
$\bar{a}_{m-7}$	.231*	.084	−.007	.140*	.103	.205*	.111	.133
	(.037)	(.057)	(.060)	(.070)	(.076)	(.057)	(.059)	
$\bar{a}_{m-8}$	.233*	.082	.024	−.040	.271*	.250*	.045	.135
	(.036)	(.055)	(.058)	(.068)	(.073)	(.055)	(.057)	
$\bar{a}_{m-9}$	.212*	.074	.017	.101	.267*	.200*	.074	.055
	(.032)	(.049)	(.052)	(.060)	(.065)	(.049)	(.051)	
$\bar{a}_{m-10}$	.211*	−.019	.017	.110	.250*	.164*	.110	.157
	(.036)	(.056)	(.059)	(.068)	(.074)	(.056)	(.057)	
$\bar{a}_{m-11}$	.278*	.140*	.014	−.025	.370*	.100	.043	.080
	(.037)	(.056)	(.060)	(.069)	(.075)	(.057)	(.058)	
$\bar{a}_{m-12}$	.222*	.132*	.017	.055	.311*	.008	.184*	.071
	(.036)	(.055)	(.058)	(.068)	(.073)	(.055)	(.057)	
d_{m-13}	.203*	.082*	.050*	.131*	.189*	.058*	.144*	.143
	(.007)	(.010)	(.011)	(.012)	(.013)	(.010)	(.010)	

NOTE: See last row in table 6A-3 for sources of dependent variables.

TABLE 6A-2. INPUT-OUTPUT MODEL WHEN NO BANK EFFECTS ARE REMOVED: TIME DEPOSIT COEFFICIENTS

	Cash	State and Local	Mortgage	Comm. and Indust.	Consumer	Shorts	1–5s	Other
$\bar{s}_w$	.199	−.254	.629*	.828*	−.224	.315	−.477	−.016
	(.192)	(.292)	(.309)	(.359)	(.390)	(.294)	(.303)	
$\bar{s}_{w-1}$	−.013	.460	.345	.541	.297	.081	−.403	−.308
	(.183)	(.280)	(.296)	(.344)	(.373)	(.282)	(.290)	
$\bar{s}_{w-2}$	−.165	−.082	.493	.041	.422	.495	.180	−.384
	(.189)	(.288)	(.305)	(.355)	(.385)	(.290)	(.299)	
$\bar{s}_{sm}$	−.051	−.124	.142	.254	.654	.362	.044	−.281
	(.166)	(.253)	(.267)	(.311)	(.337)	(.255)	(.262)	
$\bar{s}_{m-2}$	.187	−.332	.181	.627*	.330	.090	−.108	.025
	(.137)	(.210)	(.222)	(.258)	(.280)	(.211)	(.217)	
$\bar{s}_{m-3}$	−.293	−.028	.586*	.407	.954*	.194	−.218	−.602
	(.158)	(.241)	(.255)	(.297)	(.322)	(.243)	(.250)	
$\bar{s}_{m-4}$	−.264	.000	.472	.344	−.189	.871*	−.264	.030
	(.165)	(.253)	(.267)	(.310)	(.337)	(.254)	(.261)	
$\bar{s}_{m-5}$	.146	−.327	.175	.418	.783*	.066	−.116	−.145
	(.132)	(.201)	(.213)	(.248)	(.268)	(.203)	(.208)	
$\bar{s}_{m-6}$	−.220	−.000	.594*	.252	.630*	.391	−.282	−.365
	(.142)	(.216)	(.229)	(.266)	(.288)	(.218)	(.224)	
$\bar{s}_{m-7}$	−.103	.023	.617*	.171	.300	.313	.016	−.337
	(.171)	(.261)	(.276)	(.321)	(.348)	(.262)	(.270)	
$\bar{s}_{m-8}$	.087	−.362	−.072	.621*	.400	.189	.122	.015
	(.141)	(.215)	(.227)	(.264)	(.286)	(.216)	(.222)	
$\bar{s}_{m-9}$	−.261	.045	1.068*	.001	.774*	.149	−.386	−.390
	(.161)	(.246)	(.260)	(.302)	(.328)	(.247)	(.254)	
$\bar{s}_{m-10}$	.039	−.363	.524	.766*	.274	.072	−.236	−.076
	(.167)	(.255)	(.269)	(.313)	(.340)	(.256)	(.264)	
$\bar{s}_{m-11}$	−.087	−.431	.331	.504	.363	.297	.071	−.048
	(.155)	(.237)	(.250)	(.291)	(.316)	(.238)	(.245)	
$\bar{s}_{m-12}$	−.243*	.033	.552*	.266	.770*	.043	−.268	−.153
	(.122)	(.187)	(.197)	(.229)	(.249)	(.188)	(.193)	
s_{m-13}	.044*	.035*	.459*	−.009	.078*	.012	.128*	.253
	(.006)	(.009)	(.010)	(.011)	(.012)	(.009)	(.009)	

TABLE 6A-3. INPUT-OUTPUT MODEL WHEN NO BANK EFFECTS ARE REMOVED:
OTHER COEFFICIENTS

	Cash	State and Local	Mort-gage	Comm. and Indust.	Con-sumer	Shorts	1–5s	Other
			Call Report Dummy Variables					
4-12-61	.016*	−.014	−.010	.001	−.010	.017*	.002	−.002
	(.005)	(.007)	(.008)	(.009)	(.010)	(.007)	(.008)	
6-30-61	.010*	−.002	−.009	.002	−.008	.018*	−.002	−.009
	(.005)	(.007)	(.008)	(.009)	(.010)	(.008)	(.008)	
9-27-61	.015*	.005	−.004	−.005	−.010	.020*	−.005	−.016
	(.005)	(.007)	(.008)	(.009)	(.010)	(.007)	(.008)	
12-30-61	.035*	−.010	−.001	−.006	−.016	.008	.012	−.022
	(.004)	(.006)	(.007)	(.008)	(.Q08)	(.006)	(.007)	
3-26-62	.015*	−.008	−.006	.002	−.018	.018*	.002	−.005
	(.005)	(.007)	(.008)	(.009)	(.010)	(.007)	(.008)	
6-30-62	.010*	.002	−.006	.003	−.006	.013	−.001	−.015
	(.005)	(.007)	(.008)	(.009)	(.010)	(.008)	(.008)	
9-28-62	.011*	.010	−.006	−.004	−.010	.017*	−.010	−.008
	(.005)	(.007)	(.008)	(.009)	(.010)	(.007)	(.008)	
12-28-62	.030*	−.009	−.004	−.011	−.012	.008	−.003	.001
	(.004)	(.007)	(.007)	(.008)	(.009)	(.007)	(.007)	
3-18-63	.024*	.001	−.006	−.009	−.023*	.010	−.005	.008
	(.005)	(.008)	(.008)	(.009)	(.010)	(.008)	(.008)	
6-29-63	.009*	.004	−.007	.000	−.006	−.001	.002	−.001
	(.005)	(.007)	(.008)	(.009)	(.010)	(.007)	(.007)	
				Overflow				
De-mand	.002	−.010	.007	.015	−.021	.015	.013	−.021
	(.009)	(.013)	(.014)	(.016)	(.017)	(.013)	(.014)	
Time	−.001	−.002	.047*	.065*	−.044	.066*	.022	−.133
	(.012)	(.019)	(.020)	(.023)	(.025)	(.019)	(.020)	
				Capital				
c_t	.154*	.131*	−.103*	.492*	.291*	.198*	−.106*	−.057
	(.028)	(.042)	(.044)	(.052)	(.056)	(.042)	(.043)	
				Summary Statistics				
R^2	.441	.076	.646	.207	.099	.121	.051	N.A.
S_ε	.036	.054	.058	.067	.073	.055	.056	N.A.
F	31.585*	3.276*	72.827*	10.424*	4.395*	5.518*	2.102*	N.A.
Mean	.164	.069	.140	.150	.165	.082	.100	.130
Item Num-ber(s) in Table 5-1	1	3	27, 28, 29, 30	36	37, 38, 39, 40, 41	44, 45, 46, 49	47, 50	Residual

TABLE 6A-4. INPUT-OUTPUT MODEL WHEN NO BANK EFFECTS ARE REMOVED: TOTAL RESERVES

Demand Deposits		Time Deposits		Call Report Dummy Variables	
$\bar{d}_w$	.164*	$\bar{s}_w$	−.197	4-12-61	.010*
	(.027)		(.130)		(.003)
$\bar{d}_{w-1}$	.038	$\bar{s}_{w-1}$	−.138	6-30-61	−.000
	(.029)		(.125)		(.003)
$\bar{d}_{w-2}$	.208*	$\bar{s}_{w-2}$	.019	9-27-61	.014*
	(.030)		(.129)		(.003)
$\bar{d}_{sm}$	.170*	$\bar{s}_{sm}$	−.020	12-30-61	.013*
	(.025)		(.113)		(.003)
$\bar{d}_{m-2}$	.131*	$\bar{s}_{m-2}$	−.011	3-26-62	.006
	(.023)		(.093)		(.003)
$\bar{d}_{m-3}$	.088*	$\bar{s}_{m-3}$	−.212*	6-30-62	.001
	(.024)		(.108)		(.003)
$\bar{d}_{m-4}$	.091*	$\bar{s}_{m-4}$	−.043	9-28-62	.007*
	(.025)		(.113)		(.003)
$\bar{d}_{m-5}$	.111*	$\bar{s}_{m-5}$	−.115	12-28-62	.017*
	(.023)		(.090)		(.003)
$\bar{d}_{m-6}$	.095*	$\bar{s}_{m-6}$	.003	3-18-63	.006
	(.021)		(.096)		(.003)
$\bar{d}_{m-7}$	.128*	$\bar{s}_{m-7}$	−.046	6-29-63	.002
	(.025)		(.116)		(.003)
$\bar{d}_{m-8}$	.152*	$\bar{s}_{m-8}$	.036	Overflow	
	(.025)		(.096)	Demand	.020*
$\bar{d}_{m-9}$	.126*	$\bar{s}_{m-9}$	−.091		(.006)
	(.022)		(.110)	Time	−.006
$\bar{d}_{m-10}$	.079*	$\bar{s}_{m-10}$	−.204		(.008)
	(.025)		(.114)		
				Capital	
$\bar{d}_{m-11}$	.196*	$\bar{s}_{m-11}$	.037	c_t	.112*
	(.025)		(.106)		(.019)
$\bar{d}_{m-12}$	.149*	$\bar{s}_{m-12}$	−.142	Summary Statistics	
	(.025)		(.083)	R^2	.252
d_{m-13}	.091*	s_{m-13}	.034*	S_ε	.024
	(.005)		(.004)	F	10.368*
				Mean	.081
				Item Number(s) in Table 5-1	58, 59

CHAPTER 7

Estimates for the Input-Output Model from a Sample of Mutual Savings Banks

This chapter reports tests of the input-output model of mutual savings bank portfolio behavior. They were performed using data from 201 savings banks located in Connecticut, Massachusetts, New York City, and the rest of New York State. As explained in chapter 5, each of these geographic regions is studied separately.

The first section describes preliminary experiments that were performed on a pilot sample of ten large New York City banks. Section 2 reports and evaluates structural estimates for the four populations of savings banks. The third section discusses further experiments that were executed in an attempt to interpret these estimates. The last section summarizes the findings of this chapter and raises some important research questions for interpreting capital markets in which mutually chartered firms participate.

Empirical results reported in this chapter were chronologically the earliest attempts at estimating bank input-output models.[1] The experiments reported in section 1, therefore, are of additional interest because they describe the preliminary empirical filtering that underlies the specifications described in chapter 4.

1. PILOT STUDIES

A number of important preliminary questions were considered while designing the statistical model of this chapter. These were:

1. How many consecutive monthly deposit changes should be used to explain monthly first differences in savings bank portfolios?
2. What, if any, allowance should be made for seasonal variations in bank asset acquisitions?
3. Is the estimated structure the same for different banks?
4. Is the estimated structure invariant over the sample period?

Crude answers to these questions were obtained by studying a pilot sample of ten mutual savings banks located in New York City. This sample was not randomly drawn, but it appeared representative and

---

1. Preliminary versions of results reported in this chapter were presented by Hester [1965].

included banks ranging in size from $50 million to more than $1 billion in total assets.[2]

The first question is critical for what follows, since only sixty monthly balance sheets were available for each bank. Computer software and budget restrictions required that all banks be assumed to have identical deposit change horizons. For cost reasons the adaptive-expectations model discussed in chapter 9 was to be estimated in the same computer run as the input-output model. Since a seasonal deposit forecasting term was believed essential, the maximum number of observations available for any bank was forty-seven, and this only if banks made all portfolio adjustments in response to a one-month deposit forecast. The argument of the model, however, suggested that banks would respond to deposit flows, forecasted or otherwise, with a pronounced lag. If portfolios reached equilibrium after responding to seven consecutive monthly deposit forecasts, forty-one observations could be retained. Interviews with savings bankers led us to believe that this horizon was realistic.

To check this assumption first differences of mortgage loans, the primary savings bank asset, were regressed on current and different numbers of past consecutive monthly changes in regular savings deposits for each pilot sample bank. Table 7-1 reports multiple correlation coefficients obtained in regressions having one, five, and eight monthly deposit change coefficients. With the exception of bank 8, increasing the adjustment horizon from five to eight months resulted in a negligible improvement in fit.[3] Bank 8 had a multiple correlation of .841 when seven months were studied. It was concluded that eight monthly changes would suffice to describe the relation between deposits and assets.

The second question is important because the model does not predict the presence of seasonal determinants. If seasonal determinants are found, they probably reflect variations in the demand for mortgage loans associated with seasonal fluctuations in house construction and suggest the presence of simultaneous equations problems. The question was studied by examining residuals for regressions referred to in table 7-1 and by introducing monthly dummy variables in pooled regressions computed

---

2. Pilot sample banks were retained in the New York City sample studied in the remainder of this chapter. This procedure permits more efficient estimates of parameters; it also implies that the specifications studied are not independent of data resources for those banks. The pilot sample represented about 25 percent of the New York City data.

3. The improvement in the multiple correlation coefficient by increasing the number of deposit variables from five to eight was significant at the 1 percent level for bank 8; it was not significant at the 1 percent level for the nine other banks. In section 3 alternative horizons of up to fifteen months are considered for each of the samples.

for 470 pilot sample bank-month observations. Individual bank residuals suggested a weak tendency to overpredict mortgage loans in April. However this tendency did not come through when changes in individual bank assets were regressed on eight deposit changes and eleven seasonal dummies in the pooled sample. More generally, an analysis of variance test for seasonality in the cases of six savings bank assets permitted the hypothesis that seasonal factors were present to be rejected at the 1 percent level.[4]

TABLE 7-1. MORTGAGE LOAN MULTIPLE CORRELATION
COEFFICIENTS FOR DIFFERENT ADJUSTMENT HORIZONS

	Horizon (in months)		
Bank	*1*	*5*	*8*
1	.415	.550	.559
2	.539	.839	.861
3	.630	.749	.775
4	.876	.910	.924
5	.740	.836	.869
6	.655	.773	.783
7	.790	.825	.840
8	.774	.797	.857
9	.566	.791	.809
10	.913	.917	.923

NOTE: All regressions were estimated from 47 monthly observations on a bank spanning the period February 1960 through December 1963.

The third and fourth questions were studied by comparing different regressions of monthly changes in mortgage loans on the contemporaneous and the seven consecutive past monthly changes in a bank's regular savings deposits. An intercept was included in each regression to allow for a linear time trend, and 470 pilot sample bank–time period observations were used. To examine the third question separate mortgage loan equations were estimated for each bank and for the pooled sample. An analysis of covariance indicated that a hypothesis that different banks have the same

4. The six assets were cash, United States government securities, state and local securities, other securities, mortgage loans, and other loans. An undetected computer program error invalidated the test for seasonal factors in all other assets. Observations in this experiment were drawn from the period of August 1960 through December 1963.

mortgage loan equation cannot be rejected; the computed F-ratio was less than unity.

The fourth question was examined by breaking the pooled sample into two subsamples; the first refers to mortgage loan changes recorded in the period of February 1960 through January 1962, and the second concerns mortgage loan changes in the subsequent twenty-three months. An analysis of covariance indicated that the hypothesis of intertemporal stationarity must be rejected at the 1 percent level of significance. This disconcerting result was ultimately found to recur in the four different populations of savings banks, and it is discussed extensively in the third and fourth sections of this chapter.

2. Structural Estimates of the Input-Output Model

In this section, four large pooled cross-section, time-series samples are employed to estimate parameters for the input-output model. Utilizing results from the pilot experiments, it is assumed in this section that savings banks reach equilibrium eight months after a deposit shock. Forty-one observations are available for each bank, and no fewer than thirty-two banks are represented in each of the samples. Thus, 1,312, 3,649, 1,599, and 1,681 observations, respectively, are studied in the Connecticut, Massachusetts, New York City, and New York State regressions.

Tables 7-2 through 7-5 report regression results for these samples. Given the number of observations, it is not surprising that all but one regression have F-ratios that are significant at the 1 percent level. Multiple correlation coefficients tend to be quite high for first differences in mortgage loans in all four samples. They are also high in the case of "other loans" for Connecticut, Massachusetts, and New York State banks, but not for the much larger banks in the New York City sample. These loans consist of heterogeneous nonmortgage loans, and, while small in volume, they are quite sensitive to deposit flows for banks outside of New York City. The fact that New York City banks do not have a similarly strong relationship suggests that many close substitutes exist for other loans in the New York money market.

In the case of Massachusetts banks, the multiple correlation coefficient for first differences in United States government securities is also high. This reflects the fact that Massachusetts imposes state deposit taxes that effectively discourage its banks from investing in corporate securities. Since deposits invested in certain United States government securities are exempt from these taxes, Massachusetts banks are induced to place essentially all secondary reserves and short-term investments in this class of

TABLE 7-2. CONNECTICUT MUTUAL SAVINGS BANK INPUT-OUTPUT COEFFICIENTS

	Cash	United States Government Securities	State and Local Securities	Other Securities	Mortgage Loans	Other Loans	Other Assets
Intercept	-4.522	-40.638	7.820	7.125	46.568	-7.797	-8.553
$\bar{m}_t$	.0894*	.4251*	-.0096	.2083*	.1362*	.1409*	.0096
	(.0197)	(.0349)	(.0076)	(.0328)	(.0261)	(.0124)	(.0087)
$\bar{m}_{t-1}$	.0223	-.0584	-.0003	-.0213	.0972*	-.0349*	-.0045
	(.0195)	(.0346)	(.0076)	(.0326)	(.0259)	(.0123)	(.0086)
$\bar{m}_{t-2}$	-.0424*	-.0632*	.0001	.0054	.1448*	-.0799*	.0353*
	(.0113)	(.0200)	(.0044)	(.0188)	(.0150)	(.0071)	(.0050)
$\bar{m}_{t-3}$	-.0137	-.1356*	-.0003	.0697*	.1158*	-.0439*	.0078
	(.0113)	(.0201)	(.0044)	(.0189)	(.0150)	(.0072)	(.0050)
$\bar{m}_{t-4}$	-.0197	-.0218	-.0263*	.0077	.0962*	-.0232*	-.0128*
	(.0117)	(.0208)	(.0045)	(.0196)	(.0155)	(.0074)	(.0052)
$\bar{m}_{t-5}$	-.0500*	-.0350	-.0217*	-.0510*	.1353*	.0300*	-.0074
	(.0128)	(.0227)	(.0050)	(.0213)	(.0170)	(.0081)	(.0057)
$\bar{m}_{t-6}$	.0236	-.1940*	.0134	-.0663*	.1450*	.0737*	.0047
	(.0196)	(.0348)	(.0076)	(.0327)	(.0260)	(.0124)	(.0087)
$\bar{m}_{t-7}$	-.0032	.0106	.0032	-.1103*	.1273*	-.0252*	-.0026
	(.0195)	(.0345)	(.0075)	(.0325)	(.0258)	(.0123)	(.0086)
$\bar{c}_t$	.0912*	.2794*	.0093	.2021*	.2198*	.1464*	.0516*
	(.0190)	(.0337)	(.0074)	(.0317)	(.0252)	(.0120)	(.0084)
Summary Statistics							
R^2	.065	.160	.041	.130	.469	.421	.093
F	9.948*	27.46*	6.131*	21.64*	127.6*	105.4*	14.83*
S_ϵ	390.3	691.8	151.1	650.5	516.9	246.5	172.5

NOTE: The number of observations in each regression is 1,312. In this and subsequent tables in this chapter, an asterisk indicates that a coefficient is significantly different from zero at the 5 percent level in a two-tailed test, and intercepts indicate thousands of dollars per month.

TABLE 7-3. MASSACHUSETTS MUTUAL SAVINGS BANK INPUT-OUTPUT COEFFICIENTS

	Cash	United States Government Securities	State and Local Securities	Other Securities	Mortgage Loans	Other Loans	Other Assets
Intercept	−.703	−63.326	−4.384	−6.020	76.734	−.505	−1.790
$\bar{m}_t$	.0705*	.6238*	.0012	.0080	.0644*	.2191*	.0136*
	(.0132)	(.0262)	(.0055)	(.0098)	(.0230)	(.0111)	(.0058)
$\bar{m}_{t-1}$	−.0863*	.2205*	−.0021	.0069	−.0295	−.1175*	.0072
	(.0131)	(.0261)	(.0055)	(.0097)	(.0229)	(.0110)	(.0057)
$\bar{m}_{t-2}$	−.0390*	−.1060*	−.0010	.0229*	.1937*	−.0806*	.0099*
	(.0090)	(.0178)	(.0037)	(.0066)	(.0156)	(.0075)	(.0039)
$\bar{m}_{t-3}$	.0671*	−.2952*	.0017	−.0212*	.2840*	−.0282*	−.0082*
	(.0090)	(.0178)	(.0037)	(.0066)	(.0156)	(.0075)	(.0039)
$\bar{m}_{t-4}$	−.0493*	.0001	−.0020	−.0115	−.0925*	−.0382*	.0082*
	(.0089)	(.0178)	(.0037)	(.0066)	(.0156)	(.0075)	(.0039)
$\bar{m}_{t-5}$	−.0308*	−.0538*	.0012	.0025	.0476*	.0193*	.0143*
	(.0091)	(.0180)	(.0038)	(.0067)	(.0158)	(.0076)	(.0040)
$\bar{m}_{t-6}$	.0890*	−.1443*	.0015	−.0187	−.0022	.0936*	−.0194*
	(.0136)	(.0270)	(.0057)	(.0101)	(.0237)	(.0114)	(.0059)
$\bar{m}_{t-7}$	−.0110	−.0873*	.0001	−.0087	.1513*	−.0422*	−.0017
	(.0135)	(.0268)	(.0056)	(.0100)	(.0235)	(.0113)	(.0059)
$\bar{c}_t$	.0502*	.6877*	.0046	−.0119*	.1280*	.1274*	.0142*
	(.0064)	(.0128)	(.0027)	(.0048)	(.0112)	(.0054)	(.0028)
			Summary Statistics				
R^2	.121	.516	.001	.011	.424	.389	.029
F	55.63*	430.2*	.528	4.508*	298.1*	257.0*	11.86*
S_ε	273.0	542.3	113.4	202.0	475.0	229.0	119.2

NOTE: The number of observations in each regression is 3,649.

TABLE 7-4. NEW YORK CITY MUTUAL SAVINGS BANK INPUT-OUTPUT COEFFICIENTS

	Cash	United States Government Securities	State and Local Securities	Other Securities	Mortgage Loans	Other Loans	Other Assets
Intercept	-31.476	-282.187	-23.008	-419.453	797.426	-4.722	-38.684
$\bar{m}_t$	.0765*	.2522*	.0013	.2504*	.2076*	.1778*	.0384*
	(.0244)	(.0355)	(.0079)	(.0363)	(.0433)	(.0344)	(.0161)
$\bar{m}_{t-1}$	-.0693*	.0586	.0046	-.0182	.0642	-.0677	.0301
	(.0247)	(.0359)	(.0080)	(.0367)	(.0438)	(.0348)	(.0163)
$\bar{m}_{t-2}$	-.0938*	-.1043*	-.0129	.1098*	.0820*	.0413	-.0243
	(.0232)	(.0337)	(.0075)	(.0345)	(.0412)	(.0327)	(.0153)
$\bar{m}_{t-3}$	.1224*	-.0719	-.0175*	-.1385*	.2038*	-.1363*	.0333*
	(.0255)	(.0370)	(.0082)	(.0378)	(.0451)	(.0359)	(.0168)
$\bar{m}_{t-4}$	-.0726*	.0327	-.0342*	-.0594	.1666*	.0090	-.0461*
	(.0244)	(.0355)	(.0079)	(.0362)	(.0433)	(.0344)	(.0161)
$\bar{m}_{t-5}$	.0550*	.0806*	-.0111	-.0590	-.0147	.0268	-.0745*
	(.0229)	(.0333)	(.0074)	(.0340)	(.0406)	(.0323)	(.0151)
$\bar{m}_{t-6}$	.0116	-.1228*	.0218*	.0937*	.0301	-.0992*	.0667*
	(.0248)	(.0360)	(.0080)	(.0368)	(.0440)	(.0349)	(.0164)
$\bar{m}_{t-7}$	-.0164	-.1317*	.0147	.0906*	.0056	.0281	.0091
	(.0241)	(.0350)	(.0078)	(.0357)	(.0427)	(.0339)	(.0159)
$\bar{c}_t$	.0734*	.1865*	.0384	-.0792	.4653*	.0874*	.2276*
	(.0314)	(.0456)	(.0101)	(.0466)	(.0556)	(.0442)	(.0207)
			Summary Statistics				
R^2	.168	.057	.045	.132	.282	.056	.100
F	35.58*	10.75*	8.238*	26.75*	69.48*	10.37*	19.59*
S_ε	1,703.3	2,473.8	550.1	2,527.0	3,017.5	2,398.6	1,123.4

NOTE: The number of observations in each regression is 1,599.

Table 7-5. New York State Mutual Savings Bank Input-Output Coefficients

	Cash	United States Government Securities	State and Local Securities	Other Securities	Mortgage Loans	Other Loans	Other Assets
Intercept	9.066	−13.988	1.204	−52.806	61.087	−2.277	−2.157
$\bar{m}_t$	.2109*	.1948*	.0039	.0797*	.3289*	.0947*	.0862*
	(.0294)	(.0454)	(.0118)	(.0375)	(.0415)	(.0142)	(.0271)
$\bar{m}_{t-1}$	−.0986*	.1350*	−.0365*	.0613	.0629	−.1131*	−.0110
	(.0279)	(.0431)	(.0112)	(.0356)	(.0394)	(.0135)	(.0257)
$\bar{m}_{t-2}$	−.0051	−.1147*	−.0241*	.0143	.0951*	−.0298*	.0639*
	(.0218)	(.0336)	(.0087)	(.0278)	(.0307)	(.0105)	(.0200)
$\bar{m}_{t-3}$	−.0718*	.0846*	−.0102	−.0896*	.1360*	.0422*	−.0899*
	(.0237)	(.0365)	(.0095)	(.0302)	(.0334)	(.0114)	(.0218)
$\bar{m}_{t-4}$	.0362	−.1132*	−.0028	.0907*	.0524	−.0448*	−.0199
	(.0238)	(.0367)	(.0095)	(.0303)	(.0335)	(.0115)	(.0219)
$\bar{m}_{t-5}$	−.0313	−.0211	−.0205*	−.0109	.1611*	.0263*	−.1046*
	(.0224)	(.0346)	(.0090)	(.0286)	(.0317)	(.0108)	(.0206)
$\bar{m}_{t-6}$	−.0450	−.1688*	.0157	.1031*	.0375	.0233	.0364
	(.0282)	(.0435)	(.0113)	(.0360)	(.0398)	(.0136)	(.0259)
$\bar{m}_{t-7}$	−.0081	−.1626*	.0119	−.1025*	.2052*	.0170	.0388
	(.0278)	(.0429)	(.0111)	(.0355)	(.0392)	(.0134)	(.0256)
$\bar{c}_t$	.0485	.1745*	.0343*	.1285*	.2943*	.1202*	.2022*
	(.0253)	(.0391)	(.0101)	(.0323)	(.0357)	(.0122)	(.0233)
				Summary Statistics			
R^2	.070	.063	.047	.045	.447	.384	.072
F	14.01*	12.44*	9.140*	8.656*	149.9*	115.7*	14.35*
S_ε	453.5	700.1	181.7	578.6	640.0	218.2	417.2

Note: The number of observations in each regression is 1,681.

assets.[5] The portfolio models of chapter 3 predict that in such circumstances these investments should be very sensitive to a bank's deposit history. Banks in the other areas may invest without penalty in both United States government and private sector securities. For such banks there is little reason to expect any *one* of these securities to be closely related to deposit flows, but total securities should be.

Although all variables are measured as first differences, intercepts are estimated in an attempt to eliminate an obvious nonstationarity in savings bank portfolio behavior. The nonstationarity is that sample banks invested approximately 100 percent of their growth in total assets in mortgage loans during the five years ending December 31, 1963, but on that date only about 70 percent of savings bank assets were held as mortgage loans. Thus, the inclusion of intercepts is a crude device that is essential if the approach of chapters 2 and 3 is to apply. Such intercepts clearly cannot persist indefinitely; slowly growing banks would eventually be predicted to hold negative quantities of certain of their assets. Intercepts serve to eliminate unidentified nondeposit-flow events which were affecting portfolios during this particular sample period. The specification assumes that these events had a constant effect in every month and that, once eliminated, estimated deposit flow coefficients measure dynamic portfolio adjustment patterns that would be observed in other time periods.

The intercepts suggest that all four groups of banks were shifting out of United States government securities, other loans, and other assets and into mortgage loans during the forty-one-month period ending December 1963. Three of the four groups of banks were shifting out of cash and other securities as well. The units for intercepts are thousands of dollars per month. Intercepts for individual assets vary across samples, in part because of differences in average bank size.

An interpretation of this pattern is that commercial banks and other competitors were forcing savings banks to raise the average rate of interest paid on deposits. Because of the long maturity of mortgage loans, returns realized from existing savings bank assets rose very slowly. Since new mortgage loans were the highest yielding assets available to savings banks, these banks shifted heavily into mortgage loans.[6]

---

5. For a discussion of this point see National Association of Mutual Savings Banks [1962, p. 130].

6. Mortgage loan interest rates were falling during all of this period. Therefore, it is not correct to argue that savings banks were reaching for newly attractive high yields on such loans. It is probably more accurate to argue that savings banks and savings and loan associations were forced by this competitively induced cash flow shortfall to drive mortgage loan interest rates down. In this connection see Brainard and Tobin [1963] and Hester [1969].

As noted in chapter 4, the fact that a bank's total assets are equal to the sum of its liabilities and net worth imposes a number of restrictions on parameters reported in tables 7-2 through 7-5. In each table the row sums of coefficients pertaining to contemporaneous first differences in regular savings deposits, $\bar{m}_t$, and in all other deposits, liabilities, and capital, $\bar{c}_t$, theoretically should be unity. Row sums of intercepts and coefficients of lagged first differences in savings deposits should be zero. These conditions are satisfied to a high order of precision for Connecticut and Massachusetts banks and, apart from a minor discrepancy in the intercept, for New York State banks as well. In the case of New York City banks, somewhat greater aberrations were detected, which are apparently a consequence of (1) failing to prescale variables and/or (2) the fact that raw data were subject to a less-than-perfect set of balance sheet checks.[7] No row sum of New York City bank coefficients differed from its theoretical value by as much as 0.005, but the sum of the seven intercepts was -2.104. This discrepancy is very unlikely to affect any of the substantive conclusions of this chapter.

Estimated deposit coefficients tend to be erratic but broadly conform with predictions of the theory in chapter 3. Thus, all four sets of banks have significant positive cash changes in response to contemporaneous deposit inflows. With the exception of quarterly echoes, which may reflect deposit interest withdrawals, other coefficients in the cash equations are negative or insignificant as the theory predicts.

During the first two months after a deposit inflow, banks in Connecticut and the two New York samples are predicted to invest approximately 32 percent of the inflow in United States government securities. Because of previously mentioned legal restrictions, Massachusetts banks are estimated to place about 84 percent of their flow in these securities during this time interval. In subsequent months banks dispose of these securities, and the proceeds are invested in other less liquid assets, again as the theory predicts.

---

7. The first-mentioned source of error is likely to be important only in the case of the large New York City banks where occasional sizable deposit changes may result in insidious rounding errors within a computer. The second source refers to the fact that savings bank balance sheets were required to balance only up to a discrepancy of 0.25 percent in each month as explained in chapter 5. This threshold check level was selected because raw data were recorded in thousands of dollars, and for small banks a deviation slightly smaller than this magnitude could have occurred in the raw data quite frequently and innocently due to reporting rounding. It was a careless oversight on our part not to have imposed a much more restrictive standard on the New York City sample, where no such small banks were present. However, the costs of attempting to rectify this error were prohibitive when it was finally recognized.

State and local securities are quite poorly described by the model; in the case of Massachusetts banks the regression is not statistically significant when judged by an F-test. No uniform coefficient pattern recurs among the three samples with significant regressions. This is a very sensible result because in most instances savings banks should not have been acquiring these securities. During the sample period savings banks were favored by the federal income tax statutes to such an extent that typically they paid no taxes. Because interest paid on these securities is tax-exempt, their before-tax yields were very low. Securities whose interest is taxable dominate state and local securities in savings bank portfolios.

Other securities consist primarily of corporate bonds, equipment obligations, and equity securities. Apart from Massachusetts, savings banks are observed to acquire significant amounts of these assets within a month or so after a deposit inflow. Connecticut and New York City banks place about 20 percent and upstate New York institutions put about 14 percent of a deposit inflow into such securities. Coefficients on lagged deposit flows exhibit considerable instability from month to month and no uniformity across samples. Connecticut banks appear to view them as secondary reserves that are slightly less liquid than United States government securities; beginning about five months after a deposit inflow, they tend to be sold in order to acquire mortgage loans. Both groups of New York banks, on the other hand, seem to view them as "final" assets which will be traded frequently, but held in their equilibrium portfolios. No explanation for this difference in Connecticut and New York bank behavior is apparent.

Mortgage loans are acquired by all groups of banks simultaneously with a deposit inflow and then in larger quantities subsequently as the theory predicts. Both groups of New York banks acquire large volumes of mortgage loans almost immediately, 21 percent and 33 percent of a deposit inflow, whereas Connecticut and Massachusetts banks get 14 percent and 6 percent, respectively, in the first month. Connecticut banks add to their mortgage loans quite steadily at the rate of about 12 percent of the inflow per month over the whole period. The other three samples tend to concentrate acquisitions between three and five months after a deposit inflow, with a substantial further block being acquired in the last reported month for New York State and Massachusetts banks. New York City banks have a very high proportion of insured mortgages, which are often purchased in the national market through mortgage bankers, and this may account for their relatively more rapid adjustment in mortgage loans.

As noted above, adjustment paths of other loans appear to resemble those hypothesized for a combination of cash and short-term government securities in all four samples of banks. Thus, between 9 percent and 22 percent of a deposit inflow is lent during the month of the inflow. These loans are apparently of a very short-term character, for they tend to disappear within the next few months, and the resulting funds are placed in United States government securities, other securities, and mortgage loans. The composition of other loans is unclear although they probably include construction loans and short-term commercial advances.

Residual other assets, reported in the last column of each table, tend to increase in the month of a deposit inflow but otherwise have no very interesting pattern. Both sets of New York banks have adjustment paths that imply considerable trading activity in these assets; for other banks their level is quite unresponsive to deposit flows. The very heterogeneous character of these assets discourages further attempts at interpretation.

TABLE 7-6. ESTIMATED EQUILIBRIUM SHARES OF A DEPOSIT INFLOW

Asset Acquired	Connecticut	Massachusetts	New York City	New York State
Cash	.0063	.0102	.0134	−.0128
U.S. govt. sec.	−.0723	.1578	−.0066	−.1660
State and local sec.	−.0415	.0006	−.0333	−.0626
Other securities	.0422	−.0198	.2694	.1461
Mortgage loans	.9978	.8018	.7452	1.0791
Other loans	.0375	.0253	−.0202	.0158
All other assets	.0301	.0239	.0327	−.0001
Check sum	1.0001	.9998	1.0006	.9995

Table 7-6 reports estimates of the share of an initial deposit inflow that will be held in each of the seven assets at the end of an assumed eight-month adjustment period. The table is computed by summing deposit coefficients appearing in each column of tables 7-2 through 7-5. The check sum illustrates the precision to which the previously described balance sheet constraints are satisfied over the eight-month interval. All numbers in table 7-6 should be construed as point estimates.

The first and last rows of table 7-6 indicate that at the end of eight months essentially all of the deposit inflow has disappeared from cash and residual other assets into income-earning assets. This outcome seems quite sensible in terms of the theory of chapter 3. With the possible exception of New York State banks, the result is consistent with the proposition that savings banks have a small positive marginal long-term propensity to hold cash against deposits.

The negative entries in the second row of this table suggest that the estimated structure is not invariant over time.[8] Evidently, incorporating intercepts in each equation did not suffice to eliminate the previously reported nonstationary portfolio behavior by some savings banks. In particular, estimates for both Connecticut and New York State banks imply that they *sell* sizable quantities of government securities in response to a deposit *inflow*.[9] This result is not predicted by the theory and is considered in great detail in the subsequent sections. New York City banks appear to acquire essentially no government securities in response to an inflow. In long-run equilibrium Massachusetts banks are estimated to hold about 16 percent of a deposit inflow as government securities. Both of these latter results are consistent with a hypothesis of invariant portfolio behavior.

State and local securities also exhibit a lack of invariance, since small negative long-run equilibria were found for the Connecticut and the two New York bank samples. Given the general theoretical issue of why banks should be observed to hold such assets, this violation does not seem qualitatively important.

Estimated equilibria for other securities vary widely across the four samples, and for the untypical taxation case of Massachusetts, the equilibrium is slightly negative. Since prime corporate security yields typically exceed yields on United States government securities, it is not surprising that the three other groups of banks should have preferred corporate securities, but the explanation of differences among equilibria is not apparent.

Mirroring the lack of stationarity in United States government securities, Connecticut and New York State banks are estimated to place about 100 percent of a deposit inflow in mortgage loans when in equilibrium. This result is what one would expect to observe if savings banks were

8. In this discussion invariance implies that no asset has a long-run negative response to a savings deposit inflow. A pattern with a negative response could not continue indefinitely for a bank that grows at a constant arithmetic rate; eventually it would have none of that asset. A bank growing at a sufficiently high geometric rate can avoid depleting its stock of the asset if the adjustment path implies initial large positive holdings. An apparent lack of invariance was also reported in the preceding chapter when studying the relation of cash holdings to time deposit flows. As was explained, that relation probably reflects a complementarity between time deposit investments and demand deposit liquidity requirements.

9. No attempt was made to test the statistical significance of these negative equilibrium shares because it was found that the absolute value of the negative shares was an increasing function of the length of the assumed adjustment period. See the subsequent section for details.

operating in a world where a perfect secondary market existed for mortgage loans; it is not a result to be expected in the environment envisioned in chapters 2 and 3. Massachusetts and New York City banks, on the other hand, are observed to have equilibrium mortgage loan shares that are consistent with the theory's predictions. The estimated equilibrium mortgage loan share for New York City banks is almost identical with their observed share of mortgage loans at the end of the sample period.[10] A number of hypotheses that might account for these intersample differences are considered in the subsequent section.

Equilibrium shares of other loans and other assets also vary slightly across samples, but their sum is positive for each of the four groups of banks. Banks outside New York City tend to have larger equilibrium levels of other loans.[11]

The coefficients on the variable measuring first differences in bank net worth and all other liabilities, $\bar{c}_t$, are also equilibrium levels, since banks are assumed to respond instantaneously to such predictable flows. The plausibility of these estimates is very difficult to assess because of the heterogeneous character of the measured flows. For example, interest on savings deposits was paid into deposit accounts at quarterly or semiannual intervals during the sample period. No doubt a large part of the variance of $\bar{c}_t$ reflects movements in accrued interest, which, depending upon withdrawal propensities of depositors, will be placed in more or less liquid assets. Other components of $\bar{c}_t$ include additions to savings club accounts and retained earnings and are likely to have different equilibrium asset shares. In tables 7-2 through 7-5 all four groups of banks are found to invest relatively large fractions of these flows in mortgage loans and/or United States government securities. At least two groups of banks place statistically significant amounts in each of the seven asset categories.

One final remark concerns variations in the reported standard errors of estimate. They are measured in thousands of dollars and vary across samples very roughly in proportion to average bank size. With the exception of other securities and other loans, the rank correlation of standard errors with the mean bank sizes reported in chapter 5 is unity. The reported estimates of this section are likely to be somewhat inefficient owing to the presence of heteroskedasticity. As noted earlier, however, this fact is not very damaging since the samples being studied are quite large.

10. See table 5-8.
11. Banks in the same three samples were previously reported to use other loans quite extensively when effecting short-term portfolio adjustments. This was attributed to imperfections in capital markets served by those banks.

3. FURTHER STUDIES OF THE MUTUAL SAVINGS BANK SAMPLES

Results reported in tables 7-2 through 7-6 broadly conform to predictions of the theory of chapter 3 but fail to exhibit the important property of invariance in two samples. The present section attempts to expose the nature of this nonstationarity in greater detail and reports tests of a number of subsidiary hypotheses that might account for the anomaly. In addition, the estimated structural equations are used to predict sample savings bank portfolios outside of the period from which the relationships have been estimated.

Before pursuing these two topics, however, it is instructive to compare the mutual savings bank results with those obtained for corresponding assets held by commercial banks.[12] Figures 7-1 and 7-2 report plots of estimated adjustment paths for mortgage loans and government securities respectively. The commercial bank paths have been constructed from the time deposit coefficients reported in table 6-2. The commercial bank government security path was constructed by summing the columns labeled "Shorts" and "1-5s"; an arithmetic average of the first four coefficients was used to estimate the immediate month impact of time deposit inflows on assets. The mortgage loan path is a plot of mortgage loan coefficients, with the first four elements of the column again averaged into a single element. Savings bank paths have been constructed for each sample by plotting the cumulative column sum of deposit coefficients for mortgage loans and government securities, reported in tables 7-2 through 7-5.

The plots illustrate the change in a bank's mortgage loans or government securities that is predicted in response to a single permanent deposit inflow to a commercial or savings bank. In every case a large fraction of the inflow initially appears in government securities, and then, as time passes, these securities are converted into mortgage loans. The change in all other assets can be inferred from the two figures for each class of intermediary; it is the difference at each point of time between unity and the sum of the corresponding path ordinates. Two features of the plots should be noted. First, both groups of intermediaries appear to adjust to their long-run equilibria in about the same time span. Thus, the fraction

12. None of the primary mutual savings bank assets exactly corresponds to commercial bank assets studied in chapter 6. Thus a smaller fraction of commercial bank mortgage loans is insured by government agencies than is the case for mutual savings banks. Similarly, the maturity distribution of government debt is likely to vary between the two classes of intermediaries and is not available in any detail for savings banks.

of commercial bank time deposits held as mortgage loans and government securities is essentially at the equilibrium level after nine months have passed; after seven months both assets are quite close to equilibrium levels. In the pilot sample experiments reported in section 1 it was estimated that approximately seven lagged monthly changes were necessary to describe adjustments of savings bank mortgage loans to equilibrium. In the present section this result is confirmed for those samples where stability was found—that is, for Massachusetts and New York City banks.

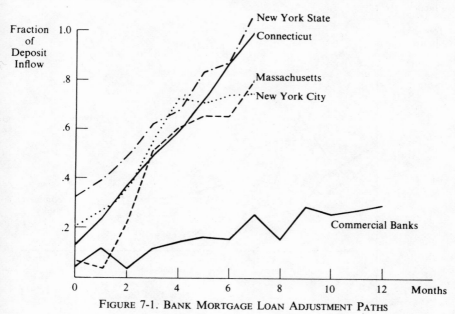

FIGURE 7-1. BANK MORTGAGE LOAN ADJUSTMENT PATHS

Second, while the adjustment spans are similar, the estimated equilibrium portfolio shares differ greatly between commercial bank time and savings deposits and mutual savings bank deposits.[13] Commercial banks have about one-third as large a percentage investment in mortgage loans as savings banks. Relative to savings banks, they hold more government securities (except perhaps in Massachusetts) and clearly hold large amounts of the other assets listed in table 6-2. Apparently this difference in portfolio behavior is a consequence of legal restrictions on portfolio composition and/or differences in management objective functions,

13. The equilibrium shares should be interpreted as estimates for the mean sample bank in each case.

because in the next chapter we report that the two types of deposits have very similar autoregressive structures. Both types of institutions undoubtedly face the same structure of brokerage charges. Savings banks are subject to more stringent legal restrictions on their assets and liabilities than commercial banks, but restrictions will not entirely explain the observed differences [National Association of Mutual Savings Banks, 1962, pp. 104–05].

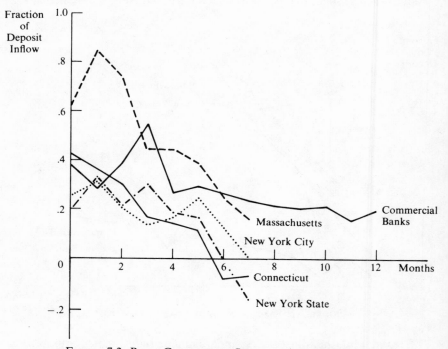

FIGURE 7-2. BANK GOVERNMENT SECURITY ADJUSTMENT PATHS

At this point it is desirable to return to the diverse results of section 2 and to consider subsidiary hypotheses that may account for differences among the samples of savings banks. These hypotheses are:

1. The pilot sample determination of the adjustment time span was faulty.
   (a) Different time spans are appropriate for different samples.
   (b) The existence of a fixed-adjustment span depends upon the existence of invariance in the structure.
   (c) The estimated time paths are insensitive to the assumed span.

2. Important structural shifts occurred during the period under study.
   (a) The shifts invalidated the intercept adjustment for nonstationarity.
   (b) The shifts implied that no stationarity exists in the matrix of estimated deposit coefficients.

Hypothesis 1a can be studied by extending the horizon beyond eight monthly changes and testing whether or not the inclusion of additional deposit change variables significantly improves descriptions of first differences in savings bank assets. When the number of deposit change variables was expanded from eight to eleven, at least five asset regressions were significantly improved at the 1 percent level in F-tests for each of the Connecticut, Massachusetts, and New York City bank samples. For New York State banks, only other security and mortgage loan regressions were significantly improved. Essentially the same pattern of significant improvements was obtained when the number of consecutive deposit changes was expanded from eleven to fifteen. Evidently the pilot sample determination of the adjustment span was misleading. However, the seriousness of this disconcerting outcome is not great, as can be ascertained when hypotheses 1b and 1c are examined.

TABLE 7-7. ESTIMATED EQUILIBRIUM SHARES OF A DEPOSIT INFLOW OVER EXTENDED HORIZONS

Asset Acquired	Connecticut	Massachusetts	New York City	New York State
		11-Month Horizon		
Cash	−.0051	−.0024	.0204	−.0189
U.S. govt. sec.	−.0966	.1917	−.0144	−.1550
State and local sec.	−.0318	−.0002	−.0253	−.0697
Other securities	.0201	−.0171	.2691	.1123
Mortgage loans	1.0605	.7908	.7163	1.1197
Other loans	.0292	.0120	.0015	.0158
All other assets	.0234	.0249	.0331	−.0047
Check sum	.9997	.9997	1.0007	.9995
		15-Month Horizon		
Cash	−.0052	.0034	.0039	.0016
U.S. govt. sec.	−.0891	.1453	.0260	−.1765
State and local sec.	−.0269	−.0012	−.0298	−.0672
Other securities	−.0335	.0059	.1738	.0778
Mortgage loans	1.1138	.8058	.7938	1.1518
Other loans	.0161	.0110	.0006	.0127
All other assets	.0250	.0299	.0325	−.0009
Check sum	1.0002	1.0001	1.0008	.9993

Table 7-7 reports evidence concerning hypothesis 1b; it shows estimated equilibrium asset shares when deposit inflow horizons are eleven and fifteen months. For every asset in the invariant Massachusetts and New York City bank samples, the equilibrium shares are not meaningfully affected by extending the horizon from eleven to fifteen months. Furthermore, these shares do not differ appreciably from their counterparts estimated for an eight-month horizon, which are reported in table 7-6.

On the other hand, equilibria for the nonstationary Connecticut and New York State samples appear to move as the time horizon is extended from eight to fifteen months. In particular, equilibrium shares of mortgage loans are an increasing function of the length of the adjustment horizon. Therefore, hypothesis 1b is accepted; the existence of a fixed adjustment span depends upon the existence of invariance.

Hypothesis 1c is most conveniently examined by referring to figures 7-3 through 7-6, which exhibit adjustment paths for mortgage loans and government securities estimated for different horizons. As before, adjustment paths for the sum of the remaining five assets can be calculated for each horizon by subtracting the sum of the plotted ordinates from unity.

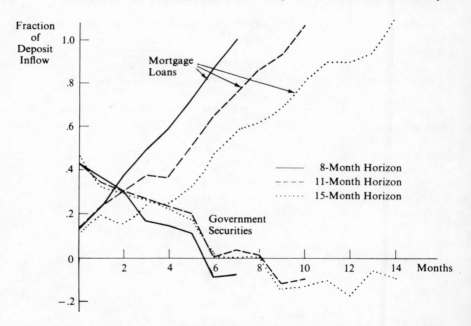

FIGURE 7-3. CONNECTICUT MORTGAGE LOAN AND GOVERNMENT SECURITY ADJUSTMENT PATHS: DIFFERENT HORIZONS

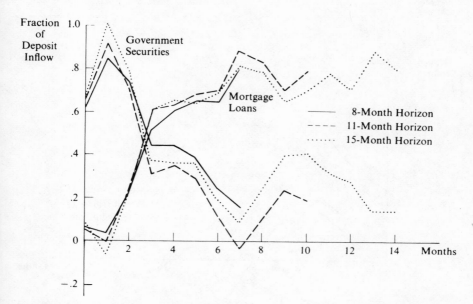

FIGURE 7-4. MASSACHUSETTS MORTGAGE LOAN AND GOVERNMENT SECURITY
ADJUSTMENT PATHS: DIFFERENT HORIZONS

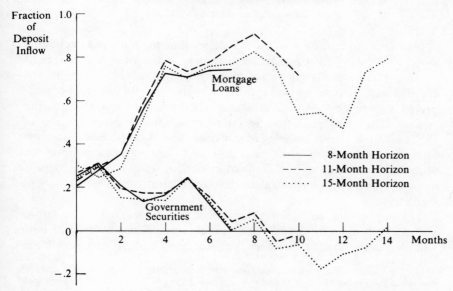

FIGURE 7-5. NEW YORK CITY MORTGAGE LOAN AND GOVERNMENT SECURITY
ADJUSTMENT PATHS: DIFFERENT HORIZONS

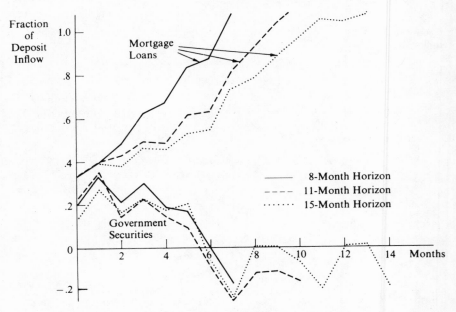

FIGURE 7-6. NEW YORK STATE MORTGAGE LOAN AND GOVERNMENT SECURITY
ADJUSTMENT PATHS: DIFFERENT HORIZONS

Inspection of figures 7-4 and 7-5 shows that for both Massachusetts
and New York City banks the adjustment paths over the first eight
months are essentially unaffected by varying the horizon. Therefore, the
eight-month horizon results reported in tables 7-3 and 7-4 can be interpreted as reliable short-run estimates, regardless of the horizon being
studied. The price paid for the faulty pilot sample determination of
the horizon for these samples of banks is very slight.[14] Both the most
interesting part of the adjustment path and the long-run equilibria are
remarkably insensitive to this misspecification. Additional early deposit
change variables describe relatively minor erratic movements about
equilibria.

The adjustment paths for Connecticut and New York State banks
displayed in figures 7-3 and 7-6 reveal a very different story. For both
samples, as the horizon increases the adjustment path for mortgage loans

14. The loss of explanation from ignoring very early deposit changes is quite small; R^2
was typically improved by 1 or 2 percent when three or four additional deposit change variables were added. Such improvements are statistically significant with 1,000 degrees of
freedom, but not of great quantitative import. The pilot sample determination missed these
minor improvements because only 470 observations were available.

rotates clockwise from a nearly common origin on the vertical axis. The rate at which these banks are estimated to convert a given deposit inflow into mortgage loans is a decreasing function of the assumed length of the adjustment span. The adjustment path for government securities, on the other hand, does not exhibit similar instability. Therefore, compensating counterclockwise shifts in the adjustment paths of some or all of the five remaining assets must occur in order to maintain the balance sheet identity.

Figures 7-7 and 7-8 report cash and other security adjustment paths for the Connecticut and New York State banks, respectively. In both samples it is apparent that the path of other securities fluctuates with the length of the adjustment span and varies inversely with the mortgage loan path.

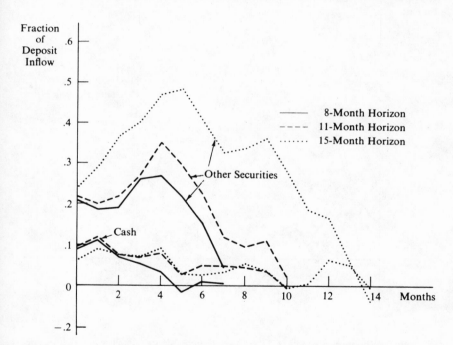

FIGURE 7-7. CONNECTICUT CASH AND OTHER SECURITY ADJUSTMENT PATHS: DIFFERENT HORIZONS

The cash adjustment paths, on the other hand, are largely unaffected over the first six or eight months by the choice of an adjustment horizon. No complete explanation is available for why other securities and mortgage loan paths should be jointly sensitive to choice of horizon. It does seem plausible that both cash and government security paths should be more stable, since the theory suggests that their shapes are primarily a function of time invariant brokerage fees and other transactions costs. Furthermore, because of the balance sheet identity, one or more of the remaining four assets must compensate for the path of mortgage loans. Apparently, the single compensating asset is other securities.[15] The conclusion is that hypothesis 1c is accepted for New York City and Massachusetts, but rejected for New York State and Connecticut banks.

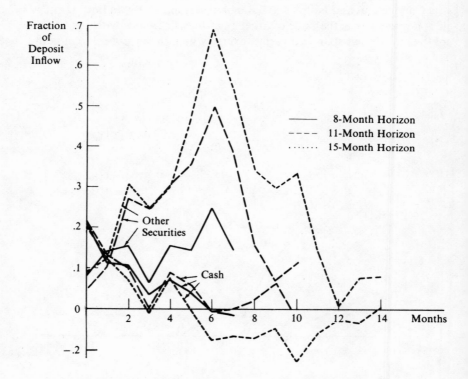

FIGURE 7-8. NEW YORK STATE CASH AND OTHER SECURITY ADJUSTMENT PATHS: DIFFERENT HORIZONS

15. The adjustment path of the sum of the remaining three assets, state and local securities, other loans, and residual other assets, appears to be quite flat and is insensitive to variations in horizon over the first eight months.

The second set of hypotheses concerns the residuals of equations reported in tables 7-2 through 7-5 and whether the reported coefficient structure is stationary in successive cross sections. Figures 7-9 and 7-10 report time series of the mean estimated mortgage loan residual for each of the four samples of savings banks. The time paths are similar in that all four groups acquired somewhat less than the predicted volume of mortgage loans in late 1960 and early 1961, when the economy was passing through the trough of a recession, and somewhat more than the predicted amounts during late 1963. This pattern is more evident in the two New York samples and is almost nonexistent in the case of Massachusetts. It suggests that savings bank portfolios are only slightly sensitive to the level of aggregate economic activity after the effects of deposit flows have been removed; this is consistent with the maintained hypothesis that bank behavior can be studied fruitfully without specifying credit demand equations. Furthermore, the presence or absence of invariance does not seem to be related to residual patterns, since New York State and Connecticut mortgage loan residuals are not very different from those of Massachusetts and New York City banks. Finally, no evidence of strong seasonality appears in any of the residual series.

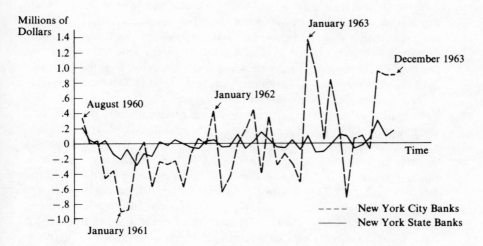

FIGURE 7-9. MEAN MORTGAGE LOAN RESIDUALS: NEW YORK CITY AND NEW YORK STATE BANKS

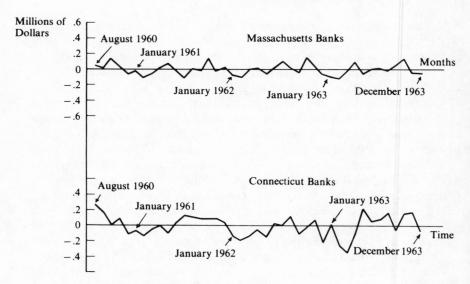

FIGURE 7-10. MEAN MORTGAGE LOAN RESIDUALS: MASSACHUSETTS AND CONNECTICUT BANKS

Since the balance sheet identity implies that the sum of the residuals must equal zero, some or all of the six other assets must be fluctuating inversely with mortgage loans. To avoid redundant reporting of results, attention will be restricted to New York City banks, where the mortgage loan residuals suggest the greatest cyclical sensitivity. Figures 7-11 and 7-12 report time series of residuals from cash, United States government security, other security, and other loan regressions for these banks.

In figure 7-11 other security residuals are predominantly positive until the middle of 1961, positive again during the middle of 1962 and 1963, and negative elsewhere. Government security residuals are predominantly positive in 1961 and negative in 1962. Together, these two assets have positive residuals in 1960 and early 1961 and negative residuals during late 1962 and 1963. Unexplained variations in first differences of mortgage loans were largely offset by unexplained variations in first differences of securities.[16] Residuals of first differences in cash, reported in figure 7-12, have no discernible trend or cyclical sensitivity. Residuals of first differences in other loans also move quite erratically over time, although they tend to be negative until the middle of 1961 and positive during most

16. It is tempting, but erroneous, to conclude from this result that securities and mortgage loans are substitutes. They may be substitutes, but it is not possible to identify substitutes without further restrictive assumptions.

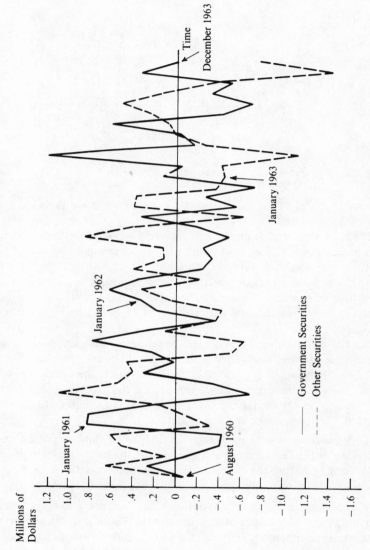

Millions of
Dollars

FIGURE 7-11. MEAN GOVERNMENT AND OTHER SECURITY RESIDUALS: NEW YORK CITY BANKS

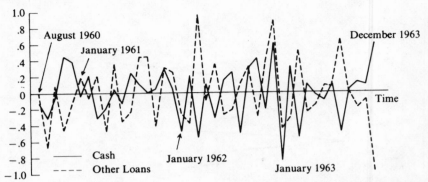

Millions of
Dollars

FIGURE 7-12. MEAN CASH AND OTHER LOAN RESIDUALS: NEW YORK CITY BANKS

of 1962. This pattern might be evidence of a weak procyclical fluctuation in loan demand. The overall conclusion from studying residual plots is that the rather arbitrary intercept adjustment for nonstationarity was not perfect, since mild cyclical fluctuations in residuals are apparent for at least four of the seven assets studied. Formally, hypothesis 2a must be accepted. However, residual patterns do not suggest gross misspecification of the structure.

For reasons of computer economy, hypothesis 2b is examined using only the sample of New York City banks. Separate equations were estimated for each of the forty-one monthly cross sections. Since only thirty-nine bank observations are available for each cross section, coefficients are expected to be somewhat erratic. Two formal hypotheses are considered using the analysis of covariance model:

1. Cross-section equations exactly analogous to those reported in table 7-4 do not differ from one another across the forty-one months.
2. After eliminating the effects of time intercept variations, cross-section equations do not differ from one another across the forty-one months.

In order to test the second hypothesis, it is necessary to eliminate noise attributable to the intercept approximation. These hypotheses are tested for cash, government security, other security, and mortgage loan regression equations. Results, reported in table 7-8, show that both hypotheses are rejected. Before eliminating time period means, each of the four asset equations varied significantly among cross sections.[17] After eliminating

17. This finding confirms the presence of nonstationarity, which was first detected in pilot experiments on mortgage loans reported at the beginning of this chapter.

these means, the hypothesis that cash equations did not vary across time could not be rejected. However, analogous hypotheses were rejected in the cases of government security, other security, and mortgage loan equations.

TABLE 7-8. ANALYSIS OF COVARIANCE OF NEW YORK CITY EQUATIONS

	Cash	U.S. Government Securities	Other Securities	Mortgage Loans
(1) Pooled sum of squares	46.103	97.242	101.473	144.681
(2) Sum of cross-section sum of squares	29.424	48.665	40.134	62.462
(3) Sum of cross-section means squared	6.485	4.375	5.484	12.303
F_1 (Hypothesis 1)	1.685**	2.967**	4.543**	3.913**
F_2 (Hypothesis 2)	1.144	3.000**	4.596**	3.697**

NOTE: Two asterisks indicate that the corresponding ratio is significantly different from unity at the 1 percent level.

For reasons that are not entirely clear, savings banks varied their acquisitions of assets in response to deposit inflows in different months over the sample period. This seemingly erratic pattern must be attributed to a number of factors that vary over time and are not included in the structural equations. Promising candidates include interest rates on both savings deposits and various assets, uncertainty about cash flows, and, perhaps, changing objective functions of mutual institutions.[18]

To gain further insight into this cross-section variation, it is instructive to examine the time series of estimated equilibrium shares constructed from the forty-one regression equations. Attention is restricted to first differences in mortgage loans, which are plotted in figure 7-13. The pooled regression suggested that eventually about 75 percent of a deposit inflow would appear in New York City bank mortgage loans. This share clearly varied considerably over time. No evidence of seasonal contamination appears in the series of estimated equilibrium shares. Also, no similarity

18. It should be recalled that nonstationarity was not detected in the commercial bank sample considered in the preceding chapter when an analogous covariance analysis was performed.

exists between mean bank mortgage loan residuals, reported in figure 7-9, and the series of equilibrium shares. The series of shares was less erratic in 1962 and 1963 than it was in earlier months, but it shows no easily interpretable pattern.

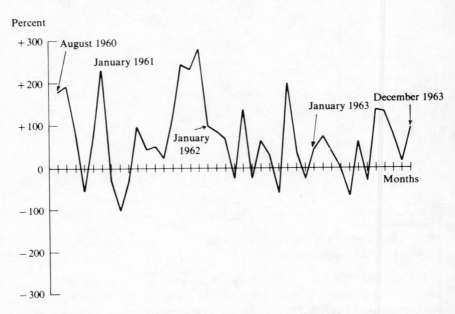

FIGURE 7-13. MORTGAGE LOAN EQUILIBRIA ESTIMATED FROM MONTHLY CROSS SECTIONS: NEW YORK CITY BANKS

In late 1959 and early 1960, savings banks, particularly those in New York City, were subjected to large deposit fluctuations because of the issuance of a four-year, ten-month Treasury note bearing a coupon of 5 percent in October 1959. Large amounts of these "magic fives" were purchased by individuals who substituted them for savings deposits in their portfolios. This unprecedented loss of deposits was widely discussed in the financial press. An interpretation of figure 7-13 is that this event shocked savings banks into making radical portfolio changes in the expectation that this event might recur. When it did not, savings banks returned to a portfolio policy more easily described by the input-output model.

4. BACKCASTING WITH THE INPUT-OUTPUT MODEL

For previously explained reasons of computational economy, only the last forty-one of fifty-nine available monthly observations on each sample bank were used to estimate the input-output structure. Since only eight monthly deposit changes are required to apply this structure, a total of eleven monthly asset changes for each bank can be studied that have not been used to estimate the reported coefficients. The following paragraphs describe the success with which the structure predicted events in this turbulent eleven-month period, September 1959 through July 1960.[19]

For selected assets, table 7-9 reports mean monthly forecast errors (actual-predicted values) for a bank in each of the four populations. To provide perspective, table 7-10 shows the observed mean changes in the same assets by these banks. It is apparent that forecasting errors are large in relation to the observed movements, with the possible exception of mortgage loans. Cash forecasting errors tend to be large and erratic with the exception of New York City banks, where very large errors occur at the semiannual dividend months of December and June. New York City banks were shifting from a semiannual to a quarterly dividend interval during the sample period. The simple input-output model is not capable of describing such structural shifts.

With the exception of the untypical Massachusetts banks, the estimated equations overpredict changes in government securities. The estimated negative intercepts in security equations were not sufficient to track the rapid liquidation of United States government securities during the eleven-month period. Apparently the structure changed between the forecasting and estimation periods. This is not surprising given the crude adjustment for nonstationarity that was attempted.

The very large negative errors in forecasting security changes by New York City and Massachusetts banks in October 1959 suggest that they may have been very strongly affected by the issuance of the previously mentioned magic fives. The simultaneous positive cash errors together with the negative adjustment in the following month suggest that these banks slightly overreacted to the crisis. New York State and Connecticut banks apparently were not similarly affected.

Other security and mortgage loan errors appear random for each bank population and do not suggest an interesting interpretation or uniformity across groups of banks on a given date. Because of the balance

19. In addition to the magic-fives episode, the yield curve on Treasury securities experienced a severe and sudden fluctuation. It was predominantly downward sloping at the end of 1959, but by June 1960 it was upward sloping.

Table 7-9. Forecast Errors of Mean Monthly Asset Changes: September 1959–July 1960
(in thousands of dollars per bank)

Asset	9/59	10/59	11/59	12/59	1/60	2/60	3/60	4/60	5/60	6/60	7/60
					Connecticut Banks (32 banks)						
Cash	26	-44	84	76	6	91	-29	-168	5	112	78
U.S. govt. sec.	-128	-105	-83	-92	-50	-64	-353	-170	-194	-353	-178
Other securities	-21	10	-157	214	0	43	-215	293	-44	59	-9
Mortgage loans	83	104	91	-141	149	-69	566	-8	173	211	343
					Massachusetts Banks (89 banks)						
Cash	-16	133	-60	-9	-19	-10	21	-28	-13	-10	14
U.S. govt. sec.	-53	-205	27	-51	95	126	4	83	-51	3	32
Other securities	-1	-48	-45	-4	-22	45	-22	-2	13	10	27
Mortgage loans	-23	111	37	85	-3	-120	-98	44	23	-33	48
					New York City Banks (39 banks)						
Cash	-521	639	-230	1,345	-1,098	74	-95	-78	203	1,563	-758
U.S. govt. sec.	178	-1,676	-128	-29	-726	-432	-206	-1,302	-770	-462	-1,151
Other securities	135	541	-327	-540	351	-218	364	563	720	89	951
Mortgage loans	-35	656	366	-405	1,531	445	-314	35	-378	-79	-243
					New York State Banks (41 banks)						
Cash	-117	26	71	115	-194	85	48	-133	318	-107	-27
U.S. govt. sec.	117	91	-145	-226	134	-113	44	-181	-415	-339	-151
Other securities	-177	-86	132	163	28	28	127	147	-37	97	57
Mortgage loans	24	-25	-60	-40	-30	63	-148	46	125	298	67

Cumulative 11-Month Forecast Error

	Connecticut	Massachusetts	New York City	New York State
Cash	237	3	1,044	85
U.S. govt. sec.	-1,770	10	-6,704	-1,184
Other securities	173	-49	2,629	479
Mortgage loans	1,502	71	1,579	320
Remainder	-142	-35	1,452	300

TABLE 7-10. MEAN MONTHLY CHANGES IN SELECTED ASSETS: SEPTEMBER 1959–JULY 1960
(in thousands of dollars per bank)

Asset	9/59	10/59	11/59	12/59	1/60	2/60	3/60	4/60	5/60	6/60	7/60
Connecticut Banks (32 banks)											
Cash	34	−63	98	42	26	85	2	−200	23	79	93
U.S. govt. sec.	−170	−196	−112	−282	18	−151	−277	−262	−225	−570	−111
Other securities	−2	−38	−153	83	116	102	−122	254	9	−54	92
Mortgage loans	379	395	308	6	474	157	826	226	441	387	657
Massachusetts Banks (89 banks)											
Cash	11	69	−60	32	−40	11	66	−73	−13	31	−4
U.S. govt. sec.	−40	−934	−232	44	122	199	176	16	46	82	107
Other securities	−15	−51	−53	−22	−31	38	−36	−4	10	−3	17
Mortgage loans	204	206	216	267	130	63	98	168	207	192	247
New York City Banks (39 banks)											
Cash	−140	−277	163	1,962	−2,155	478	333	−920	445	2,161	−1,511
U.S. govt. sec.	−206	−2,741	−517	138	−791	−596	−522	−1,427	−667	−1,078	−1,255
Other securities	331	−487	−280	−460	−51	−525	779	−637	332	111	555
Mortgage loans	1,320	908	1,082	1,205	2,203	1,709	1,531	1,074	1,010	1,262	1,316
New York State Banks (41 banks)											
Cash	−128	−31	100	188	−264	76	141	−173	339	−51	−55
U.S. govt. sec.	67	−154	−226	−240	10	−178	123	−236	−448	−344	−236
Other securities	−188	−104	78	172	1	−15	109	168	−16	62	61
Mortgage loans	386	296	303	295	275	332	261	320	473	657	433

sheet identity and the negative errors on government securities, however, their cumulative sum is positive for all but Massachusetts banks.

TABLE 7-11. ROOT MEAN SQUARED FORECAST ERRORS
(in thousands of dollars)

Region	Cash	U.S. Government Securities	Other Securities	Mortgage Loans
Connecticut	80.61	189.93	138.30	230.68
Massachusetts	46.49	87.18	27.54	68.30
New York City	787.78	822.43	500.94	570.45
New York State	138.43	206.58	111.21	114.50

Table 7-11 reports root mean squared forecast errors computed from each row of table 7-9. As might be expected, these statistics are smaller than the individual bank standard errors reported in tables 7-2 through 7-5. Together, tables 7-2 through 7-5 and 7-11 strongly suggest that errors in bank portfolio equations are not statistically independent and/or that the structure of the model changed between the eleven-month forecast period and the forty-one month estimation period. This inference can be drawn because, if neither were true, an application of the law of large numbers would predict substantially smaller average forecast errors than were observed. We have already noted that misspecification is evident in the government securities equation. It is therefore not surprising that all groups of government security forecasts have very large root mean squared errors, given the number of banks in each sample. Seemingly large root mean squared errors are also evident in cash forecasts for banks in the Massachusetts and the two New York samples and in mortgage loan forecasts for banks in Connecticut and Massachusetts.

As noted in chapter 4, the question of lack of independence of error terms is important for evaluating the promise of cross-section techniques in describing aggregative relations. If every bank had an identical positive or negative residual on a given date, there would be little point in using cross-section techniques to study aggregative capital markets. This worst of all possible worlds situation is not even approximately present in the savings bank samples; residuals vary substantially in size and sign on a given date. Unfortunately, it is not possible to measure lack of independence formally unless a maintained hypothesis of correct specification is adopted. In the present instance this assumption is difficult to defend because of the crude intercept adjustment. Therefore, no further evidence on this issue will be offered.

5. Summary and the Question of Mutuality

Many results are reported in the preceding sections; the task now is to order them in terms of importance and potential for future research. The principal findings are:

(1) Portfolio behavior by mutual savings banks in the four regions examined cannot be described by the same input-output model that characterized commercial banks in the preceding chapter. Mortgage loans as a fraction of deposits rose markedly at savings banks in all regions during the five years being studied. The commercial bank model allowed for a small amount of fluctuation in equilibria by permitting adjustment paths to shift up or down on different dates through the use of dummy variables. However, when equilibria shift greatly, as in the savings bank samples, adjustment paths are likely to "twist" and not merely shift vertically. Therefore, the earlier model is inappropriate.[20]

(2) A somewhat more general first-difference formulation of the input-output model can be specified which permits equilibria to change linearly over time. An intercept in each equation was used to measure this linear drift. In general, the modified formulation described savings bank behavior successfully with parameters that broadly conform to theoretical expectations. However, a number of anomalous empirical results were also detected which suggest that additional theoretical specification will be required before the structure can be applied confidently.

(3) The most serious discrepancy between theory and result concerns a lack of invariance that was found in two of the four bank samples. This means that, after the intercept adjustment for nonstationary equilibria, regression estimates of the coefficients implied that a savings bank eventually would *decrease* its holdings of at least one asset in response to a deposit *increase*. The lack of invariance became more severe as the adjustment period lengthened; therefore, the result is not a consequence of underestimating the time necessary for a savings bank to reach equilibrium.

(4) Apart from this implausible result, coefficient estimates were broadly similar across the four samples of savings banks, except for Massachusetts where a local tax law gave government securities a preferred status over other short-maturity assets as a secondary reserve. Thus, all banks had initial increases in cash and government securities, which eventually were liquidated in favor of mortgage loans. The timing

---

20. After encountering lack of invariance, the commercial bank model was estimated with savings bank data. Results were generally inferior to those reported above, and the effort was abandoned.

of these adjustments was broadly similar to that found in chapter 6 for commercial bank time deposits. The equilibrium change in mortgage loans in response to a savings deposit inflow, however, was much larger than had been estimated for commercial bank time and savings deposits.

(5) The problem of lack of invariance was explored in considerable detail in the preceding section. Principal findings were:

a. The adjustment span is slightly longer than the eight months found in the pilot sample, but very little information is lost by truncating the span at eight months.

b. Whenever a lack of invariance occurred, the adjustment paths of mortgage loans and other securities shifted inversely to one another as the adjustment span lengthened. Paths of none of the remaining assets appeared to shift. No explanation for this phenomenon is evident.

c. Residuals for mortgage loans and securities (both government and other) do not appear entirely random nor do they exhibit conspicuous seasonality. Mortgage loan residuals tend to be slightly negative during the recession years of 1960 and 1961 and slightly positive in 1962 and 1963 for the two New York samples. The security residuals had the inverse of this pattern.

d. An analysis of covariance for New York City banks was performed by estimating the model from cross sections for each of the forty-one available months. This analysis suggested that some asset adjustment paths varied over time. Because only twenty-nine degrees of freedom were available in each cross section, it was not possible to discern a systematic pattern.

(6) Finally, the estimated equations were used to forecast savings bank portfolio behavior outside of the period from which they were estimated. This forecast period, September 1959 through July 1960, was a period of wide fluctuations in interest rates and represents a formidable test for the model. With the interesting exception of Massachusetts, the structure overpredicted first differences in government securities and underpredicted first differences in other securities and mortgage loans. Errors were larger than might have been expected from standard errors reported in Tables 7-2 through 7-5.

The differences between commercial and savings bank versions of the input-output model are quite striking. Even when modified, the model was much less successfully applied to mutual savings banks than was the corresponding version to commercial banks. It is important that explanations be sought for why the model performs so differently for these seemingly similar financial intermediaries. A number of possibilities exist.

Savings bank portfolio behavior may differ from commercial bank behavior because (1) these intermediaries are regulated by different supervisory agencies; (2) by tradition and/or regulation some assets appear in one intermediary's portfolio, but not in the other's; (3) savings banks have different charters and presumably objective functions than commercial banks; and (4) the liabilities of savings banks are more homogeneous (less diversified) than commercial banks.

Some explanations can be dismissed at the outset. First, since both data sets span approximately the same time interval, March or August 1961 through December 1963, differences in behavior cannot be explained by differences in general economic conditions. In particular, variations in market interest rates (and presumably expectations of market interest rates) cannot explain differences in portfolio behavior unless they concern assets that only one of the intermediaries holds. During the three years under consideration, most interest rates were remarkably stable. Exceptions were rises in short-term rates, for example, interest rates on Treasury bills, on four- to six-month prime commercial paper, and most interest rates paid on savings deposits and savings and loan shares. Mortgage loan interest rates declined slightly, while most other long-term interest rates rose very modestly.

Regulatory agencies supervising commercial and savings banks were very passive during this three-year span. Regulation Q was relaxed whenever it began to bind. In addition, the tax environments of both sets of banks were essentially unchanged throughout the period. It is very doubtful that erratic portfolio behavior by savings banks can be traced to changing regulations by the various state banking commissioners because regulations were not markedly altered.

The second possible explanation of portfolio differences concerns the fact that savings and commercial banks hold different assets. For example, savings banks have common stocks and corporate bonds, which commercial banks are not allowed to hold, while commercial banks are distinctive in making commercial and industrial loans. If interest rates on these intermediary-specific assets moved differently than other rates, it is likely that portfolio behavior would differ. It happens that a very sharp decline in stock market prices occurred during 1962, reaching a low point in June of that year. Inspection of figure 7-11 indicates that, while New York City banks did acquire more other securities at this time, residuals were not extreme. We tentatively conclude from this and from the stability of other asset interest rates that differences in legal investments do not account for the observed savings bank portfolio behavior.

The third possible explanation concerns the fact that mutual savings banks do not have a well-defined objective function, as noted in chapter 2. If we accept the premise that stock chartered commercial banks attempt to maximize the expected value of some function of discounted net income and that mutually chartered savings banks do not, then there is no reason to expect that portfolios of these two intermediaries will respond similarly to a common set of market conditions. In chapter 2 it was argued that mutual institutions would not be interested in net income to the same extent as stock institutions, but that they would attempt to maintain their share of the savings flow and would seek safety to a greater extent. Is the observed pattern consistent with this prediction?

First, recall that in table 6-3 commercial banks were shifting their portfolios into mortgage loans, consumer loans, and other assets while shifting out of short-term government securities. While these shifts were small, commercial banks were acquiring assets with high and falling yields and disposing of assets with low and rising yields, just as savings banks. Second, commercial bank time deposit adjustment paths were far more erratic than demand deposit paths. Since time deposits constituted a small fraction of commercial bank liabilities, this picture may be consistent with a hypothesis that a commercial bank with only time deposits would exhibit behavior equally as erratic as that of savings banks. Third, commercial bank time deposits did have a negative implied reserve requirement. In chapter 6 this was attributed in part to a liquidity effect associated with the cash flow from time deposit financed assets. An alternative interpretation now appears to be that this result reflected a true lack of invariance. The two interpretations cannot be distinguished with available data. Therefore, existing evidence does not strongly support a hypothesis that mutuality is the sole source of lack of invariance in savings bank portfolio equations—although lack of invariance was certainly more conspicuous in mutual firms.

Tentatively, it appears that both groups of institutions were quite far out of equilibrium in 1960 in the sense that neither had invested savings deposits efficiently nor had paid interest on them which reflected their true opportunity value. Growing competition from savings and loan associations and short-term debt instruments threatened to pull these deposits away from banks unless deposit interest rates rose. In order to be able to meet this competition, both groups of banks were forced to pay higher interest rates on deposits and realize greater earnings from such deposits by investing them in higher yielding and probably more risky assets. Therefore, government and other securities were liquidated in favor of mortgage loans. This relation became clear in the savings bank study partly because the liability structure of savings banks is far more homogeneous and because the long maturity of mortgage loans made a more drastic response essential if cash flows were to be maintained. It is probably also true that mutual institutions respond to competitive pressures with a greater lag than stock institutions [Hester, 1967a].

No static explanation other than misguided monopoly power can be suggested for why banks preferred low interest rate mortgage loans in 1963 instead of high interest rate mortgage loans in 1961. A host of dynamic stories can be suggested, but they will not be developed here.

CHAPTER 8

On Forecasting Bank Deposits

In this chapter results from applying the autoregressive deposit forecasting model are reported for both commercial and mutual savings banks.[1] These results support the contention of chapter 2 that a distinction should be made between variability and predictability of deposits. The evidence indicates that banks with highly variable deposits can still make relatively accurate deposit predictions.

The first section describes preliminary experiments that were performed on a pilot sample of commercial banks. The second summarizes results from applying the model to the full sample of commercial banks. The third examines the relation between forecasted and actual deposits for banks of different sizes on different dates. The fourth section describes deposit forecasting experiments performed on a pilot sample of mutual savings banks, and the fifth summarizes the deposit forecasting results for the full sample of savings banks.

1. EXPERIMENTS WITH A PILOT SAMPLE OF COMMERCIAL BANKS

Three questions were raised in chapter 4 concerning characteristics of the model for forecasting an individual commercial bank's demand and time deposits. First, what degree of smoothing should be incorporated in the forecasting model? Second, what should be the order of the time and demand deposit autoregressive processes? Third, are these processes stationary over time? These questions were studied with a small pilot sample of commercial banks, stratified by size but not randomly selected, from the sample of 201 commercial banks described in chapter 5.

The pilot sample consisted of nine banks ranging in total deposits from less than $2 million to more than $300 million on January 6, 1960. For simplicity, the banks were selected from the front of one deposit tape. To avoid heteroskedasticity, all the weekly deposit figures were deflated by a bank's total assets on the call report of April 12, 1961.

1. Preliminary versions of results reported in this chapter were presented in Hester [1965] and Hester and Pierce [1967b].

A number of banks in the pilot sample were found to experience very large weekly percentage changes in both their demand and time deposits.[2] Often these shocks were completely offset in the weeks following the shock. Banks experiencing such shocks are not likely to forecast future deposits in the same way as other banks. They will expend considerable effort to ascertain the sources of these extraordinary shocks. Unfortunately outside investigators cannot duplicate their efforts; therefore, it is assumed that a threshold percentage change in deposits exists which distinguishes extraordinary shocks from usual week-to-week shocks. So long as a bank's change in deposits is less than this percentage threshold, no smoothing occurs. If a large shock is experienced, the bank is assumed to expect a "synthetic" deposit change that is equal to the average weekly percentage change experienced by the bank in 1960. Smoothing continues until the percentage difference between the observed level of a bank's deposits and the synthetic level of deposits is less than the threshold.[3]

Experiments were performed with a number of thresholds ranging to a 25 percent absolute change in one week. A 25 percent threshold was finally adopted on the grounds that it appeared to eliminate extreme shocks without excessively frequent smoothing.[4] In all but a few cases, smoothing was necessary for fewer than eight consecutive weeks; data for most banks were not smoothed at all.

The commercial bank autoregressive processes were given in expression (4.3.4) and are repeated in (8.1.1):

$$(8.1.1) \quad \bar{d}_t = \theta_0 + \sum_{\tau=1}^{T} \theta_\tau \bar{d}_{t-\tau} + \theta_{52} \bar{d}_{t-52} + \varepsilon_t, \qquad \tau \neq 52, \quad \text{and}$$

$$\bar{s}_t = \varphi_0 + \sum_{\tau=1}^{T} \varphi_\tau \bar{s}_{t-\tau} + \varphi_{52} \bar{s}_{t-52} + v_t, \qquad \tau \neq 52,$$

where the individual bank subscript and the total asset deflator have been suppressed for ease of reading, the ~ underscore indicates that the variable may have been smoothed, and ε_t and v_t are generated by independent white-noise processes.

2. Demand deposits are defined as the sum of demand deposits due to banks, United States government demand deposits, and other demand deposits; these components are described in table 5-2. Time deposits are item 7 in that table.

3. The synthetic level was constructed by taking a bank's deposit level immediately before a large shock and successively incrementing it by the 1960 average weekly change. A similar technique was used to smooth deposit changes before estimating the input-output model in chapter 6.

4. Obviously such procedures cannot be rigorously defended; their adoption represents subjective judgments about what is a sensible and insightful approach.

To determine the order of the autoregressions, processes of three, seven, eleven, fifteen, nineteen, and twenty-three consecutive weeks were tried, ignoring the seasonal correction which was always present. With each span all demand deposit regressions yielded F-values that were significant at the 5 percent level; all but one bank's regressions were significant at the 1 percent level as well. As each new "block" of four weekly changes was added, F-tests were employed to test the hypothesis that the additional four parameters improved the description of a bank's deposit changes. When the order of the autoregression was extended from three to seven, three bank equations were significantly improved at the 5 percent level. Further increases of the order to eleven, fifteen, nineteen, and twenty-three coefficients successively improved the equations of three, three, one, and two banks. Given the dampening of significance after fifteen weeks, it was concluded that an autoregression of order nineteen would prove satisfactory when applied to the full sample of 201 banks. To facilitate computations, as mentioned in chapter 4, it has been assumed that autoregressions for each deposit type are of the same order for all banks.

Time deposit regressions were much less successful. Only six of the nine banks had a significant regression when three lags were studied, and the only consistently significant coefficient was the seasonal. Adding additional lags did not improve the description of weekly changes in time deposits. Consequently an autoregression of order three was assumed for all banks.

To examine whether the introduction of such factors as negotiable certificates of deposit (CDs) or changing seasonal relations had altered the autoregressive process, residuals were computed for each of the pilot sample time deposit regressions. In one experiment the net number of positive residuals was tabulated for each half year after December 31, 1960, and they are plotted in figure 8-1.[5] Two features of this diagram deserve comment. First, banks with more than $50 million in deposits on January 6, 1960, had a substantially larger number of negative residuals than smaller banks during 1961, before CDs were introduced in large quantities. The autoregressive model systematically overestimated deposit growth at large banks until CDs appeared. Second, over the entire period the total number of negative residuals at large banks considerably exceeded the number of positive residuals. The average value of their positive residuals was substantially larger than the average absolute value of their negative residuals. Both features are a probable consequence of the introduction of negotiable certificates of deposit and tend to confirm the apprehension that the time deposit process was not stationary between

5. One bank's residuals are not reported because its time deposits were smoothed for part of the period.

1960 and 1964. There was no evidence, however, that changes in seasonality added to this nonstationarity of the time deposit process.

An identical analysis of residuals from demand deposit regressions was also performed. No unusual pattern of residuals was observed for individual banks of different sizes over time. It was concluded that the stationarity assumption for demand deposits was well-satisfied in the pilot sample of banks.

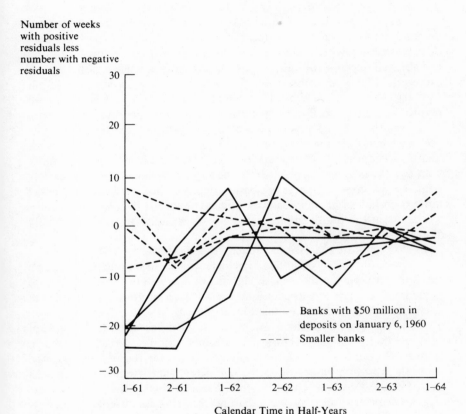

FIGURE 8-1. NET SIGNS OF INDIVIDUAL PILOT-SAMPLE BANKS IN DIFFERENT HALF YEARS

2. REGRESSION RESULTS FROM THE SAMPLE OF 201 COMMERCIAL BANKS

Autoregressive structures estimated for each of the 201 banks (including pilot sample banks) very successfully described bank deposit histories. Approximately 90 percent of the 201 demand deposit regressions and 70 percent of the 186 time deposit regressions had F-ratios that were significant at the 5 percent level.[6] The incidence of nonsignificant demand deposit regressions seemed to be unrelated to bank size, except that banks with total deposits in excess of \$50 million invariably had significant demand deposit equations. Nonsignificant time deposit regressions were disproportionately frequent for very small and very large banks.

Table 8-1 reports the number of regression coefficients with t values exceeding 1.96 in absolute value for different parameters and different January 6, 1960, bank sizes. The average number of significant demand deposit regression coefficients per bank is an increasing function of bank size even though the proportion of banks having significant total regressions is not. Ignoring the seasonal coefficient, θ_{52}, the average bank had three significant coefficients, but the group of large banks had more than five. As expected, deposit shocks in the recent past were more closely related to the current change in a bank's deposits than were earlier shocks; more than half of all significant coefficients concern the five most recent weeks. As in the pilot sample, statistical significance drops off markedly after θ_{15}.

In time deposit regressions, apart from the seasonal coefficient, φ_{52}, the average number of significant coefficients was about one per bank; no relation between the number of significant coefficients and bank size is evident. Contrary to expectation, the greatest number of significant coefficients occurred in the most recent period.

Mean values of coefficients are reported for different bank size groups in table 8-2. Demand deposit coefficients exhibit the expected sign pattern. Substantially negative coefficients exist for recent past periods; then, the absolute values of coefficients somewhat irregularly approach zero. For most groups of banks, estimated values of $\theta_4, \theta_5, \theta_8, \theta_9, \theta_{13}$, and θ_{17} are somewhat more positive than neighboring coefficients, suggesting the existence of regular monthly deposit inflows. Between 35 percent and 55 percent of a bank group's year-ago-week's deposit change reappears in the current weekly deposit change; bank seasonal flows are clearly very important.

6. Fifteen banks in the sample of 201 had no time deposits and were excluded from the summary reported in table 8-1.

TABLE 8-1. FREQUENCY OF SIGNIFICANT COMMERCIAL BANK
FORECASTING COEFFICIENTS

Coefficient	Bank Size[a]						Total
	0–2	2–5	5–10	10–25	25–50	Over 50	
Demand Deposits	(number of banks)						
θ_1	4	17	17	19	5	5	67
θ_2	5	26	26	21	6	10	94
θ_3	5	18	18	25	7	9	82
θ_4	2	7	7	7	4	7	34
θ_5	3	4	8	6	2	4	27
θ_6	1	8	6	8	2	2	27
θ_7	2	5	7	7	3	4	28
θ_8	3	6	5	5	1	5	25
θ_9	2	4	4	4	1	0	15
θ_{10}	3	6	8	8	6	8	39
θ_{11}	1	6	2	3	0	0	12
θ_{12}	2	3	5	8	6	9	33
θ_{13}	1	6	6	3	3	1	20
θ_{14}	2	3	7	2	2	2	18
θ_{15}	0	8	2	3	3	1	17
θ_{16}	0	2	5	3	4	4	18
θ_{17}	0	2	2	0	1	2	7
θ_{18}	0	2	1	1	1	1	6
θ_{19}	0	7	2	3	1	0	13
θ_{52}	15	46	54	33	15	14	177
Total Number of Banks in Group	15	61	58	38	15	14	201
Time Deposits							
φ_1	5	30	31	20	7	10	103
φ_2	0	11	17	8	1	2	39
φ_3	1	5	5	5	0	1	17
φ_{52}	5	24	33	16	7	6	91
Total Number of Banks in Group	12	52	56	37	15	14	186

NOTE: A coefficient is defined to be significant if it differs from zero at the 5 percent
level in a two-tailed test.
[a] Bank size refers to the amount of deposits (in millions of dollars) that a bank held
on January 6, 1960.

TABLE 8-2. MEAN DEPOSIT COEFFICIENTS FOR DIFFERENT BANK SIZE GROUPS

Coefficient	0–2	2–5	5–10	10–25	25–50	50–100	100–300	Over 300	Overall
					Bank Size[a]				
θ_0 (trend)	.000	.001	.000	.001	.001	.001	.001	.000	.001
θ_1	−.087	−.076	−.066	−.136	−.089	−.139	−.094	−.121	−.089
θ_2	−.129	−.150	−.147	−.164	−.161	−.115	−.247	−.155	−.152
θ_3	−.109	−.107	−.118	−.181	−.167	−.083	−.207	−.193	−.132
θ_4	−.028	−.047	−.025	−.078	−.105	−.151	−.143	−.161	−.057
θ_5	−.007	−.028	−.010	−.084	−.093	−.111	−.081	−.077	−.041
θ_6	−.060	−.073	−.057	−.100	−.079	−.037	−.103	−.117	−.073
θ_7	−.059	−.047	−.051	−.089	−.103	−.069	−.114	−.108	−.065
θ_8	−.025	−.024	−.032	−.033	.023	−.073	−.074	−.071	−.028
θ_9	−.034	.016	.014	.019	.010	.047	−.003	.005	.012
θ_{10}	−.033	−.046	−.072	−.086	−.068	−.101	−.195	−.183	−.069
θ_{11}	.010	−.030	−.030	−.048	−.003	−.002	.031	.029	−.025
θ_{12}	.009	−.044	−.064	−.081	−.087	−.163	−.164	−.170	−.064
θ_{13}	.003	.053	.030	.035	.085	.058	.092	.071	.043
θ_{14}	−.006	−.028	−.041	−.043	−.026	.001	−.065	−.065	−.033
θ_{15}	−.049	−.051	−.033	−.060	−.030	−.070	−.065	−.052	−.047
θ_{16}	−.067	−.053	−.050	−.061	−.018	−.080	−.055	−.121	−.054
θ_{17}	−.018	−.009	.009	−.008	.014	.090	−.022	.016	.001
θ_{18}	−.002	−.007	−.003	−.014	.002	−.053	−.079	.009	−.009
θ_{19}	−.015	−.055	−.052	−.033	.002	−.030	−.003	−.053	−.041
θ_{52} (seasonal)	.443	.341	.373	.428	.482	.441	.565	.535	.396
rpd	.586	.554	.556	.445	.528	.481	.386	.397	.520
φ_0 (trend)	.001	.000	.000	.000	.000	.001	.000	.001	.000
φ_1	.040	.036	.004	.056	.142	.212	.284	.062	.050
φ_2	−.029	−.049	−.063	−.064	−.023	−.022	−.048	.017	−.050
φ_3	−.014	.000	−.011	.024	.018	.000	.052	−.005	.003
φ_{52} (seasonal)	.143	.140	.230	.152	.137	.158	.208	−.009	.167
rps	.997	.987	.935	1.016	1.159	1.234	1.404	1.080	1.003

Values of the mean deposit retention ratio, *rpd*, as defined in expression (2.4.6), are related to bank size; large banks have lower demand deposit retention ratios than others. This relation is probably a consequence of differences in markets served by large and small banks. Large banks are found in large metropolitan areas and tend to be more interrelated than small banks. Small banks tend to serve more isolated suburban or small-town markets. Being more isolated, they are somewhat like monopoly banks who noticeably benefit from the process of "creating" money. Small banks tend to retain about 55 percent of an initial deposit shock, whereas banks with more than $100 million in deposits retain only about 40 percent.

It would be quite surprising if individual bank portfolios did not reflect these differences in deposit retention. Incorporating deposit forecasting equations in portfolio models should improve empirical descriptions of bank behavior.

Time deposit coefficients vary considerably across different sizes of banks. Positive coefficients on lagged time deposit changes were expected, but they were not expected in the first few time periods. Positive values of φ_1 apparently result from autocorrelation of time deposit shocks at a bank; they should be interpreted with considerable caution. Seasonality in time deposit changes is only about one-third as strong as in demand deposit changes. As expected, the overall retention ratio for time deposits, *rps*, is about unity.

Finally, standard errors of estimate and multiple correlation coefficients of demand and time deposit regressions are of interest. Mean values of these statistics and of the standard deviations of actual demand and time deposit changes are reported for different sizes of banks in table 8-3.[7] As bank size increases, there is a decrease in the standard error of estimate of changes in demand deposits, and the multiple correlation coefficient rises. While the standard deviation of actual demand deposit changes also declines with bank size, the standard error of estimate tends to decline more rapidly. Thus, the demand deposit changes of large banks are both less variable and relatively more predictable than are the demand deposit changes of small banks. The improvement in deposit predictability with increases in bank size clearly is not negligible. Portfolio managers of large banks may be able to exploit this greater demand deposit predictability profitably.

The results for the time deposit prediction regressions generally are less useful. While standard errors of estimate of time deposit changes are very low relative to demand deposits, the standard deviations of time deposit

7. It should be recalled that the deposit change data for each bank were deflated by the value of its total assets on April 12, 1961.

TABLE 8-3. SUMMARY STATISTICS FOR DEMAND AND TIME DEPOSIT EQUATIONS

Bank Size[b]	Demand Deposits[a]				Time Deposits[a]			
	Standard Error of Estimate (1)	Standard Deviation of Actual Changes (2)	Ratio of (1) to (2)	Multiple Correlation Coefficient	Standard Error of Estimate (3)	Standard Deviation of Actual Changes (4)	Ratio of (3) to (4)	Multiple Correlation Coefficient
0–2	3.138%	3.502%	.896	.557	.577%	.619%	.932	.279
2–5	4.671	5.608	.833	.545	.420	.438	.959	.352
5–10	2.308	2.711	.851	.568	.401	.433	.926	.367
10–25	2.281	2.794	.816	.610	.298	.321	.928	.360
25–50	1.788	2.295	.779	.673	.263	.270	.974	.321
50–100	1.782	2.216	.804	.652	.276	.296	.932	.368
100–300	1.751	2.613	.670	.769	.299	.313	.955	.375
over 300	1.491	2.211	.674	.759	.338	.340	.994	.183

[a] Weekly changes as a percentage of total bank assets.
[b] Bank size refers to the amount of deposits (in millions of dollars) that a bank held on January 6, 1960.

changes are also relatively very low. Multiple correlation coefficients for time deposit changes are small for all size groups. The pattern of the summary statistics across size groups is not as clear as for demand deposits. There is no evidence that large banks enjoy more predictable time deposits than do small banks. For banks with up to $50 million in total deposits, the standard error of estimate of time deposit changes declines as bank size increases. The relative improvement, however, is not as great as for demand deposits. For banks with total deposits in excess of $50 million, both the standard error of estimate and the standard deviation of changes rise with bank size. Further, the standard error of estimate also rises relative to the standard deviation of time deposit changes. Finally, for banks under $50 million, there is no interesting relationship between the standard error of estimate and the standard deviation of actual changes.

This pattern of results is not surprising in light of the introduction of certificates of deposit during the period. It is difficult for small banks to compete in the CD market, so their savings and time deposits remained largely of the passbook variety over the period. The variance of these deposits is small, and their changes are relatively predictable using an autoregressive process. Large banks, on the other hand, came to be significant issuers of CDs during the period. Thus, large banks experienced a higher variance of time deposit changes; these changes were not easily described with an autoregressive model, although individual banks may have predicted them with considerable accuracy.

3. Some Remarks on the Quality of Forecasts Produced by These Equations

Forecast statistics reported in tables 8-4 through 8-6 require some interpretative comments. The statistics were compiled from deposit forecasts that are subsequently used when estimating the adaptive-expectations model. In that model it is assumed that with the passage of each week a bank makes new forecasts of the levels of demand and time deposits expected to prevail during the week of a call report. It is assumed that a bank's maximum forecast horizon is fifty-two weeks. Thus, using the autoregressive structures whose estimation is described in section 2, fifty-two separate forecasts were made for the demand and time deposit levels expected to prevail during the week of each call report. Each forecast was generated recursively from a sequence of deposit changes that was known to the bank at the time of the forecast. The forecasted changes were converted to levels and divided by the value of total assets shown on the relevant call report.[8] Following the convention of chapter 6, except for the three weeks just prior to the call report, weekly forecasts were averaged into successive four-week "months." In table 8-4 all forecasts were made for a call report six months in the future.[9] Several forecast horizons are considered in the remaining tables. Because data were available only for the period from January 6, 1960, through July 1, 1964, year-ago levels of deposits were not always available for the first four dates reported in table 8-4. Therefore, mean values of changes for each of the fifty-two weeks have been used to estimate corresponding unobserved 1959 deposit changes in order to generate forecasts.

The results reported in table 8-4 indicate that the average forecast errors for demand deposits are considerably larger than those for time deposits. This result is not surprising, since demand deposits are much more variable than time deposits. In addition, for the six-month forecasting horizon, it appears that the regression equations have not completely accounted for seasonal variations in demand deposits. This is concluded because on all September and December dates the equations underestimated changes in demand deposits for almost all sizes of banks. This defective deseasonalization appears to be unavoidable, given the available deposit data. Time deposit forecast errors do not exhibit any obvious seasonal pattern.

Root mean squared forecast errors are reported in tables 8-5 and 8-6. The errors are again expressed as a percentage of each bank's total assets on the call report to which the forecast applies.[10] For each horizon, statistics are reported for banks in eight size classes and for the pooled sample. For each size class, forecast errors decline for both demand and time deposits as the interval between forecast and realization shortens. The decline is monotonic for the demand deposit forecasts for all banks combined and is nearly so for each size class taken separately. The decline in forecast errors for time deposits is monotonic for all size classes. It is interesting to note that demand deposit forecasting errors, relative to total assets, are larger for small banks than for large. Also, the accuracy of forecasts decays more rapidly for small banks than for large banks as the forecast horizon lengthens.

8. It should be noted that these are not "pure" forecasts because the autoregression coefficients were estimated using these same data.

9. The number of banks varies both across size classes and over time. Small mean forecast errors may reflect good performance by the model and/or the law of large numbers. Table 8-1 reports information about the size distribution of banks.

10. As explained at the beginning of the section, summary statistics were computed from forecasts of deposits for weeks in which there were call reports. Therefore, there is no direct relation between standard errors of estimate reported in table 8-3 and forecast errors reported in this section.

TABLE 8-4. MEAN SIX-MONTH DEPOSIT FORECAST ERRORS

Date to which Forecast Applies	Bank Size[a]							
	0–2	2–5	5–10	10–25	25–50	50–100	100–300	Over 300
Demand Deposits								
4/12/61	−.736	3.924	3.181	2.846	3.653	2.839	−.035	1.474
6/30/61	1.129	2.253	1.341	2.405	.750	1.042	.708	.537
9/27/61	−5.442	−3.294	−3.520	−2.526	−3.097	−1.635	−.962	−1.628
12/30/61	−4.492	−2.786	−3.293	−3.720	−2.813	−2.343	−4.855	−3.333
3/26/62	4.885	5.004	3.822	1.676	3.534	1.836	−.591	1.480
6/30/62	3.330	2.652	2.796	.139	−.349	.166	.301	−.197
9/28/62	−4.210	−2.859	−2.527	−2.529	−2.530	−.099	−2.171	1.109
12/28/62	−3.063	−1.804	−2.148	−2.822	−2.768	−2.492	−2.662	−1.369
3/18/63	3.633	3.462	2.880	1.403	2.343	.297	1.159	−1.580
6/29/63	−.568	.357	.282	.358	.350	1.348	.565	−.501
12/20/63	−2.761	−1.636	−1.666	−.916	−.135	.393	−.719	.079
Time Deposits								
4/12/61	−.124	.127	−.104	−.253	−.899	−.436	−.512	−1.344
6/30/61	−.218	−.191	−.108	−.232	−.934	−.408	−.034	−.532
9/27/61	−.169	−.398	−.327	−.271	.174	−.113	−.137	−.447
12/30/61	.484	−.031	.497	.385	.511	.937	−.323	−1.124
3/26/62	−.292	−.298	−.013	−.137	.051	−.406	−.272	−2.823
6/30/62	−1.868	−.466	−.536	−.922	−1.287	−1.856	−.046	−.666
9/28/62	−1.029	−.443	−1.085	−.510	−.709	−1.758	−.835	−.588
12/28/62	−.301	.013	−.267	.023	.363	−.915	.875	−.479
3/18/63	−.147	−.148	−.227	−.696	−.156	−1.715	−.396	−1.047
6/29/63	.255	.336	−.391	−1.028	−.635	−1.582	−1.627	−1.477
12/20/63	.546	−.066	.179	.135	.223	.078	−2.395	−2.671

NOTE: Errors are defined to be predicted minus actual deposits expressed as a percentage of a bank's total assets.
[a] Bank size refers to the amount of deposits (in millions of dollars) that a bank held on January 6, 1960.

TABLE 8-5. ROOT MEAN SQUARED FORECAST ERRORS: DEMAND DEPOSITS

Forecast Horizon	Bank Size[a]								All Banks
	0–2	2–5	5–10	10–25	25–50	50–100	100–300	over 300	
1 week	2.185	1.839	1.542	1.482	1.385	1.287	1.178	1.150	1.635
2 weeks	3.246	2.570	2.412	2.224	1.879	1.356	1.895	1.572	2.396
3 weeks	3.532	3.101	2.840	2.600	2.129	1.420	2.029	1.638	2.803
2 months	4.002	3.562	3.211	2.986	2.374	1.617	2.093	1.654	3.189
3 months	4.488	4.389	4.345	3.458	2.986	1.961	2.382	1.906	3.980
4 months	5.589	5.289	4.965	3.906	3.212	2.149	2.585	1.950	4.645
5 months	7.141	5.847	5.379	4.236	3.498	2.526	2.822	1.999	5.162
6 months	6.950	6.129	5.837	4.251	3.580	2.574	2.768	2.053	5.392
7 months	7.184	6.818	6.277	4.527	3.656	2.471	2.770	1.801	5.825
8 months	7.256	7.280	6.507	4.679	3.747	2.531	2.887	2.001	6.092
9 months	6.382	7.443	6.730	4.634	3.637	2.778	2.830	2.072	6.153
10 months	6.448	7.708	7.053	4.440	3.544	2.648	2.772	2.095	6.325
11 months	6.353	7.976	7.096	4.526	3.617	2.433	2.818	1.890	6.438
12 months	6.860	8.242	7.021	4.510	3.484	2.456	2.848	1.772	6.532

NOTE: Following the convention of chapter 6, months are averages of 4 weekly forecasts. Errors are expressed as a percentage of a bank's total assets.

[a] Bank size refers to the amount of deposits (in millions of dollars) that a bank held on January 6, 1960.

TABLE 8-6. ROOT MEAN SQUARED FORECAST ERRORS: TIME DEPOSITS

Forecast Horizon	Bank Size[a]								All Banks
	0–2	2–5	5–10	10–25	25–50	50–100	100–300	over 300	
1 week	.326	.246	.346	.438	.183	.167	.112	.177	.320
2 weeks	.534	.452	.422	.486	.312	.251	.285	.259	.435
3 weeks	.722	.590	.520	.585	.359	.301	.353	.357	.547
2 months	1.040	.728	.719	.650	.464	.489	.450	.806	.708
3 months	1.268	1.029	1.145	1.061	.858	.850	.911	1.199	1.073
4 months	1.477	1.267	1.361	1.275	1.098	1.285	1.218	1.457	1.305
5 months	1.484	1.399	1.488	1.412	1.229	1.465	1.408	1.730	1.434
6 months	1.642	1.466	1.552	1.490	1.321	1.725	1.394	2.026	1.521
7 months	1.811	1.669	1.705	1.676	1.444	2.101	1.525	2.205	1.702
8 months	2.203	1.796	1.828	1.951	1.571	2.251	1.587	2.338	1.875
9 months	2.274	1.883	1.847	1.833	1.647	2.387	1.626	2.562	1.904
10 months	2.439	1.999	1.963	1.939	1.675	2.703	1.737	2.701	2.025
11 months	2.673	2.062	2.091	2.167	1.732	2.888	1.988	2.854	2.164
12 months	2.770	2.095	2.096	2.053	1.796	2.952	2.095	2.916	2.171

NOTE: Following the convention of chapter 6, months are averages of 4 weekly forecasts. Errors are expressed as a percentage of a bank's total assets.

[a] Bank size refers to the amount of deposits (in millions of dollars) that a bank held on January 6, 1960.

The time deposit results do not display such patterns when different sizes of banks are compared. The root mean squared errors rise almost equivalently for all bank sizes as the horizon is extended. Indeed forecasts of time deposits for large banks are no better than forecasts of demand deposits, even though time deposits have a much smaller weekly variance. Forecasts of time deposits at small banks, on the other hand, are more accurate than those for demand deposits.

The results reported in this section clearly indicate that there is an important distinction to be made between deposit variability and deposit predictability. Earlier studies emphasized the former to the exclusion of the latter. The evidence reported here shows that highly variable deposit flows can be highly predictable flows. If asset transactions costs are a function of the size and advance notice of the transaction, it is important for a bank to predict future deposit movements accurately. The fact that the pattern of predicted deposit flows is highly variable is, of course, also important.

It is interesting to note that the predictions were particularly successful for the demand deposits of large banks. While on the average small banks retain a larger proportion of a given deposit inflow than do large banks, deposit changes are much more difficult to predict for small banks.

Finally, over the period studied, time deposits were not subject to nearly as much variability as were demand deposits. Banks' inability to predict time deposit changes with a high degree of precision was not very damaging because these deposits simply did not change very much.

4. EXPERIMENTS WITH A PILOT SAMPLE OF MUTUAL SAVINGS BANKS

The three questions of section 1 concerning (1) the degree of deposit smoothing to be incorporated in the model, (2) the order of the auto-regressive structure, and (3) the stationarity of the process over time are investigated in this section using a small pilot sample of mutual savings banks. The pilot sample was drawn from the large sample of mutual savings banks described in chapter 5 and consists of the 10 New York City savings banks described in section 1 of chapter 7. It should be recalled that the sample was not randomly selected but contains banks ranging from $50 million to more than $1 billion in total assets.

No large monthly percentage changes were encountered in the pilot sample data, and no smoothing was necessary. Large deposit shocks also were not observed in the full sample considered later.

Several versions of the forecasting model of (4.3.4) were estimated for each of the banks in the pilot sample. The most elaborate version involved seven lagged monthly deposit changes and the year-ago change to give

$$(8.4.1) \qquad \bar{m}_t = \psi_0 + \sum_{i=1}^{7} \psi_i \bar{m}_{t-i} + \psi_{12} \bar{m}_{t-12} + \mu_t.$$

The results of the experimentation can be summarized as follows: The seasonal coefficient, ψ_{12}, was significant at the 1 percent level for all ten banks. When four lags were considered, ψ_1 was significantly positive three times out of ten, ψ_3 was significantly positive six times out of ten, and ψ_2 and ψ_4 were not significantly positive for any of the banks. When the full seven lags were used, ψ_6 was significant three times out of ten, and ψ_5 and ψ_7 were not significant. The prevalence of significant coefficients at quarterly intervals apparently reflects the practice of paying interest at quarterly and/or semiannual intervals.

These results suggested the following model for the full sample:

$$(8.4.2) \qquad \bar{m}_t = \psi_0 + \psi_1 \bar{m}_{t-1} + \psi_3 \bar{m}_{t-3} + \psi_{12} \bar{m}_{t-12} + \mu_t.$$

A crucial assumption necessary to justify the deposit prediction model is that its structure be stable over time. To test this hypothesis, the ten sample banks were pooled to yield a total of 470 observations. The pooled data were divided into two parts; the first concerned deposit changes from February 1960 through January 1962, and the second concerned changes for the remaining twenty-three months. An analysis of covariance revealed that the hypothesis of no change in structure must be rejected at the 1 percent level. This result is discouraging for the application of the prediction model. As stated in chapter 7, one of the most turbulent periods in savings bank deposit history had occurred during 1959 with the issuance of the magic fives. This event may well have obscured an underlying structure.

5. REGRESSION RESULTS FROM A SAMPLE OF TWO HUNDRED SAVINGS BANKS

Table 8-7 reports a summary of results obtained by using (8.4.2) and the full sample of two hundred mutual savings banks.[11] The regression model

---

11. The forecasting equation for one Massachusetts savings bank was improperly estimated because of a data coding error. The error was corrected in time for that bank to be included in the input-output analysis of chapter 7, but it was not used in calculations reported in this and the following chapter.

is quite successful in describing first differences in deposits; only a few individual bank equations were not significant at the 1 percent level. The mean squared multiple correlation coefficient is about .64.

TABLE 8-7. FREQUENCY OF SIGNIFICANT SAVINGS BANK FORECASTING
COEFFICIENTS

Region	Number of Banks	ψ_1	ψ_3	ψ_{12}
Connecticut	32	3	2	28
Massachusetts	88	26	13	83
New York City	39	5	35	37
New York State	41	1	29	41
Total	200	35	79	189

NOTE: A coefficient is defined to be significant if it differs from zero at the 5 percent level in a two-tailed test.

It is apparent from table 8-7 that drawing a pilot sample only from New York City banks was not a good strategy. The large number of significant values of ψ_3 apparently reflects a quarterly interest payment period useful for predicting New York City and New York State bank deposit flows, but not flows elsewhere. This misspecification of the process for banks outside New York makes their forecasting equations inefficient, but is not the fatal flaw for applying the adaptive-expectations model. As will be seen in chapter 9, the adaptive-expectations model was not successful for any group of savings banks.

Estimates of ψ_1 were also surprisingly nonsignificant given the results in the pilot study. This variable probably could also have been omitted from the forecasting equation. The success of the model was in large part attributable to the coefficient on the seasonal, ψ_{12}, whose sign was uniformly positive as expected.

These results suggest that for banks outside New York the deposit change structure is an extremely simple one composed only of a constant and a seasonal term. New York banks give evidence of a somewhat more complex structure. Overall, savings bank forecasting equations are quite similar in appearance to commercial bank time deposit equations.

The results reported in this chapter indicate that the application of the autoregressive model for explaining changes in demand deposits at commercial banks was reasonably successful. The results are plausible, and the structure appears to have been stationary through time. The autoregressions performed less well when applied to commercial bank time deposits and to deposits at mutual savings banks. The usefulness of incorporating deposit forecasts in models of bank portfolio selection is considered in the next chapter.

CHAPTER 9

The Adaptive-Expectations Formulation

In this chapter deposit forecasts of individual commercial banks are used to describe variations in bank portfolios.[1] The regression analysis utilizes the same sample of 184 commercial banks that was studied in chapter 6. The underlying statistical model for the adaptive-expectations approach was described in chapter 4, and the deposit forecasts were evaluated in chapter 8.

Deposit forecasts for mutual savings banks were also studied in chapter 8. However, savings banks are not considered in this chapter because the forecasting equations lacked an interesting structure. Attempts to estimate the structure of the adaptive-expectations model for mutual savings banks were not successful because successive coefficients fluctuated erratically. The principal reason for the failure is that deposit changes in mutual savings banks do not have a well-defined autoregressive structure, apart from a pronounced seasonal change; and, therefore, monthly forecasts are highly correlated.

It is assumed that a commercial bank has a forecast horizon of about one year. The bank is assumed to use weekly averages of all deposit data available to it to make a series of forecasts of changes in the average level of its demand and time deposits for each of fifty-two consecutive weeks, exploiting the recursive structure of the forecasting equations described in the preceding chapter. As new data become available each week, the bank revises its forecasts for the succeeding fifty-two weeks. Therefore, the change in its deposits in the week of a call report, j, is actually forecasted on fifty-two separate dates. In order to economize on the number of variables used in the portfolio analysis, forecasts made in the distant past for a call report have been converted to four-week averages.

The adaptive-expectations model is used to study three questions. Do estimates of the lag structure describing the relation between the history of a bank's deposit forecasts and current portfolio composition support the theoretical approach of this monograph? Are the lag structures and steady-state values for demand deposit forecasts different from those for

1. Preliminary versions of results reported in this chapter were presented in Hester and Pierce [1967b].

savings and time deposit forecasts? Does the adaptive-expectations approach provide a better explanation of bank portfolio selection than the competing input-output formulation?

1. ESTIMATES OF THE STRUCTURE OF THE MODEL

Coefficient estimates for the adaptive-expectations model were obtained by applying the method of ordinary least squares to the 1,843 individual bank observations that were studied in chapter 6. All variables have been deflated by a bank's total assets on a corresponding call report, and all variables are measured about individual bank means. Coefficients again have been normalized so that regression lines go through the means of the average bank in the sample.

The results from the analysis of bank asset aggregates are reported in tables 9-1, 9-2, and 9-3; except for the absence of overflow variables, coefficients have similar interpretations to those reported in tables 6-1, 6-2, and 6-3.[2] As before, the three tables must be read together because the coefficients in any column come from the same regression. In tables 9-1 and 9-2 coefficients in all but the last row refer to revisions of forecasts of the average levels of demand and time deposits made for the week of some call report. The superscript on a deposit variable refers to the time span between the date of some forecast or forecast revision and the date of a call report. The first coefficient in each table refers to the difference between the deposit forecast made one week prior to the call report and the actual deposit level for the week of the call report. The next two coefficients refer to weekly deposit forecast revisions, and the next one to a revision over a two-week period. The next eleven refer to successive revisions over four-week periods.[3] The last row of coefficients in each table refers to a forecast of deposit levels which was made about fifty weeks before a call report.

Standard errors are reported below each coefficient. No test statistics are reported for "other assets" because these coefficients were obtained from an identity or, equivalently, by pooling a number of regression coefficients of some other minor bank assets.

Table 9-3 shows the values of coefficients of dummy call report variables. Their pattern is similar to that reported in table 6-3 and, thus, requires no further comment.

2. See section 3 of chapter 4 for a discussion of this approach.
3. The first such four-week period consists of an average of deposit forecasts made in the fifth, sixth, seventh, and eighth weeks and thus is centered at six and a half weeks. Therefore, the first monthly change refers to a change over about three weeks. Subsequent averages are centered at four-week intervals.

TABLE 9-1. ADAPTIVE-EXPECTATIONS MODEL FOR ASSET AGGREGATES: DEMAND DEPOSIT COEFFICIENTS

	Cash	State and Local	Mortgage	Comm. and Indust.	Consumer	Shorts	1–5s	Other
$\bar{d}^w$	.441*	.048*	.049*	.083*	.092*	.192*	−.065	.160
	(.030)	(.021)	(.013)	(.023)	(021)	(.048)	(.038)	
$\bar{d}^{w-1}$	.358*	.017	.064*	.124*	.106*	.174*	.026	.131
	(.032)	(.022)	(.014)	(.025)	(.022)	(.050)	(.040)	
$\bar{d}^{w-2}$	.200*	.054*	.061*	.102*	.067*	.302*	.131*	.083
	(.040)	(.028)	(.018)	(.031)	(.028)	(.063)	(.050)	
$\bar{d}^{sm}$	.342*	.043	.069*	.072*	.125*	.256*	.042	.051
	(.038)	(.026)	(.017)	(.030)	(.027)	(.060)	(.048)	
$\bar{d}^{m-2}$	.269*	.041	.039*	.150*	.137*	.281*	−.017	.100
	(.031)	(.022)	(.014)	(.024)	(.022)	(.050)	(.039)	
$\bar{d}^{m-3}$	.231*	.044	.066*	.057*	.077*	.294*	.125*	.106
	(.033)	(.022)	(.014)	(.025)	(.023)	(.052)	(.041)	
$\bar{d}^{m-4}$	.220*	.047*	.084*	.186*	.146*	.138*	.147*	.032
	(.033)	(.022)	(.014)	(.025)	(.023)	(.051)	(.041)	
$\bar{d}^{m-5}$	.186*	−.002	.080*	.053	.152*	.263*	.126*	.142
	(.038)	(.026)	(.017)	(.029)	(.026)	(.060)	(.047)	
$\bar{d}^{m-6}$	.149*	.038	.101*	.146*	.165*	.232*	.092*	.077
	(.033)	(.022)	(.014)	(.025)	(.023)	(.051)	(.040)	
$\bar{d}^{m-7}$	.259*	.066*	.072*	.148*	.120*	.146*	.145*	.044
	(.038)	(.026)	(.017)	(.029)	(.026)	(.060)	(.047)	
$\bar{d}^{m-8}$	.257*	.045	.089*	.095*	.171*	.126*	.061	.156
	(.036)	(.024)	(.016)	(.028)	(.025)	(.056)	(.044)	
$\bar{d}^{m-9}$	.216*	.051*	.101*	.143*	.154*	.196*	.091*	.048
	(.030)	(.021)	(.013)	(.023)	(.021)	(.048)	(.038)	
$\bar{d}^{m-10}$	.193*	.031	.097*	.139*	.186*	.113*	.125*	.116
	(.026)	(.017)	(.011)	(.020)	(.018)	(.040)	(.032)	
$\bar{d}^{m-11}$	224*	.081*	.070*	.154*	.185*	.047	.105*	.134
	(.026)	(.017)	(.011)	(.020)	(.018)	(.040)	(.032)	
$\bar{d}^{m-12}$	.230*	.091*	.095*	.146*	.190*	.009	.147*	.092
	(.024)	(.017)	(.011)	(.019)	(.017)	(.039)	(.030)	
d^{m-13}	.209*	.067*	.097*	.148*	.187*	.113*	.099*	.080
	(.010)	(.007)	(.004)	(.008)	(.007)	(.016)	(.012)	

NOTE: See last row in table 9-3 for sources of dependent variables. In this and subsequent tables in this chapter, an asterisk indicates that a coefficient differs significantly from zero at the 5 percent level in a two-tailed test.

	Cash	State and Local	Mortgage	Comm. and Indust.	Consumer	Shorts	1–5s	Other
$\bar{g}^w$	.421*	.114	.112	.090	−.034	.256	−.183	.224
	(.150)	(.102)	(.066)	(.116)	(.104)	(.236)	(.186)	
$\bar{g}^{w-1}$	.181	.095	.082	.048	.038	.492*	−.361	.425
	(.156)	(.106)	(.068)	(.120)	(.108)	(.245)	(.193)	
$\bar{g}^{w-2}$	.153	−.022	.255*	.047	.313*	.092	.195	−.033
	(.172)	(.118)	(.076)	(.134)	(.120)	(.271)	(.214)	
$\bar{g}^{sm}$	.326*	−.062	.131*	.198	.250*	.323	−.012	−.154
	(.137)	(.094)	(.060)	(.106)	(.095)	(.216)	(.170)	
$\bar{g}^{m-2}$	.070	.149*	.016	.123	.065	.224	.073	.280
	(.099)	(.068)	(.044)	(.077)	(.069)	(.156)	(.123)	
$\bar{g}^{m-3}$	−.017	.081	.042	.299*	.016	−.023	.275*	.327
	(.111)	(.076)	(.049)	(.086)	(.077)	(.174)	(.137)	
$\bar{g}^{m-4}$	−.024	.096	.303*	.133	.224*	.252	−.120	.136
	(.107)	(.073)	(.047)	(.083)	(.074)	(.168)	(.132)	
$\bar{g}^{m-5}$	.091	.156*	.048	.112	.084	.357*	−.028	.180
	(.096)	(.066)	(.042)	(.074)	(.067)	(.151)	(.119)	
$\bar{g}^{m-6}$	−.057	−.027	.133*	.244*	.203*	.049	.047	.408
	(.100)	(.068)	(.044)	(.078)	(.070)	(.158)	(.124)	
$\bar{g}^{m-7}$	.144	−.011	.250*	.217*	.043	−.048	.165	.240
	(.120)	(.082)	(.053)	(.093)	(.084)	(.189)	(.149)	
$\bar{g}^{m-8}$	.066	.132	.228*	.291*	.040	.026	−.095	.312
	(.098)	(.067)	(.043)	(.076)	(.068)	(.154)	(.121)	
$\bar{g}^{m-9}$	.090	.152*	.040	.016	.244*	−.048	.070	.436
	(.096)	(.065)	(.042)	(.074)	(.067)	(.151)	(.119)	
$\bar{g}^{m-10}$	−.027	.036	.260*	.218*	.189*	.135	−.080	.269
	(.094)	(.064)	(.041)	(.073)	(.065)	(.148)	(.116)	
$\bar{g}^{m-11}$	.138	.105	.303*	.139	−.021	−.032	.162	.206
	(.098)	(.067)	(.043)	(.076)	(.068)	(.154)	(.121)	
$\bar{g}^{m-12}$	−.049	.123*	.146*	.195*	.245*	.002	−.091	.429
	(.071)	(.049)	(.031)	(.055)	(.049)	(.112)	(.088)	
g^{m-13}	−.008	.079*	.269*	.160*	.139*	−.018	.084*	.295
	(.024)	(.016)	(.010)	(.018)	(.017)	(.037)	(.030)	

	Cash	State and Local	Mort-gage	Comm. and Indust.	Con-sumer	Shorts	1–5s	Other
				Call Report Dummy Variables				
4-12-61	.024*	−.002	−.009*	−.006*	−.013*	.004	.023*	−.021
	(.003)	(.002)	(.001)	(.002)	(.002)	(.005)	(.004)	
6-30-61	.015*	.004*	−.007*	.000	−.008*	−.002	.022*	−.024
	(.003)	(.002)	(.001)	(.002)	(.002)	(.005)	(.004)	
9-27-61	.018*	.002	−.008*	−.003	−.014*	.008	.027*	−.030
	(.003)	(.002)	(.001)	(.002)	(.002)	(.005)	(.004)	
12-30-61	.033*	−.009*	−.008*	−.003	−.017*	.008	.017*	−.021
	(.003)	(.002)	(.001)	(.002)	(.002)	(.004)	(.003)	
3-26-62	.019*	−.003	−.007*	−.001	−.010*	.005	.005	−.008
	(.003)	(.002)	(.001)	(.002)	(.002)	(.005)	(.004)	
6-30-62	.016*	.005*	−.006*	.003	−.004	−.002	.003	−.015
	(.003)	(.002)	(.001)	(.002)	(.002)	(.005)	(.004)	
9-28-62	.015*	.004*	−.008*	−.001	−.009*	.010*	−.004	−.007
	(.003)	(.002)	(.001)	(.002)	(.002)	(.005)	(.004)	
12-28-62	.026*	−.008*	−.008*	−.005*	−.013*	.006	.002	.000
	(.003)	(.002)	(.001)	(.002)	(.002)	(.004)	(.004)	
3-18-63	.024*	−.001	−.005*	.001	−.009*	−.006	−.003	−.001
	(.003)	(.002)	(.001)	(.002)	(.002)	(.005)	(.004)	
6-29-63	.013*	.006*	−.005*	.002	−.004	−.013*	.004	−.003
	(.003)	(.002)	(.001)	(.002)	(.002)	(.005)	(.004)	
				Capital				
f^C	.186*	.055*	.108*	.139*	.195*	.136*	.100*	.081
	(.011)	(.008)	(.005)	(.009)	(.008)	(.018)	(.014)	
				Summary Statistics				
R^2	.205	.121	.202	.053	.146	.108	.147	N.A.
S_ε	.024	.016	.010	.018	.016	.037	.029	N.A.
F	10.391*	5.538*	10.221*	2.238*	6.921*	4.881*	6.948*	N.A.
Mean	.164	.068	.140	.149	.165	.083	.099	.132
Item Num-ber(s) in Table 5-1	1	3	27, 28, 29, 30	36	37, 38, 39, 40, 41	44, 45, 46, 49	47, 50	Residual

NOTE: The number of observations in each regression is 1,843.

While the pattern of coefficients is erratic, the general time profile of portfolio adjustment indicated by the adaptive-expectations model is evident. Changes in deposit forecasts made in weeks just prior to a call report appear primarily in adjustments in cash and short-term government securities. Distant forecast revisions, made long before a call report, primarily affect holdings of less liquid assets. A comparison of coefficients of the earliest forecasts of deposit levels suggests that relatively larger fractions of savings and time deposits flow into mortgage loans, state and local securities, and "other" assets than is the case for demand deposits. This behavior is to be expected in light of the greater predictability of savings and time deposits.[4] In an analysis of covariance, the set of savings and time deposit coefficients was significantly different at the 5 percent level from the set of demand deposit coefficients for all assets reported in these tables.

Revisions of forecasts of call report deposit levels made on intermediate dates, however, are related to portfolio composition in a very erratic manner. The uneven pattern of the coefficients probably reflects in part the imperfect deseasonalization of deposit forecasts mentioned in chapter 8. In part, it also reflects more conventional short-run (nonseasonal) errors in variables. If this argument is correct, further averaging of the deposit forecasts might yield a pattern of portfolio response more in accord with a priori expectations.

Some rough evidence in support of this argument can be offered. When deposit forecasts are averaged together, the response pattern better approximates that predicted by theory. The original weekly forecasts were converted to twelve-week averages except for the three weekly forecasts made just prior to a call report, which were combined with the actual value of deposits during the week of the call report to form a four-week average. The results for this smoothed adaptive-expectations model are reported in table 9-4.[5] The first coefficients for demand and time deposits may be interpreted as referring to a final deposit forecast revision that is made about two weeks before a call report. The next three coefficients for each deposit type may be thought of as referring to

---

4. Very early demand deposit forecasts have coefficients that are remarkably similar to those on "capital" for different assets. The likely reason for this similarity is that capital was defined in chapter 4 to be the difference between the sum of a bank's demand and time deposits and its total assets on a call report. Much of the interbank variation in bank capital consists of short-term liabilities, which are similar to demand deposits. A similar pattern is evident in table 6-3.

5. Coefficients were estimated for the ten call report dummy variables and for bank capital but are not reported because they do not differ appreciably from those presented in table 9-3.

TABLE 9-4. COEFFICIENTS FOR SMOOTHED ADAPTIVE-EXPECTATIONS MODEL

	Cash	State and Local	Mort-gage	Comm. and Indust.	Con-sumer	Shorts	1–5s	Other
				Demand Deposits				
Most recent	.363* (.027)	.050* (.017)	.064* (.011)	.114* (.020)	.123* (.018)	.329* (.040)	.018 (.032)	−.061
One-quarter	.137* (.023)	.024 (.015)	.076* (.010)	.133* (.017)	.118* (.015)	.212* (.034)	.135* (.027)	.185
Two-quarter	.201* (.023)	.046* (.015)	.092* (.010)	.128* (.017)	.144* (.015)	.200* (.034)	.089 (.027)	.100
Three-quarter	.189* (.023)	.041* (.015)	.098* (.010)	.136* (.017)	.176* (.015)	.100* (.035)	.114* (.027)	.146
Earliest	.193* (.010)	.063* (.007)	.101* (.004)	.145* (.007)	.184* (.007)	.115* (.015)	.096* (.012)	.103
				Time Deposits				
Most recent	.210* (.072)	.055 (.047)	.081* (.031)	.176* (.053)	.128* (.048)	.197 (.108)	.084 (.085)	.069
One-quarter	−0.34 (.055)	.104* (.036)	.136* (.024)	.172* (.041)	.134* (.037)	.215* (.084)	.049 (.066)	.224
Two-quarter	.131* (.055)	.026 (.036)	.169* (.023)	.233* (.041)	.118* (.037)	.108 (.083)	.061 (.065)	.244
Three-quarter	.082 (.053)	.116* (.035)	.193* (.023)	.155* (.040)	.183 (.036)	.023 (.081)	−.010 (.064)	.258
Earliest	.031 (.024)	.086* (.016)	.264* (.010)	.172* (.018)	.147* (.016)	−.009 (.036)	.088* (.028)	.221
				Summary Statistics				
R^2	.118	.107	.165	.028	.123	.091	.131	N.A.
S_ε	.025	.016	.011	.018	.017	.037	.029	N.A.
F	12.168*	10.889*	17.987*	2.607*	12.832*	9.131*	13.766*	N.A.

quarterly revisions made three, six, and nine months earlier. The last co-efficients refer to forecasts of deposit levels made about a year before a call report. The following statements describe this smoothed adaptive-expectations model:

(1) Forecast revisions of demand deposits made near the call report have a larger impact on cash asset holdings than do revisions made at

earlier dates. Revisions made more than one quarter prior to the call report have no noticeable impact on the cash asset position. Estimated marginal cash assets held against forecasted demand deposits are about 19 percent in the long run. Time deposit coefficients in the cash regression are a little more erratic; in the long run the share going into cash is about 3 percent.

(2) The percentages of a bank's assets placed in state and local securities, one- to five-year government securities, and other residual assets are not very regularly related to forecasts of demand or time deposits. There is also no regular pattern in the estimated commercial and industrial loan coefficients for time deposit forecasts.

(3) Mortgage loans and consumer loans are considerably more responsive to more distant demand and time deposit forecasts than they are to revisions made during weeks just prior to a call report. Commercial and industrial loans display a similar pattern for demand deposit forecasts. For example, a $1 revision in a demand deposit forecast made just prior to a call report is associated with a $.06 change in mortgage loans, whereas the same $1 revision in preceding weeks is associated with a $.10 average change in mortgage loans. The changes in mortgage loans for recent and more distant $1 revisions in time deposit forecasts are $.08 and $.26, respectively.

(4) The relationship between both demand and time deposit forecasts and holdings of short-term government securities reflects the hypothesized pattern. Holdings of these assets are considerably more responsive to revisions in deposit forecasts made just prior to a call report than they are to revisions made in the more distant past.

2. EVALUATION OF THE SUCCESS OF THE ADAPTIVE-EXPECTATIONS MODEL

The estimates of the structure of the adaptive-expectations model are interesting and encouraging. The hypothesis that the history of deposit forecasts has no significant impact on bank portfolios is rejected. These results are, however, inferior to results reported in chapter 6 for the input-output formulation when judged by conventional regression summary statistics. With the single exception of commercial and industrial loans, F-ratios are lower (and standard errors of estimate are higher) in table 9-3 than in table 6-3. For individual asset regressions, demand and time deposit coefficients are much more erratic in the adaptive-expectations model than in the input-output specification. This superiority of the input-output model occurred even though there is clear evidence that autoregressive structures differed markedly across banks.[6]

In evaluating the adaptive-expectations model, it is important to stress several important differences between the two models. First, the adaptive-expectations model, through its autoregressive forecasting equations, requires the estimation of many more parameters than does the input-output formulation. Second, when applying the adaptive-expectations model, an investigator must utilize deposit forecasts that differ by some unknown amount from the actual forecasts used by the banks in the sample. The input-output model, on the other hand, uses actual deposit data.

Third, if individual bank portfolio equations have the same period of adjustment, the input-output version requires a much shorter history of deposit changes to describe a bank's portfolio composition than does the adaptive-expectations formulation. As tables 6-1 and 6-2 indicate, deposit shocks that occur more than one year prior to a call report are unrelated to a bank's asset structure on that report. The recursively generated forecasts of the adaptive-expectations model utilized actual deposit data two years before the call report.

In principle the same cutoff date for lagged actual deposit changes could be imposed when specifying the two models, but this modification is not likely to prove illuminating.[7] With the possible exception of mortgage loans, the estimated coefficients of the input-output model strongly suggest that individual banks respond completely to a shock within one calendar year. The erratic coefficients reported in tables 9-1 and 9-2 provide no sharp evidence about the length of the deposit sequence to be used in the adaptive-expectations formulation.[8]

Of all the differences between the two models, the probable existence of errors in variables in the adaptive-expectations formulation seems the most serious. Individual banks unquestionably have more information about their current and future deposits than is contained in a time series of past deposit shocks. The method of deseasonalization that is used in the model is also crude. The evidence provided in chapter 8 indicates that seasonal variations were not completely removed from the demand deposit equations.

6. The estimation procedure favored the adaptive-expectations model to some extent because the forecasting equations used parameter estimates based on samples which could not actually be available to banks applying the method.

7. The wide disparity in the number of lagged actual deposit changes required by the two models is primarily a result of the use of year-ago deposit changes to capture seasonal deposit movements in the expectations model.

8. At one point experiments were conducted that shortened the sequence of forecasts by up to two months. The results were not materially affected in these experiments.

In chapter 8 time deposit forecasting equations were found to be less successful than forecasting equations for demand deposits. To determine the importance of time deposit forecast errors, coefficients were estimated for a hybrid model composed of demand deposit forecasts and actual time deposit data, that is, the matrices $_fD$ and S, respectively. The fit of this hybrid model was generally not better than that of the adaptive-expectations model. Time deposit forecast errors do not appear to be the cause of the relatively poor showing of the expectations model.

As indicated in chapter 8, year-ago changes in deposits were not available for generating deposit forecasts for the first four call reports, and estimates of the unobserved 1959 changes were inserted in their place. This procedure clearly introduces an additional potential source of error. To test the hypothesis that this procedure distorted coefficient estimates in the adaptive-expectations model, the sample was separated into observations for the first five call reports and for the remaining six. The estimates for the two subsamples were not materially different from each other, and there was no evidence that the estimates of the 1959 deposit changes were an important source of error.

The exercise was not in vain, however; information about the auto-regressive structure of deposit changes helps to interpret bank behavior. An example illustrates the point. It was reported in chapter 6 that there was no evidence that large banks hold less excess cash and other liquid assets than small banks. The estimates of the deposit equations reported in chapter 8 provide a rationale for this finding. Large banks have more predictable demand deposits than small banks, and their time deposits are more easily controlled through the issue of CDs. But large banks, on average, also show evidence of lower deposit-retention ratios than small banks. An interpretation is that the greater deposit predictability is offset by lower deposit retention to produce the observed result.

Finally, the empirical results of this chapter suggest that economic theories which rely heavily on unobservable expectations constructs may be very difficult to verify with conventional regression techniques. There are strong theoretical reasons for believing that banks should try to forecast their future deposit flows. This theoretical assertion is confirmed by interviews with bankers who indicate that these forecasts are, in fact, made. The present investigators were unusually fortunate in being able to study a large body of clean, disaggregated data concerning quite well defined variable classifications and decision-making units. The data yielded plausible and very significant estimates of the parameters of deposit-generating processes at individual banks. Yet, when these estimates were used to generate forecasts for the portfolio model, the parameter estimates were inferior to estimates from the simpler, mechanistic input-output formulation. That formulation does not deny the existence of forecasting; but if banks forecast, it implies that they have identical autoregressive forecasting equations. In such a circumstance it would not be possible to identify parameters of *the* forecasting equation. Perhaps even more detailed data in greater quantities would permit the promise of expectations models to be realized, but that must remain an open question. It is very unlikely that econometric research in other applied areas will be endowed, in the near future, with a comparable volume and quality of data. Distributed lags may be reliably identified, but one should be very cautious when working with "proxies" for expectations.

Chapter 8 presents evidence that analysis of data for individual firms can yield quite reliable forecasts. Unfortunately, the costs of estimating the "best" forecasting equation for each decision unit in a large sample of firms are prohibitive. As a result, it was necessary to make simplifying assumptions. For example, it was necessary to assume that deposit changes were generated by an autoregressive process of the same order for all banks in the sample.

Possibly a detailed time-series analysis of an individual decision-making unit, essentially a case study, would provide insights into the formation and role of expectations. This approach is plagued by the difficulty of finding the "representative" decision unit. The promise of using aggregative data to estimate the structure of expectations models seems to be much more limited. It is notoriously difficult to justify aggregation when distributed lags exist in micro-equations [Theil, 1954].

The results reported in this chapter illustrate the importance of having an adequate alternative against which results from expectations models can be compared. The input-output formulation served this purpose well.

CHAPTER 10

Bank Earnings, Costs, and Rates of Return

This chapter reports estimates of parameters of a model that explains cross-section variations in four measures of bank income. As suggested in section 4 of chapter 4, coefficients of the asset and liability variables are to be interpreted as the marginal interest rates that an average sample bank could earn if it could substitute a dollar of the asset or liability for a dollar of vault cash. The underlying statistical model was described in chapter 4.

The first section reports a number of preliminary tests and procedures that have been adopted in this chapter. Section 2 contains an evaluation of interest rates estimated for different assets and liabilities and compares them with market interest rates and with interest rates that have been estimated in earlier studies. Section 3 reports an analysis of residuals obtained from the estimated equations and a set of subsidiary tests utilizing the residuals.

1. Procedures and Preliminary Tests

A bank's call reports must be averaged together if they are accurately to describe the portfolio that generated its income in a year. Four call reports were available in 1960, 1961, and 1962, and three in 1963. Average balance sheets were constructed from the observed balance sheets using weights to reflect the information that each call report contained about the bank's portfolio. For example, in the year 1960 the March 15 call report received a weight of 0.375, the June 15 and the October 3 reports each received a weight of 0.250, and the December 31 report had a weight of 0.125.[1] All call report variables had been deflated by total assets on the date of a report. In this chapter call report variables were multiplied by a bank's total assets on that call report and then divided by its total assets at year end before averaging. Banks disappearing before the end of a year

---

1. In 1961 and 1962 the two enclosing year-end call reports received weights of 0.125, and the three other reports within the year were weighted by 0.250. In 1963 weights were 0.125 for the December 1962 report, 0.250 for the March 1963 report, 0.375 for the June report, and 0.250 for the December 1963 report.

were discarded because no statement of income and dividends was available. A total of 762 bank-year observations were available for the First Federal Reserve District banks; 200 in 1960, 199 in 1961, 187 in 1962, and 176 in 1963.

In chapter 4 four issues were raised for further consideration in the present chapter. They are (1) the decision to suppress intercepts; (2) the degree of disaggregation of loan, deposit, and United States government security measures; (3) the justifiability of the linear specification; and (4) the intertemporal stationarity of the estimated structure.

The procedure for examining these issues was to pool all 762 observations into a large sample and then estimate a highly aggregated version of the underlying equation for each of the four income measures. Analyses of covariance relating to the first two issues were performed using this aggregated specification as a basis for testing the null hypotheses. Subsequently, the linear specification and intertemporal stationarity issues were evaluated with an appropriately disaggregated version. The design of experiments was strongly influenced by results obtained by Hester and Zoellner [1966].

Table 10-1 shows results obtained for the aggregated model. The definitions of variables are indicated by the last column of the table which refers to table 5-1. All regressions are highly significant, and coefficients are generally in agreement with a priori expectations. Thus, the coefficients of the first four assets and the two deposit liabilities have the expected signs and magnitudes in all but the gross operating income case, where positive coefficients were expected on deposits. Coefficients on residual assets and liabilities seem implausible. Two analyses of covariance were performed to determine whether even this low level of disaggregation was warranted. The tests indicate that at the 5 percent level of significance for each of the four income measures (a) the five asset variables do not have the same coefficients, and also (b) the three liability variables do not have the same coefficients.

The first issue concerns the possible statistical significance of intercepts for the regressions in table 10-1. The four equations were re-estimated with an intercept, and the results are reported in table 10-2. The intercept was not significantly different from zero at the 5 percent level in a two-tailed test for either the gross operating income or the net income after-tax regression. The hypothesis that the intercept was not different from zero was rejected in net operating income and net income before-tax regressions.

Apparently, banks have significant net income that is unrelated to asset composition and that can only be detected when direct operating

TABLE 10-1. RATES OF RETURN ESTIMATED FROM POOLED SAMPLE: AGGREGATED VERSION

Asset or Liability	Gross Operating Income	Net Operating Income	Net Income before Taxes	Net Income after Taxes	Item Number(s) in Table 5-1
Demand balances at other banks	.903 (.631)	.731 (.523)	.804 (.632)	.425 (.487)	55
United States government securities	5.346* (.572)	3.502* (.474)	2.961* (.573)	1.646* (.441)	2
State and local securities	4.283* (.574)	3.676* (.476)	3.457* (.575)	2.966* (.442)	3
Gross loans	8.814* (.517)	3.968* (.429)	3.020* (.519)	1.527* (.399)	6, 43
Miscellaneous other noncash assets	2.647* (.898)	−3.097* (.745)	−3.637* (.900)	−2.154* (.692)	4, 5, 7, 8, 9, 10, 11
Demand deposits	−1.087* (.498)	−1.332* (.413)	−.987* (.499)	−.452 (.384)	60, 61, 62, 63, 64, 65
Time deposits	−2.389* (.548)	−2.832* (.455)	−2.225* (.550)	−1.130* (.423)	66, 67, 68, 69, 70
Other liabilities	.800 (.986)	1.106 (.817)	3.456* (.988)	1.154 (.760)	residual
Reciprocal of total assets	1,838.817 (952.995)	−3,988.650* (790.253)	−1,916.103* (954.961)	1,681.629* (734.769)	12, 43
			Summary Statistics		
R^2	.522	.374	.268	.182	
S_ε	.418	.346	.418	.322	
F	91.198*	49.925*	30.704*	18.630*	
N	762	762	762	762	

NOTE: In this chapter, the coefficient of the reciprocal of total assets has a dimension of dollars per year; all other regression coefficients have a dimension of percentage per year. Also, in this chapter, an asterisk indicates that a coefficient differs significantly from zero at the 5 percent level in a two-tailed test.

Asset or Liability	Gross Operating Income	Net Operating Income	Net Income before Taxes	Net Income after Taxes	Item Number(s) in Table 5-1
Demand balances at other banks	.888	.572	.639	.370	55
	(.635)	(.524)	(.635)	(.490)	
United States government securities	5.319*	3.216*	2.665*	1.548*	2
	(.586)	(.484)	(.585)	(.452)	
State and local securities	4.249*	3.310*	3.079*	2.841*	3
	(.597)	(.493)	(.596)	(.460)	
Gross loans	8.785*	3.655*	2.696*	1.420*	6, 43
	(.536)	(.443)	(.536)	(.413)	
Miscellaneous other noncash assets	2.630*	−3.277*	−3.823*	−2.215*	4, 5, 7, 8,
	(.902)	(.745)	(.901)	(.695)	9, 10, 11
Demand deposits	−1.142*	−1.916*	−1.592*	−.652	60, 61, 62,
	(.563)	(.464)	(.562)	(.434)	63, 64, 65
Time deposits	−2.435*	−3.322*	−2.733*	−1.298*	66, 67, 68,
	(.591)	(.488)	(.590)	(.456)	69, 70
Other liabilities	.742	.490	2.819*	.944	residual
	(1.024)	(.845)	(1.023)	(.789)	
Reciprocal of total assets	1,789.642	−4,510.545*	−2,456.650*	1,503.410*	12, 43
	(981.925)	(810.347)	(980.502)	(756.607)	
Intercept	.069	.733*	.760*	.250	
			Summary Statistics		
R^2	.522	.379	.274	.183	
S_ε	.418	.345	.417	.322	
F	91.095*	51.152*	31.474*	18.737*	
N	762	762	762	762	

expenses are eliminated in a regression model. This net income is related to a bank's total assets. It probably is attributable to lock-box services, information dissemination, payroll and related data processing, and so on. It is not clear why the payment of corporate taxes should reduce the value of the intercept to insignificant levels. However, inspection of coefficients and standard errors of coefficients in net income before- and after-tax regressions suggests that variations in effective average tax rates are related to portfolio composition; this may be the clue to the puzzle. When corporate taxes are taken out of bank income, regression coefficients fall more (absolutely) than corresponding standard errors. This result would not occur if all banks faced the same average tax rate. Both progressivity in corporate tax schedules and tax law anomalies associated with capital gain carry-backs and carry-forwards could operate to obscure net income that is not asset specific in after-tax regressions. Given this ambiguous pattern, intercepts will typically be omitted from estimated relationships. However, in all cases the reported specification will also have been estimated with an intercept, and serious discrepancies resulting from inclusion of an intercept will be noted.

The second issue concerns the degree of disaggregation at which loans, demand deposits, and United States government securities should be studied. In an analysis of covariance, separate coefficients were estimated for insured real estate, other real estate, commercial and industrial, consumer installment, single payment consumer, and miscellaneous other loans. Definitions of these variables are indicated in the last column of table 10-3.[2] The hypothesis that all loan measures have the same coefficient was rejected at the 5 percent level for the first three income measures but not for the fourth. In the net income after-tax regression, the estimated marginal rates of return on the several types of loans were not significantly different from each other. The observed equalizing of rates of return on loan components apparently occurs only after banks exploit provisions of the tax laws. This after-tax result would be observed in a world in which banks were competitive and required no reward for bearing risk.

Further attempts to disaggregate loans were not made because no further appealing breakdowns were available, and in an earlier study a further loan disaggregation did not prove significant [Hester and Zoellner, 1966, p. 376]. Throughout the remainder of this chapter loans will continue to be separated into the six indicated components.

---

2. The covariance tests for disaggregation of loans, securities, and demand deposits were performed using the model reported in table 10-2 as the base. That is, only one disaggregation was performed at a time.

TABLE 10-3. RATES OF RETURN ESTIMATED FROM POOLED SAMPLE: DISAGGREGATED VERSION

Asset or Liability	Gross Operating Income	Net Operating Income	Net Income before Taxes	Net Income after Taxes	Item Number(s) in Table 5-1
Demand balances at other banks	.555	.329	.777	.449	55
	(.544)	(.532)	(.649)	(.503)	
Short-term United States government securities	4.479*	3.175*	3.253*	1.775*	44, 45, 46, 47, 49, 50
	(.506)	(.495)	(.604)	(.468)	
Long-term United States government securities	4.882*	3.146*	2.285*	1.261*	51, 52
	(.512)	(.501)	(.611)	(.473)	
Other United States government guaranteed securities	6.581*	3.096*	2.186	1.203	48, 53
	(1.302)	(1.275)	(1.555)	(1.204)	
State and local securities	3.846*	3.442*	3.515*	2.981*	3
	(.494)	(.484)	(.590)	(.457)	
Insured real estate loans	4.507*	2.427*	2.990*	1.718*	28
	(.709)	(.694)	(.846)	(.655)	
Other real estate loans	7.965*	3.593*	2.934*	1.493*	27, 29, 30
	(.518)	(.507)	(.618)	(.479)	
Commercial and industrial loans	7.156*	3.889*	3.258*	1.466	36
	(.479)	(.469)	(.572)	(.443)	
Consumer installment loans	11.175*	4.160*	3.235*	1.798*	37, 38, 39, 40
	(.467)	(.457)	(.558)	(.432)	
Single payment consumer loans	6.808*	2.290*	1.842*	.858	41
	(.568)	(.556)	(.679)	(.526)	

Table 10-3 (continued)

Asset or Liability	Gross Operating Income	Net Operating Income	Net Income before Taxes	Net Income after Taxes	Item Number(s) in Table 5-1
Miscellaneous other loans	5.986* (.554)	3.599* (.543)	2.726* (.662)	1.141* (.513)	31, 32, 33, 34, 35, 42
Miscellaneous other noncash assets	3.792* (.765)	−3.041* (.749)	−3.263* (.914)	−1.865* (.707)	4, 5, 7, 8, 9, 10, 11
Demand deposits of individuals, partnerships, and corporations	−.393 (.432)	−.931* (.423)	−.848 (.516)	−.409 (.400)	60
United States government demand deposits	−2.608* (.999)	−.830 (.978)	−1.660 (1.194)	−.730 (.924)	62
All other demand deposits	−.649 (.569)	−1.573* (.557)	−1.537* (.679)	−.402 (.526)	61, 63, 64, 65
Time and savings deposits	−1.444* (.488)	−2.440* (.477)	−2.196* (.582)	−1.108* (.451)	66, 67, 68, 69, 70
Other liabilities	1.429 (.864)	.656 (.846)	2.729* (1.032)	.848 (.799)	residual
Reciprocal of total assets	1,219.991 (824.133)	−3,633.717* (806.704)	−1,243.382 (984.298)	1,941.934* (761.963)	12, 43
		Summary Statistics			
R^2	.673	.403	.289	.195	
S_ε	.348	.340	.415	.321	
F	84.921*	27.884*	16.792*	10.027*	
N	762	762	762	762	

Disaggregation of demand deposits into deposits of individuals, partnerships, and corporations; United States government deposits; and other demand deposits yielded a significant result in the analysis of covariance for gross operating income, but not for any other income measure. The hypothesis of different coefficients is rejected. Nevertheless, because of continuing interest in the profitability of Tax and Loan Accounts of the United States government and because a significant result was obtained, demand deposits hereafter will also be analyzed in a disaggregated form.

United States government securities were broken down into bills, notes, certificates of indebtedness and bonds with maturities of less than five years; marketable bonds with a maturity of more than five years; and other nonmarketable securities and securities guaranteed by the United States government. It was not convenient to study securities with a maturity of less than one year separately because that detail was not available for Treasury notes in the 1960 and 1961 call reports. The hypothesis that all three measures have the same coefficient was rejected in gross operating income and net income before-tax regressions.

It should be noted that while the estimated after-tax rates of return on total loans and total United States government securities are significantly different from each other, there are no significant differences in after-tax rates of return among different types of loans or among different types of United States government securities. This result is important because it indicates that differences in measured gross rates of return are not reliable indicators of the relative profitability of different assets.

Parameter estimates for the disaggregated model are reported in table 10-3; they will be extensively discussed and compared in the next section. Inspection of the coefficients does not suggest, however, that coefficients of loan variables are especially large or that coefficients of security variables are particularly small. The hypothesis involving the existence of bias resulting from nonlinearities in the specification, which was suggested in chapter 4, does not appear to be supported by this result.[3]

Finally, it is necessary to test the hypothesis that relations reported in table 10-3 are stationary through time. The rejection of this hypothesis would imply that interest rates changed by more than can be accounted for by interbank variation within a year. The hypothesis is tested by estimating separate equations for each of the years and then comparing residual variation from the pooled regressions with the sum of residual variation in the annual regressions.

3. As indicated in chapter 4, these biases would occur if (1) a bank influenced the interest rates at which it borrowed or lent, or (2) the percentage of a bank's resources held in different assets were a function of interest rate differentials existing at a point in time.

In an analysis of covariance, the stationarity hypothesis could not be rejected at the 5 percent level for the gross operating income, net operating income, and net income before-tax variables; it was rejected for the net income after-tax measure. This lone lack of stationarity may result from the fact that the average size of sample banks rose substantially during the four years; progressivity in the corporate income tax structure might then cause the hypothesis to be rejected.

However, a more likely explanation is suggested in table 10-4, which

TABLE 10-4. TIME PATHS OF SELECTED RATES OF RETURN

Asset	1960	1961	1962	1963	Pool
Short-term United States government securities					
Gross operating income	4.731	5.007	5.164	3.784	4.479
Net operating income	3.663	3.890	3.396	4.497	3.175
Net income before taxes	3.105	4.591	3.658	3.771	3.253
Net income after taxes	2.259	2.992	1.496	2.296	1.775
Long-term United States government securities					
Gross operating income	5.187	5.906	5.054	4.232	4.882
Net operating income	3.453	4.797	3.411	4.741	3.146
Net income before taxes	3.939	4.733	3.336	3.531	3.285
Net income after taxes	2.825	3.710	1.671	2.460	1.261
Other real estate loans					
Gross operating income	8.211	8.611	8.579	7.368	7.965
Net operating income	3.818	4.527	4.322	5.179	3.593
Net income before taxes	2.407	4.516	3.678	4.054	2.934
Net income after taxes	1.283	3.136	1.596	2.533	1.493
Commercial and industrial loans					
Gross operating income	7.086	7.602	8.033	6.807	7.156
Net operating income	3.749	4.580	4.771	5.409	3.889
Net income before taxes	2.382	4.421	4.683	4.020	3.258
Net income after taxes	1.134	2.427	2.179	2.468	1.466
Consumer installment loans					
Gross operating income	11.176	11.804	11.900	10.608	11.175
Net operating income	4.133	5.229	4.834	5.443	4.160
Net income before taxes	2.338	4.788	4.688	3.792	3.235
Net income after taxes	1.382	3.688	2.487	2.142	1.798

NOTE: These coefficients were obtained from annual disaggregated regressions. Asset variables are defined in the preceding table.

reports selected asset rates of return in each of the four years, estimated for each of the four income measures. It appears that year-to-year variation in estimated interest rates increases as the income variable moves from net operating income toward variables that might better be characterized as "profits." Apparently, various bookkeeping adjustments such as tax carry-forwards, tax carry-backs, additions to loss reserves, charge-offs, and recoveries are major sources of variation in profits after taxes. In the third section additional evidence about such adjustments is presented.

2. Evaluation of the Results

a. Interpretation

Parameter estimates for assets in gross operating income regressions reported in table 10-3 are larger than published interest rates for the period 1960–63. For example, instead of the 4.48 percent estimated for securities with maturities under five years, Treasury three- to five-year issues actually yielded approximately 3.75 percent during these years. Because securities are carried at cost and because interest rates had fallen from 1959 heights, it is remotely possible that the estimated value for these securities accurately measures the rate of return that banks earned on book values. State and local securities actually yielded approximately 3.50 percent instead of the estimated 3.85 percent. Other estimated government security interest rates also appear to be positively biased.

As expected, consumer installment loans have the highest estimated gross interest rate, 11.2 percent per annum. These loans tend to be amortized discount loans with a maximum discount of 6 percent typically allowed by usury laws; the estimate suggests that most installment loans were bearing this maximum legal rate. Uninsured real estate (mortgage) loans, which include farm and business loans secured by real estate, were estimated to yield 8.0 percent. Commercial and industrial loans and single payment consumer loans were estimated to gross 7.2 percent and 6.8 percent, respectively, during the four years. Real estate loans insured by the FHA and VA earned an estimated 4.5 percent. While this last estimate appears low, it should be remembered that banks made many insured mortgage loans during the early fifties before the credit stringency of 1957, when FHA and VA ceilings were quite low. Also, New England is traditionally an area of low mortgage loan interest rates due to the prevalence of mutual savings banks.

Bank liabilities were expected to be positively related to gross operating income; however, all deposit variables were negatively related to gross income. There is no obvious interpretation for the significantly negative time and savings deposit and United States government demand deposit coefficients.

Results from the net operating income regressions seem quite plausible and suggest why gross income regressions may be biased. The differences between gross and net income estimates of interest rates imply very large estimates for operating costs. It is likely that the net rate of return for an asset, at the margin, is quite similar for banks serving a given market; competition will force this outcome. However, gross interest rates do not necessarily tend to equality across banks. Explicit interest rate charges and implicit services or costs for an asset can be packaged quite differently among banks that earn the same net rate of return.[4] In addition, window dressing on the June and December call reports produces an upward bias in estimates of gross returns. Because the dates of these call reports are known ahead of time, banks momentarily increase their holdings of cash and decrease their nondeposit debts by reducing their stocks of earning assets, especially United States government securities. As a result of this practice, their gross income during the year is generated by a larger average stock of earning assets than their balance sheets indicate. Thus, the regressions for gross income produce estimates of rates of return on earning assets that are biased upward. This bias is less important in the regressions for the net income measures because both revenues and costs are biased upward.

Because of these problems, in what follows net operating income interest rates will be viewed as more meaningful than gross rates. Gross rates are studied because they approximate market rates that most investigators believe are relevant for the transmission of monetary policy.

Estimated rates of return for the four security variables in net operating income regressions are quite similar although state and local securities tend to yield slightly more than United States government securities. Net rates of return on commercial and industrial loans and consumer installment loans exceed most security interest rates. Other real estate loans are estimated to net about 3.6 percent, while insured mortgages loans net only about 2.4 percent. Miscellaneous other loans, including loans to farmers and financial institutions, have a modest estimated net rate of return of 3.6 percent for sample banks. Miscellaneous other assets include the book value of a bank's premises; they have an estimated rate of return that is

4. There were not enough time-series observations to allow removal of any bank effects from the data. Some evidence on bank effects is provided in section 3 and in the next chapter.

negative. Because such assets are both heterogeneous and measured with little reference to market values, this disturbing result should not be taken too seriously.

Estimated net rates of return for deposit liabilities are all negative as expected. The estimated cost of demand deposits is approximately one-half the cost of time deposits; deposits of individuals, partnerships, and corporations cost banks about 0.9 percent per year after service charges. The estimated cost of United States government deposits was not significantly different from zero. Minor other demand deposits cost about 1.6 percent, and time and savings deposits cost about 2.4 percent per year during the period studied. Miscellaneous other liabilities were estimated to yield a positive net return that was not significantly different from zero.

The coefficient on the reciprocal of total assets in the net operating income regression is an estimate of net "fixed cost." This cost figure can be used to estimate the "break-even" size for sample banks. The estimated net fixed cost for a bank is $3,634, and the average ratio of net income to total assets during the period was 1.3 percent. Assuming that this ratio holds for all banks in the sample, the asset size for which income equals cost is approximately $280,000.[5] The smallest banks in the sample had roughly $900,000 in total assets and were, therefore, well above the break-even point.

Coefficients in net operating income and net income before-tax regressions differ because of net realized losses, bookkeeping transfers to reserves, and write-offs. By comparing these coefficients, it is possible to estimate the collective magnitude of these adjustments for each asset. For example, sample banks appear to have experienced large losses and/or write-offs (relative to standard errors) from long-term United States government securities, but not from other varieties of securities. For loan variables corresponding "losses" were about 0.9 percent per annum for installment loans, 0.6 percent for commercial and industrial loans, and 0.7 percent for conventional real estate loans. Other coefficients were similar in the two regressions.

Many asset coefficients in the net income before-tax regression are quite similar in magnitude. If the corresponding assets differ in terms of riskiness, it appears that rewards for risk taking are small relative to estimated standard errors. While these rewards may not be small in relation to observed bank earnings/asset ratios, they are too small to be reliably measured in the present statistical cost accounting analysis. Obviously it is impossible to reject the existence of some rewards.

5. Very similar results were obtained in a study of banks in the Tenth Federal Reserve District [Hester and Zoellner, 1966, p. 378].

It is also interesting to note that the estimated fixed cost for the net income before-tax regression is only one-third the size of the estimate obtained for net operating income and is not significantly different from zero. Because capital and management and other "fixed" factors vary across banks, it is not implausible to obtain an insignificant coefficient. Until write-offs and other manipulations are allowed for, banks appear to experience fixed costs.

Coefficients in the net income after-tax regression, with the notable exception of tax-exempt state and local securities, were reduced approximately 40 percent in absolute terms from values in the before-tax regression. This is an estimate of the average rate of income taxation experienced by sample banks. Coefficients of tax-exempt securities were about a standard error apart in the two regressions; they bore the highest after-tax rate of return of all assets considered. Consumer installment loans were the most "profitable" variety of loan, but their rate of return was only about one standard error higher than interest rates on most other varieties of loans. Short-term government securities were also quite profitable. The unexpected significant positive coefficient for the reciprocal of total assets probably results from the progressivity of corporate income taxes. Finally, deposit mix was an important determinant of bank profits; ceteris paribus, banks with large proportions of time deposits were less profitable. However, ceteris paribus is not relevant; as noted in chapter 6 banks were observed to place demand deposits and time deposits in quite different portfolios. In chapter 11 the profitability of demand and time deposits is compared more meaningfully.

b. Comparisons with other studies

An interesting contribution to understanding variations in bank earnings was made by the Federal Reserve Bank of Boston during the early 1960s with its "functional" cost studies.[6] These studies report costs and revenues associated with different balance sheet variables and are estimated by applying conventional cost accounting procedures to samples of small banks. While the variables studied above and those used in the Bank's studies are not identical, they are close enough to permit comparisons. Table 10-5 reports interest rate estimates that have been constructed from the Bank's analysis of an average commercial bank. Estimates of asset gross rates of return are uniformly less than rates reported in table 10-3. Deposit gross rates are positive by construction because they represent service charges that banks collect from customers. Differences between tables 10-3 and 10-5 are partly a consequence of differences in accounting

6. For details about method and coverage, see Federal Reserve Bank of Boston [1960–62].

criteria; they also reflect the previous observation that the regression procedure may not be well suited to analyzing bank gross income flows.

TABLE 10-5. INTEREST RATES FROM FUNCTIONAL COST ANALYSES

	Gross		Net	
Asset or Liability	*1961*	*1962*	*1961*	*1962*
Installment loans	9.08%	9.20%	5.49%	5.67%
Real estate loans	5.25	5.37	4.53	4.64
All other loans[a]	5.22	5.27	4.05	4.11
Investments	2.94	3.19	2.79	3.00
Demand deposits	.85	.85	−2.27	−2.30
Time deposits	.03	.03	−3.12	−3.56

SOURCE: Federal Reserve Bank of Boston, *Functional Cost Analysis: Average Participating Bank* (1962), pp. A4-A16.

[a] Commercial and industrial loans comprised the bulk of these loans.

Net rates of return from functional cost analyses, on the other hand, are quite similar to comparable net operating income estimates in table 10-3. Investments and all other loans, the bulk of which are commercial and industrial loans, have almost identical estimated rates. The conventional method imputes higher rates of return to real estate and installment loans and higher costs to both types of deposits. It suggests that bank net income is more sensitive to bank asset composition than does the statistical approach. Both methods indicate that time and savings deposits were approximately 1 percent to 1.25 percent more expensive per annum than demand deposits.

TABLE 10-6. RATES OF RETURN REPORTED IN HESTER-ZOELLNER STUDY

Asset or Liability	*Net Operating Income*	*Net Income before Taxes*
United States government securities	3.60%	3.86%
Tax-exempt securities	3.37	3.90
Gross loans	3.81	4.17
Demand deposits of individuals	−1.15	−2.02
Time deposits of individuals	−2.96	−3.31
Other noncash assets	1.85	2.93
Other deposit liabilities	−2.22	−1.66

SOURCE: Hester and Zoellner, 1966, p. 381.

NOTE: These estimates were obtained in a least-squares cost accounting analysis of a sample of Connecticut commercial banks pooled over the years 1957–63.

Table 10-6 reports results from a previous statistical cost analysis of a sample of forty-three Connecticut banks; parameters were estimated from annual data for the years 1957–63 [Hester and Zoellner, 1966]. A small number of the Connecticut banks appear in the present study, but for the most part the samples are distinct. Results in table 10-6 are best compared with estimates reported in table 10-1. The comparison indicates that the absolute differences between the two sets of estimates are always less than a standard error. This comparison suggests that (1) estimates of interest rates in the New England region can be duplicated from different independent samples, and (2) estimated interest rates may have applied to sample banks for longer than just the 1960–63 period of observation.[7]

3. ANALYSIS OF RESIDUALS

This section analyzes residuals from the four income regressions reported in table 10-3. For ease of comparison, only 700 residuals for the 175 banks that were in the sample over the entire 1960–63 period are studied. All hypotheses are tested at the 5 percent level of significance.

It is instructive to begin by examining the correlations among the residuals from the four regressions, which are reported in table 10-7. A striking feature of these results is the low correlation between the gross income residuals and those for other income measures. There is no strong tendency for banks with greater than predicted gross income to have greater than predicted net income. This result is consistent with the assertion made in section 2 that asset gross rates of return differ more widely among banks than do net rates. The correlations among residuals of the net income measures, on the other hand, are relatively high. All net income measures for a bank tend to be simultaneously underpredicted or overpredicted. An additional interesting result concerns the correlation between residuals from the net income before-tax and after-tax regressions. If the effective tax rate were the same for all banks, the correlation would be unity. The slight progressivity in the corporate income tax, the special treatment of capital gains and losses, and other tax peculiarities reduce the correlation to .86.

Residuals were analyzed to determine if they are related to such characteristics as bank size, asset growth, and deposit predictability. If there are important returns to scale, large banks should have positive

---

7. The duplication of the earlier result also suggests that inter-year variations reported previously for the sample of Connecticut banks was a consequence of measurement errors. No evidence of year-to-year coefficient variation in net operating income or net income before-tax regressions was detected in the present study. Cf. Hester and Zoellner [1966, pp. 381–83].

TABLE 10-7. CORRELATION OF RESIDUALS FROM INCOME REGRESSIONS

	Gross Operating Income	Net Operating Income	Net Income before Taxes	Net Income after Taxes
Gross operating income	1.000	.421	.258	.278
Net operating income	—	1.000	.775	.627
Net income before taxes	—	—	1.000	.863
Net income	—	—	—	1.000

NOTE: Residuals were obtained from regression equations reported in table 10-3.

residuals in either the net operating income or net income before-tax regressions. The banks in the sample were divided into the eight size categories shown in table 5-4. An analysis of variance indicated a significant relation between bank size and the residuals from the gross operating income equation. The regression tends to underpredict gross income for the larger size groups. Apparently large banks package their loans and deposits in such a way as to earn higher gross income. They also incur higher costs in doing so because no significant relation was found between the size groups and the residuals from the other three income equations.

The hypothesis that residuals are related to the growth rate of a bank's assets was rejected. No significant correlations were found between any of the four sets of residuals and the annual rate of growth of total assets measured for each bank over the entire 1960–63 period.

Two other hypotheses concern relationships between bank earnings and deposit variability and deposit predictability. Banks with predictable deposits or banks with small deposit fluctuations may acquire assets at lower cost than other banks. Low deposit variability should also reduce the costs of servicing deposits. The situation is a little unclear for time deposits because banks with small fluctuations in time deposits may pay a higher interest rate to attract such time funds.

Using the sample of 175 banks, the deposit-predictability hypotheses were tested by regressing each set of income residuals on standard errors of estimate of both the autoregressive demand and the autoregressive time deposit forecasting equations.[8] None of the regressions had significant F-ratios; the conclusion is that no relation exists between demand and time deposit predictability and bank earnings. Analogous hypotheses involving a relationship between earnings and standard deviations of demand and time deposits were also tested. No significant relation was

8. See chapter 8 for a description of these equations.

found between weekly variability in a bank's demand and time deposits and any of its four income residuals.

Some very interesting results were obtained when analyzing the relationship between net operating income residuals and the annual net write-offs of losses on loans and securities.[9] A significant correlation exists between the residuals from the net operating income regression and the net value of write-offs in a year, expressed as a percentage of bank assets. Banks with large net write-offs relative to total assets tend to have greater than predicted net operating income. Two interpretations of this result are possible. First, banks with unusually high operating incomes may obtain this income at the cost of greater risk of losses on their assets. Second, banks with unusually high incomes are adept at reducing their taxable incomes by the use of write-offs.

In order to distinguish between these two interpretations, the residuals from the net operating income equation were regressed on a bank's mean net annual write-offs of loans and securities, estimated from four years of data, and also the annual deviations from these means. The coefficients on the mean net write-offs are interpreted to measure the compensation for risk taking, and the coefficients on deviations from the means are interpreted to measure tax avoidance through write-offs. The results are reported in table 10–8. Both the mean and deviations coefficients for securities had the expected positive coefficient and were significantly different from zero at the 5 percent level. A $1.00 increase in the mean net write-off is associated with a $.37 increase in the excess of actual over predicted net operating income. A $1.00 increase in the annual deviation in security net write-offs is associated with a $.16 increase in the excess of actual over predicted net operating income.

These results substantiate a hypothesis that banks partly use security write-offs to avoid taxes and smooth income in good years and also are consistent with a widely held view that banks with good management— that is, positive income residuals—attempt systematically to exploit the tax advantages that are available through careful security trading. The results for loans are ambiguous. When considered with securities, neither the mean nor the deviations coefficient for net loan write-offs was significantly different from zero. However, when considered alone, the coefficient on the mean value of net loan write-offs was significant. We conclude that banks execute security transactions in order to reduce their tax liabilities, but they do not manipulate loan write-offs in the same manner.

9. Net write-offs are defined as losses, charge-offs, and transfers to reserves less recoveries, transfers from reserves, and profits on loans and securities. See chapter 5 for descriptions of the variables.

There is strong evidence that banks with relatively high net operating income experience relatively high losses on assets, but apparently, on average, loan recipients do not compensate banks for write-offs experienced on loan accounts when both types of assets are considered together. This result clearly requires further study.

TABLE 10-8. ANALYSIS OF NET OPERATING INCOME RESIDUALS

Intercept	$-.0005$
Mean security net write-offs	.372*
	(.114)
Deviation in security net write-offs	.156*
	(.068)
Mean loan net write-offs	.037
	(.178)
Deviation in net loan write-offs	$-.061$
	(.090)
R^2	.029
F	5.104*
S_ε	.003
N	700

NOTE: Residuals were obtained from the net operating income regression reported in table 10-3. All variables have been deflated by a bank's year-end total assets.

4. SUMMARY

The results reported in this chapter indicate that statistical cost accounting is a valuable tool for the analysis of commercial banking. Several results deserve emphasis. First, variations in bank portfolios do explain variations in bank earnings. Gross operating income and net operating income are more closely related to portfolio composition than are the remaining income measures. Second, all income regressions had large unexplained variances, and these variances were not significantly reduced by introducing such factors as bank size, asset growth, and deposit predictability. Finally, both absolute rates of return and differences in rates of return among asset and liability categories decline as the income measures go from gross operating income to net income after tax. The pattern of estimated rates of return from net operating income and income before-tax regressions illustrates the importance of asset write-offs and of special tax advantages on portfolio rates of return.

CHAPTER 11

Some Prescriptive Conclusions for Improving Commercial Bank Earnings

The models in this monograph have evolved in large part from an assumed theory of expected profit maximization by banks. In a perfectly competitive industry, this assumption could never be tested; all existing firms would be following best industry practice, and no other behavior would be observed. As noted in chapters 2 and 3, however, banking is far from being a competitive industry. Entry is limited, and banks are munificently provided with a law that prevents them from paying interest on one of their principal factor inputs, demand deposits. Banks are also widely geographically dispersed and legally limited in their choice of branch location. Therefore, relatively imperfect local banking markets are likely to recur throughout the United States. In such circumstances the invisible hand will be a clumsy paw; inefficient and poorly managed firms and noncompetitive behavior are likely to exist for long periods of time.

If the approach of this monograph is correct, it is likely that more efficient banks will exhibit behavior more in conformity with the proposed models than will other banks. This hypothesis can be tested if it is assumed that efficient banks are likely to realize relatively high profits. The major objective of this chapter is to consider this hypothesis in detail. Before turning to this question, it is instructive to consider the relative profitability of demand and time deposits carefully. The suggestion in the preceding chapter that these two liabilities differ in profitability appears to be a conspicuous example of noncompetitive bank behavior.

1. THE RELATIVE PROFITABILITY OF DEMAND AND TIME DEPOSITS

In chapter 10 it was reported that time and demand deposits differed in their relative cost of servicing; the imputed cost of time deposits uniformly exceeded that for demand deposits. This result, which was expected, does not imply that time deposits are unprofitable for banks or even necessarily that a dollar of time deposits is less profitable than a dollar of demand deposits. Equations reported in tables 6-1 and 6-2 indicate that demand and time deposits are eventually transformed into portfolios that have markedly different composition.

To measure the relative profitability of different deposit types, it is necessary to evaluate the *total*, not the *partial*, effect of a unit change in demand or time deposits on bank profits. The partial effects are given by the estimated net costs of deposits as reported in table 10-3. The total effect can be computed by multiplying a row vector of estimated equilibrium portfolio changes (both assets and the assumed changes in liabilities) in response to a permanent deposit injection by a column vector of corresponding imputed rates of return as estimated in chapter 10.

To measure the effect on a bank's profits of substituting a dollar of demand deposits for a dollar of time deposits, it is necessary to re-estimate portfolio adjustment equations so that asset categories correspond to those for which rates of return were obtained in chapter 10. Table 11-1 reports estimated demand and time deposit equilibrium shares for these asset categories.[1] The third column of the table shows the difference between the two sets of coefficients which is the predicted portfolio change that a commercial bank would make if it lost a dollar of time deposits and gained a dollar of demand deposits.[2] Table 11-2 shows the net contribution to bank income of each asset's change. It was obtained by multiplying elements of the third column in table 11-1 by the corresponding coefficients reported in table 10-3 for each of the four income variables studied. The last row of table 11-2 reports the total effect of this substitution on the four measures of bank income.

Shifting from time to demand deposits causes income flows from long-term bonds, mortgage loans, and miscellaneous other loans to decline and causes income from consumer loans to expand considerably. Such shifts cause a bank's gross operating income to fall, principally because a larger fraction of assets must be non–interest-bearing reserves. On the other hand, shifting from time to demand deposits causes the three net income measures to rise. These increases, 0.51 percent, 0.56 percent, and 0.37 percent are remarkably large and apparently reflect the high interest cost of time deposits. In chapter 5 it was reported that mean sample bank net current operating income as a percentage of total assets was 1.30 percent; corresponding means for net income before and after taxes were 1.17 percent and 0.74 percent, respectively. The mean sample bank had a ratio of demand to time deposits of about 2:1 and total deposits represented about 86 percent of bank assets. Assuming that this ratio of

1. These coefficients were obtained from a regression specification and sample identical to those used to obtain the coefficients reported in tables 6-1 through 6-3, but with different dependent variables. They correspond to the last row in tables 6-1 and 6-2. To avoid redundancy, other details about the underlying equations are not reported.

2. The sum of the changes differs from zero because of changes in cash assets, which are irrelevant to the analysis because they are assumed to earn no net interest.

deposits to total assets is maintained, a bank having no time deposits is estimated to have net income after taxes as a percentage of total assets equal to 0.86 percent; the corresponding value for a bank with no demand deposits is 0.54 percent.

TABLE 11-1. EQUILIBRIUM SHARES OF COMMERCIAL BANK ASSETS

Asset	Demand Deposits	Time Deposits	Demand less Time Deposits
Demand balances at other banks	.0956	−.0605	.1561
Short-term United States government securities	.1522	.1976	−.0454
Long-term United States government securities	.0356	.1314	−.0958
Other United States government securities	−.0115	.0342	−.0457
State and local securities	.0667	.0706	−.0039
Insured real estate loans	.0125	.0253	−.0128
Other real estate loans	.0743	.2658	−.1915
Commercial and industrial loans	.1491	.1397	.0094
Consumer installment loans	.2009	.1021	.0988
Single payment consumer loans	.0792	.0048	.0744
Miscellaneous other loans	.0255	.1171	−.0916
Miscellaneous other noncash assets	.0276	.0503	−.0227

NOTE: Definitions of assets are in table 10-3.

These results suggest that commercial banks operating in imperfect markets would not be interested in attracting time deposits if each dollar attracted meant a dollar loss in demand balances. However, commercial banks do have to contend with savings and loan associations and mutual savings banks that have no corresponding reason to avoid competition for time deposits. So long as these latter competitors have a very small share of a community's liquid savings, it would not be profitable for commercial banks to compete. The losses in income from switches from demand to time balances would likely exceed gains in income from externally attracted time deposits. However, in every local market there will be some critical share after which this inequality will be reversed, and commercial banks will compete for time deposits. Evidently this critical share was reached in many communities in the United States during the late 1950s and early 1960s. It was reached in the national money market in about 1962, when negotiable certificates of deposit first appeared in large volume in major financial centers.

There is no immediate interpretation from this argument for the pattern of time and savings deposit coefficients observed in chapters 6, 7, and 9. However, if banks successively viewed time deposits as exogenous and then partially endogenous, arguments underlying the adaptive-expectations approach suggest that behavior would change and perhaps appear erratic. Empirical studies of our portfolio models could be seriously impaired if different banks reached critical local market shares on different dates. The conclusion for profit-maximizing banks is that they should begin to compete for time deposits only after their market share has fallen sufficiently.

TABLE 11-2. IMPACT ON PROFITS OF SUBSTITUTING DEMAND DEPOSITS
FOR TIME DEPOSITS

Asset or Liability	Gross Operating Income	Net Operating Income	Net Income before Taxes	Net Income after Taxes
Demand balances at other banks	.087%	.051%	.121%	.070%
Short-term United States government securities	−.203	−.144	−.148	−.081
Long-term United States government securities	−.468	−.301	−.219	−.121
Other United States government securities	−.301	−.142	−.100	−.055
State and local securities	−.015	−.013	−.014	−.012
Insured real estate loans	−.058	−.031	−.038	−.022
Other real estate loans	−1.525	−.688	−.562	−.286
Commercial and industrial loans	.067	.037	.031	.014
Consumer installment loans	1.104	.411	.320	.178
Single payment consumer loans	.507	.170	.137	.064
Miscellaneous other loans	−.548	−.330	−.250	−.105
Miscellaneous other noncash assets	−.086	.069	.074	.042
Private demand deposits	−.542	−1.019	−.989	−.424
Time deposits	1.444	2.440	2.196	1.108
Total change in earnings	−.537	.510	.559	.370

2. COMMERCIAL BANK PROFITABILITY AND THE SUCCESS OF THE MODEL

This section builds upon results reported in chapters 6 and 10; it reports an additional "higher order" test of the arguments of chapters 2 and

3. The analysis proceeds in three stages. First, a regression equation similar to that reported in table 10-3 was estimated for net current operating income from the pooled sample of 762 bank-year observations.[3] Residuals were computed for each observation and then were averaged for each bank. The resulting set of 201 residual means measure variations in net income that by construction are independent of average portfolio composition. Among other things, they reflect differences in locational monopoly rents, scale, entrepreneurship, and portfolio adjustment paths. These sources of residual net income are not necessarily independent, but in the following discussion banks will be studied as if only differences in portfolio adjustment paths matter.

Second, the 201 residual means were sorted into ascending order and then arbitrarily divided into three subsamples. The first subsample consisted of the 60 banks with the highest residual means; hereafter it is called the "positive" sample. The second or "negative" sample consisted of the 60 banks with the lowest residual means, and the remaining 81 banks constituted the "remainder sample."[4] As was reported in chapter 5, not all of these banks were studied in the portfolio analysis of chapters 6 and 9. Accordingly, in the present chapter attention will be restricted to the 184 banks that were studied in both chapters 6 and 10. The subsamples, therefore, are somewhat smaller than just described. There are 57 positive (relatively profitable) banks, 54 negative (relatively unprofitable) banks, and 73 remainder banks. Table 11-3 shows the size distribution of the banks in the three subsamples.

The distribution suggests a slight tendency for small banks to have a disproportionately large presence in the negative sample, but scale is by no means the sole discriminant. In terms of bank call report observations, the positive and negative samples each have 560 observations; the remainder sample has 723 observations. Other characteristics of banks in the three samples are considered in section 3 below.

Third, parameters of the input-output model of chapter 6 were estimated from each of the three samples. All assets considered in chapter 6 were regressed on (1) the thirty-two deposit change and level measures, (2) the two overflow variables, (3) the ten dummy variables, and (4) capital. Individual bank effects were again removed. Table 11-4 reports the assets that were studied, summary statistics about these regressions, and

3. The specification differed from that reported in table 10-3 because the reciprocal of total assets had to be omitted for reasons of confidentiality when this chapter was being prepared.

4. Only 3 of the 201 banks fell into different subsamples when the reciprocal of total assets was subsequently added to the regression. For the purposes of this chapter the omission of the reciprocal of total assets is inconsequential.

analyses of covariance, which test the hypothesis that parameter estimates from the three subsamples came from the same population.

TABLE 11-3. NUMBER OF SUBSAMPLE BANKS IN DIFFERENT SIZE CATEGORIES

Bank Size[a]	Positive	Remainder	Negative	Total
0–2	1	6	5	12
2–5	16	19	20	55
5–10	20	22	13	55
10–25	10	15	10	35
25–50	5	3	5	13
50–100	2	4	0	6
100–300	1	2	1	4
over 300	2	2	0	4
Total	57	73	54	184

[a] Bank size refers to the amount of deposits (in millions of dollars) that a bank held on January 6, 1960.

The three sets of subsample regressions were generally significant with F-ratios that were comparable to results reported in chapter 6, once allowance is made for their smaller numbers of degrees of freedom. These F-ratios are not reported. F-ratios reported in columns (1), (2), and (3) of table 11-4 test the hypothesis that the inclusion of thirty-two current and lagged demand and time deposit variables improve descriptions of bank portfolios when compared to a model where only contemporaneous levels of bank liabilities, capital, and call report intercepts appear. These tests suggest that the input-output model can be applied successfully to all three subsamples and that knowledge of a history of deposits is especially useful in describing a bank's cash, state and local securities, mortgage loans, consumer loans, and short-term securities.[5] Judging from the F-ratios, the model does almost equally well for each of the subsamples.

However, the analyses of covariance strongly suggest that adjustment paths differ among the three subsamples. F-ratios reported in column (4) of table 11-4 indicate that adjustment paths for cash, loans to banks, consumer installment loans (especially auto loans), and short-term government securities differ significantly at the 5 percent level. Since descriptions of fluctuations in cash and particularly short-term government securities are an important concern in this monograph, these results are very encouraging from the standpoint of developing prescriptions for optimal portfolio behavior by a bank.

5. Analogous tests were described in the text of chapter 6, where it was concluded that knowledge of the history of a bank's deposits yielded substantially improved descriptions of bank portfolios when compared with a contemporaneous liability formulation.

TABLE 11-4. *F*-RATIO STATISTICS FOR SUBSAMPLE REGRESSIONS

Asset	Subsample				Item Number(s) in Table 5-1
	Positive (1)	Remainder (2)	Negative (3)	Covariance (4)	
Cash	3.750*	2.589*	2.385*	1.438*	1
State and local securities	2.396*	1.908*	1.483	1.259	3
Mortgage loans	2.681*	3.080*	3.828*	1.023	27, 28, 29, 30
Financial loans	1.635*	.825	1.571*	1.095	31, 32, 33
Commercial and industrial loans	1.081	1.002	1.313	.902	36
Consumer loans	1.710*	4.101*	1.987*	1.311*	37, 38, 39, 40, 41
Short-term govt. securities	3.138*	4.967*	3.103*	1.389*	44, 45, 46, 49
1–5-year govt. securities	1.463	1.455	1.174	1.559*	47, 50
5–10-year govt. securities	1.019	.791	1.414	1.106	51
Other assets	.759	1.119	1.102	1.292	residual
Mortgage Loan Detail					
Insured	.997	.887	1.276	.823	28
Conventional	3.433*	1.494*	1.748*	1.098	29
Nonfarm, nonresidential	1.308	1.906*	1.452	.997	30
Consumer Loan Detail					
Automobile	1.620*	2.231*	.770	1.571*	37
Other consumer installment	1.310	.863	.974	1.160	38
Repair and modernization	.803	1.089	1.319	1.084	39
Single payment	1.436	3.270*	1.370	1.029	41
Interbank Claim Detail					
Deposits due from banks	1.069	2.534*	1.345	.894	55
Total reserves	1.141	1.633*	1.311	1.169	58, 59
Loans to banks	1.743*	.594	1.653*	1.351*	31

NOTE: An asterisk indicates that the *F*-ratio is statistically significant at the 5 percent level. Degrees of freedom have been adjusted to account for the fact that bank effects have been removed. Thus in columns (1) and (3), degrees of freedom are 30/455; in column (2), 30/614; and in column (4), 90/1524.

TABLE 11-5. CASH, SHORT-TERM GOVERNMENT SECURITY, AND CONSUMER LOAN ADJUSTMENT PATHS FOR BANK SUBSAMPLES

	Cash			Short-Term Govt. Securities			Consumer Loans		
	Positive	Remainder	Negative	Positive	Remainder	Negative	Positive	Remainder	Negative
				Demand Deposits					
d_w	.556*	.491*	.497*	.215*	.326*	.300*	.098*	.004	.068
d_{w-1}	.435*	.231*	.301*	.221*	.423*	.348*	.135*	.050	.017
d_{w-2}	.222*	.277*	.387*	.328*	.251*	.256*	.143*	.046	-.024
d_{sm}	.366*	.396*	.373*	.285*	.333*	.295*	.153*	.028	-.001
d_{m-2}	.264*	.315*	.299*	.390*	.389*	.283*	.139*	.082*	-.005
d_{m-3}	.210*	.272*	.207*	.439*	.255*	.426*	.170*	.056	.032
d_{m-4}	.188*	.236*	.216*	.376*	.289*	.448*	.178*	.047	-.014
d_{m-5}	.198*	.251*	.316*	.471*	.352*	.255*	.190*	.064*	.008
d_{m-6}	.166*	.265*	.259*	.349*	.327*	.302*	.197*	.099*	.076*
d_{m-7}	.126*	.291*	.273*	.234*	.157*	.161	.220*	.094*	.066
d_{m-8}	.240*	.261*	.285*	.327*	.150*	.037	.209*	.104*	.060
d_{m-9}	.175*	.359*	.229*	.316*	.246*	.154	.162*	.140*	.094*
d_{m-10}	.197*	.273*	.349*	.192*	.110	.054	.224*	.184*	.045
d_{m-11}	.189*	.262*	.479*	.154	.025	-.240*	.276*	.160*	.117*
d_{m-12}	.259*	.334*	.330*	.138	-.004	-.120	.178*	.233*	.096*
d_{m-13}	.224*	.238*	.354*	.086*	-.002	.053	.233*	.196*	.154*

Time Deposits

$\bar{s}_w$	.450	.562	−.121	.669	.154	.562	−.102	.169	−.116
$\bar{s}_{w-1}$	.393	−.230	.372	.666	.640*	.023	.132	.150	.332
$\bar{s}_{w-2}$	.376	.237	−.085	−.580	.606	.107	.032	.162	−.007
$\bar{s}_{sm}$	.090	.410*	.405	.866	.628*	.081	.239	.006	.269
$\bar{s}_{m-2}$	.458*	.147	−.347*	.291	.412	.122	.294	.009	.199
$\bar{s}_{m-3}$	.200	−.509*	−.023	.172	−.085	.258	−.308*	.111	.028
$\bar{s}_{m-4}$	.098	−.038	−.255	.494	1.316*	.385	.280	−.037	.159
$\bar{s}_{m-5}$	.301	.296*	−.397*	.430	.367	.153	.328*	−.091	.309*
$\bar{s}_{m-6}$	.206	−.135	−.188	.676*	−.171	.110	−.167	.283*	.085
$\bar{s}_{m-7}$	.259	−.085	.262	−.673	.592	.062	−.093	−.069	.114
$\bar{s}_{m-8}$	.125	−.027	.103	.013	.346	.345	.193	−.045	.103
$\bar{s}_{m-9}$	−.158	.350	−.571*	.975*	−.455	.236	−.088	.149	.312*
$\bar{s}_{m-10}$	.288	−.270	−.085	−.517	.165	.262	.001	.397*	.158
$\bar{s}_{m-11}$	.152	−.081	−.090	.420	.230	.113	−.050	−.161	.104
$\bar{s}_{m-12}$	−.236	.074	−.457*	.632*	−.081	−.012	.214	.095	.312*
s_{m-13}	−.088	−.072	−.235*	.081	.167*	.082	.062	.110*	.095*

NOTE: An asterisk indicates that a coefficient differs significantly from zero at the 5 percent level in a two-tailed test.

It is convenient to examine differences in adjustment paths both numerically and graphically. Table 11-5 reports demand and time deposit coefficients estimated for the three subsamples of banks. Again, bank effects, call report effects, and the influence of capital and overflow variables have been removed during estimation. In view of the significance pattern in column (4) of table 11-4, attention is restricted to cash, consumer loan, and short-term government security regressions.

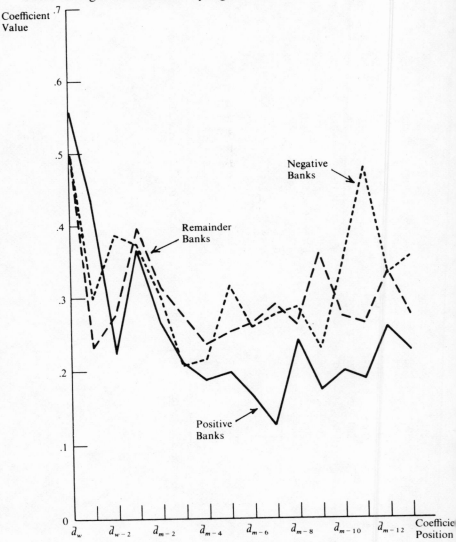

FIGURE 11-1. DEMAND DEPOSIT COEFFICIENTS FOR CASH

Demand deposit coefficients for cash, which are plotted in figure 11-1, show striking differences.[6] Positive banks exhibit a relatively smooth declining adjustment path with banks retaining a large fraction of cash, 56 percent, during the week of the inflow. This fraction declines to near the estimated equilibrium level of 22 percent after five weeks. Remainder banks show similar initial and equilibrium coefficients, 49 percent and 24 percent respectively, but they are somewhat slower in reaching the equilibrium level, and their coefficients are more erratic. Negative banks, on the other hand, have much larger equilibrium levels of cash, approximately 35 per cent, and are much more erratic. The third from last coefficient for negative banks almost equals the initial value of 50 percent. Evidently, differences in bank management of cash in response to demand deposit inflows are important in explaining variations in bank profitability. Very profitable banks control their cash as the theory of chapter 3 predicts. Other banks have distinctly more erratic cash profiles and in equilibrium have excessive cash assets.

Time deposit coefficients for cash, plotted in figure 11-2, are more erratic but also seem to differ among subsamples. While statistical significance is infrequent, the following pattern is evident. The least erratic are coefficients for positive banks; they are large initially and then decline to insignificant negative values. Remainder banks have a similar trend, but are quite irregular. Coefficients for negative banks are equally irregular and very often nonpositive. Five coefficients for negative banks are significantly different from zero, and all have this seemingly wrong sign. No doubt, the estimated negative time deposit reserve requirement, discussed in chapter 6, would have been less evident if these unprofitable banks had been excluded. Again, the behavior of the most profitable banks seems to be best predicted by the theory.

Demand deposit coefficients for short-term government securities, plotted in figure 11-3, differ less among subsamples than do cash coefficients. All three groups of banks buy some securities when deposits flow in, have a maximum incremental security/deposit ratio after about four months and then allow securities to run off. Positive banks again show the smoothest adjustment path. Initially, 22 percent of their inflow is invested in short-term securities. A maximum share of 47 percent is reached in about six months, and the equilibrium share is about 9 percent, which differs significantly from zero. Remainder and negative banks buy more securities initially and have long-run equilibria that are insignificantly different from zero. Remainder banks also exhibit a less peaked adjustment path than positive banks. The negative bank path is distinctive in that it is very erratic and that its coefficients are insignificantly positive

6. The coefficients are plotted sequentially in figures 11-1 through 11-6 without reference to the time interval that they describe. Thus, the abscissae show the position of the coefficient in table 11-5, not calendar time.

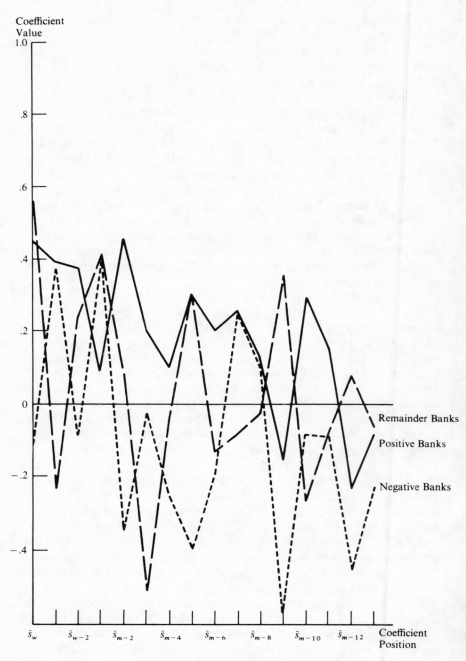

FIGURE 11-2. TIME DEPOSIT COEFFICIENTS FOR CASH

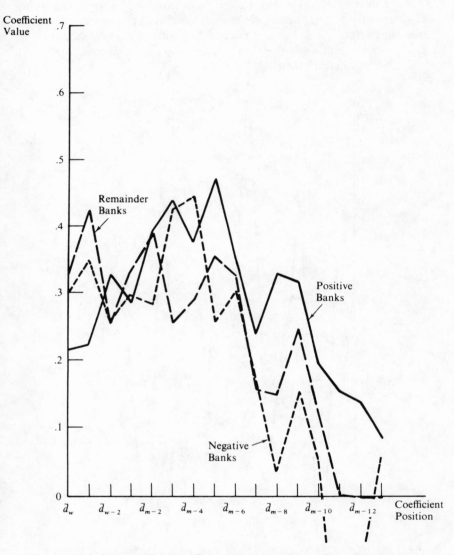

FIGURE 11-3. DEMAND DEPOSIT COEFFICIENTS FOR SHORT-TERM SECURITIES

after about seven months. Evidently, both remainder and negative banks acquire and dispose of securities prematurely; higher profits can be obtained by converting them to loans and other investments at a slower rate.

Time deposit coefficients for short-term government securities (figure 11-4) are very erratic; successive coefficients flip-flop considerably. Negative banks have the smoothest pattern of coefficients although no coefficients differ significantly from zero. Equilibrium time deposit coefficients also do not differ appreciably.

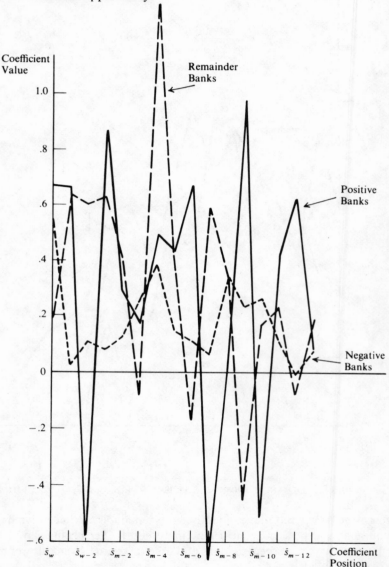

FIGURE 11-4. TIME DEPOSIT COEFFICIENTS FOR SHORT-TERM SECURITIES

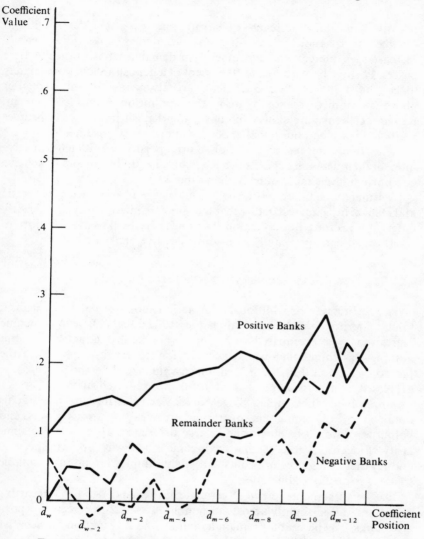

FIGURE 11-5. DEMAND DEPOSIT COEFFICIENTS FOR CONSUMER LOANS

Demand deposit coefficients for consumer loans, plotted in figure 11-5, differ suggestively across subsamples. For negative banks, the share of demand deposits invested in such loans fluctuates widely and is not regularly significant until the last three coefficients. The equilibrium level of 15 percent for negative banks is low relative to other bank samples, but high relative to their own deposit-change coefficients. It appears that negative banks failed to reach equilibrium one year after a deposit inflow. On the other hand, both positive and remainder banks quite steadily increase their incremental consumer loan/demand deposit ratios as time passes. Positive banks allocate 10 percent of a deposit inflow immediately to consumer loans; their coefficients are always significant, and after about six months essentially are at the equilibrium level of 23 percent. Remainder banks are slower in converting deposit inflows to consumer loans and reach equilibrium after about ten months. Consumer loans have high net operating income rates of return; positive banks tend to have more of their demand deposits in such loans at equilibrium and to achieve equilibrium levels more quickly than other banks.[7]

Consumer loan time deposit coefficients (figure 11-6) appear very erratic and seem of little interest in this chapter. They are infrequently significantly different from zero. Both remainder and negative banks have equilibrium levels that differ significantly from zero; positive banks do not.

3. CONCLUDING REMARKS

This section reports additional information about subsample banks and briefly interprets the findings. In chapter 10 residuals of various income regressions were compared to a number of bank characteristics, but nothing was found that would account for the results reported in the preceding section. For the record, mean values of different bank assets, expressed as a percentage of total assets, are reported in table 11-6 for the three bank subsamples. Since banks were classified from residuals obtained by regressing net operating income on various assets and liabilities, it would be surprising if large differences appeared. The similarity of means suggests (1) that the income model was properly specified and (2) that differences in profits across subsamples are not attributable to average portfolio differences.

The mean standard error of estimate in demand deposit forecasting equations varied slightly across subsamples. It was 2.35 percent for positive banks, 2.39 percent for remainder banks, and 2.43 percent for negative banks. In chapter 10 the correlation between individual bank standard errors and profit residuals was found to be insignificantly different from zero. Therefore, this weak relation does not seem worth pursuing.

7. Net operating income does not reflect adjustments for default losses and loan write-offs. It is possible, therefore, that bank profits after taxes are not augmented by rapidly acquiring consumer loans. No attempt has been made to investigate this possibility, but it does not seem likely in light of results from an experiment reported in the next section.

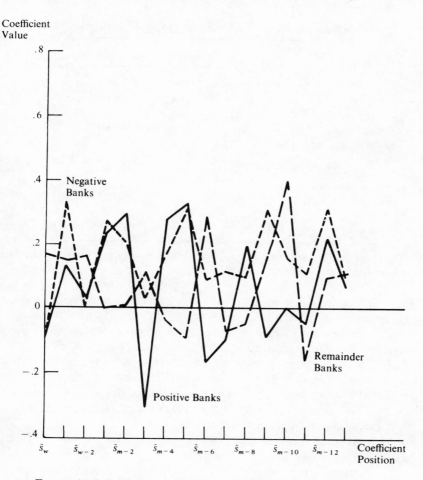

FIGURE 11-6. TIME DEPOSIT COEFFICIENTS FOR CONSUMER LOANS

Because bank growth rates and residuals were also found to be unrelated in chapter 10, no further investigation of deposit growth was attempted.

A more substantive issue concerns whether the correct measure of net income has been used to classify banks. A bank presumably wants to maximize net income after taxes rather than net current operating income. The latter measure, nevertheless, was used in this chapter since it is less subject to arbitrary accounting adjustments for tax purposes. In chapter 10 the correlation between net current operating income and net after-tax

TABLE 11-6. MEAN PORTFOLIO SHARES OF BANK SUBSAMPLES

| | Subsample | | | Item Number(s) in Table 5-1 |
Asset	Positive	Remainder	Negative	
Cash	16.5%	16.4%	16.4%	1
State and local securities	7.3	6.6	6.4	3
Mortgage loans	14.1	14.2	13.5	27, 28, 29, 30
Commercial and industrial loans	15.8	13.5	15.9	36
Consumer loans	15.3	17.7	16.1	37, 38, 39, 40, 41
Short-term govt. securities	8.1	8.4	8.3	44, 45, 46, 49
1–5-year govt. securities	10.1	10.8	10.2	47, 50
Other assets	12.8	12.4	13.2	residual
Total assets	100.0%	100.0%	100.0%	

NOTE: Means of bank assets differ slightly from those reported in table 5-5, which were estimated from the sample of 201 banks.

income was found to be .627. Table 11-7 reports mean residuals corresponding to the four measures of income, expressed as a percentage of total assets, for the three subsamples. Clearly, banks with positive (negative) net operating income residuals also tended to have positive (negative) residuals for other measures as well. Subsample mean residual variations appear quite large for the three net income measures. In chapter 5 it was reported that all sample banks had mean percentages of net operating income and income before and after taxes to total assets of 1.30 percent, 1.17 percent, and .74 percent, respectively.

In conclusion, the evidence of this chapter is consistent with the following statements and does not seem readily interpretable without them. First, markets served by commercial banks are quite imperfect owing to limited entry and to legally imposed restrictions on competition. Quite wide differences in bank efficiency are evident. Second, after eliminating effects of variations in bank portfolio composition, bank net income is strikingly related to the shapes of adjustment paths that describe how banks convert demand deposit inflows into cash, short-term securities, and consumer loans.

Positive (profitable) banks have much smoother portfolio adjustments to demand deposit shocks than other groups of banks. Like other banks, they initially hold a large percentage of a demand deposit inflow in cash, but they reduce this cash position more rapidly by purchasing both short-term securities and consumer loans. They retain their short-term securities for a longer time and appear to desire larger equilibrium shares of such securities than other banks. Profitable banks are much prompter in investing in lucrative consumer loans than other banks.

TABLE 11-7. MEAN INCOME RESIDUALS FOR BANK SUBSAMPLES

Income Measure[a]	Subsample		
	Positive	Remainder	Negative
Gross operating income	.123%	−.021%	−.072%
Net operating income	.330	.000	−.316
Net income before taxes	.312	−.007	−.285
Net income after taxes	.139	.006	−.133

NOTE: These residuals were computed from regression equations which differ from those reported in table 10-3 because they omitted the reciprocal of total assets. Mean values are unlikely to be appreciably affected by this omission. Rows in this table do not sum precisely to zero because the income regressions were estimated from the full sample of 201 banks, whereas a total of only 184 banks appear in the subsamples.

[a] Expressed as a percentage of total assets.

A comparison of results for positive and negative banks strongly supports the arguments in chapters 2 and 3, which predict that banks who maximize expected net income will exhibit the dynamic behavior observed in positive banks. Neither variations in bank deposit variability nor variations in bank size across subsamples are sufficiently pronounced to explain the observed differences.

CHAPTER 12

Bank Behavior and Macroeconomic Credit Flows

In this chapter the input-output models that were described in chapters 6 and 7 are examined from a macroeconomic perspective.[1] The objective is to study processes by which such micro-bank relations can be aggregated to macro-equations. When comparing aggregation processes, systemwide speeds of adjustment and equilibrium portfolio allocations are emphasized.

The first section describes the additional specifications that are necessary to construct macro-relations from the empirical portfolio results reported in tables 6-1, 6-2, and 7-2 through 7-5. It also shows how those results were modified to facilitate simulation experiments and intuitively suggests the nature of the aggregation processes.

The second section reports a number of simulation experiments that illustrate quantitatively how some hypothetical financial systems respond to different shocks. These experiments are based on the assumption that banks do not distinguish between reserves and other cash assets; primary emphasis is upon aggregate portfolio composition.

In the third section other experiments are described that ignore details of portfolio composition but strictly observe the distinction between reserves and other cash assets. These latter experiments utilize actual aggregate levels of member bank reserves as simulation input and yield estimates of aggregate bank deposits. They thus characterize a number of alternative "money supply functions."

The concluding section utilizes the simulation experiments to analyze problems associated with implementing monetary policy and also to account for certain unusual econometric results that have appeared in the literature.

1. AGGREGATION IN A CLOSED LINEAR SYSTEM

Since all relations considered in chapters 6 and 7 are linear, it might seem a trivial matter to construct macro-equations from individual bank

---

1. Preliminary versions of results reported in this chapter were presented in Hester and Pierce [1967a, 1970].

behavioral equations. This is not the case. Intuitively, the problem is that as one bank adjusts toward equilibrium, it necessarily disturbs the positions of other banks in the system. The dynamic adjustment paths of an individual bank and the banking system will be related but not identical; a system of many banks will reach equilibrium more slowly than will an autonomous individual bank. Additional information or assumptions *must* be used to close the system; when the system is closed, it need not behave like an individual bank.

There are at least three major nonbank actors in the aggregation process. First, in principle, the aggregate level of member bank deposits in the United States is controlled by the Federal Reserve System, which sets the volume of reserves available to the banking system and reserve requirements. Second, the public influences the process when it determines the amounts of currency, demand deposits, time deposits, and savings deposits that it will hold and when it chooses between member and nonmember bank depositories.[2] Finally, in recent years international financial and nonfinancial corporations have affected the process through the Eurodollar market and other financial innovations.

In the following discussion, no attempt will be made to analyze the ways in which international firms affect the banking system's portfolio. In addition, with the exception of the fourth section, the Federal Reserve System will play an exceedingly passive role, although this role differs in sections 2 and 3. The public and banks occupy the spotlight. A policy-induced shock to bank deposits is hypothesized to cause a dynamic expansion of credit that depends on (1) the rate at which individual banks adjust their portfolios (as estimated in chapters 6 and 7); (2) the speed at which the public effectively returns funds withdrawn from financial institutions; and (3) the shares of newly created deposits that are redeposited in commercial bank demand accounts, in commercial bank time accounts, and in savings bank accounts. The effective return speed or "turnover" rate and the redeposit shares are primarily determined by transactions habits and savings behavior of the public. Turnover also depends importantly on clearing conventions and government regulations concerning settlements of interbank transactions.

In a primitive world, banks may be thought of as executing all transactions with currency. When a bank acquires an income-earning asset, it pays for it with currency. In such a world, a banking system could not expand credit beyond an initial currency injection until its currency outlays were returned to it by the public. In modern banks, of course, assets can be acquired without currency outflows through the use of checks.

---

2. For a similar specification, see contributions by Brunner [1961] and Modigliani, Rasche, and Cooper [1970].

Until the checks are presented for collection, a bank experiences no loss of reserves (or currency). Since in most instances another bank will present the check for collection, the banking *system* rarely experiences the loss of reserves or currency that its primitive counterpart suffered. This does not imply, however, that the modern system can expand credit as fast as its constituent banks. Banks must be aware that they have received funds and believe that such funds will remain with them long enough for them to profit from a credit expansion. In the modern system the length of time it takes, on average, for a banking system to reacquire *effective* use of money it has created is the reciprocal of the turnover rate.[3] It is not fruitful to explore the determinants of turnover in great detail. They include (a) a legal structure that defines and relates cash items, deferred availability, bank float, Federal Reserve float, and so on; (b) individual banks' information about and analysis of their cash flow; (c) the proportion of credit created that is drawn down in the form of currency flows; and (d) asset transactions costs.

The turnover rate is important for describing how much time must pass before a policy-induced shock is absorbed by the system. If the deposit turnover rate approaches infinity, total financial credit will trace a path that converges as fast as the slowest adjusting financial institution. Total financial credit will follow a path that is proportional to a weighted average of the reciprocals of previously estimated deposit coefficients, where weights are the shares redeposited in different accounts. On the other hand, if the turnover rate is low, the system will be able to expand credit only very slowly. Apart from crude debit statistics, very little information exists about the rate of deposit turnover. Turnover is intensively studied in section 3 below, where estimates of the average rate of turnover of demand and time deposits are reported.[4]

While the turnover rate is crucial for understanding the speed with which a system adjusts to a shock, it is unrelated to the equilibrium toward which a stable system tends. Redeposit shares, on the other hand, are critical for understanding the equilibrium mix of financial assets. If savers in an economy place all of their incremental liquid assets in demand deposits, the economy will tend to have a portfolio that resembles the last row of asset shares in table 6-1. If instead they place half of their incremental assets in time and half in demand deposits, portfolio shares

3. A modern banking system may never reacquire effective use of money it has created. An example is when a bank lends to an individual who engages in multibank kiting of checks.
4. In principle, it is possible to view deposits created by different asset acquisitions as turning over at different velocities. No attempt is made to incorporate this possibility; the maintained hypothesis is that turnover rates are independent of bank asset choices.

will approach an equilibrium lying between the last rows of asset shares shown in tables 6-1 and 6-2.[5]

The simulations considered below concern systems that create demand, time, and savings deposits. With one exception in section 3, it will be assumed that the turnover rate is independent of interest rates and is an institutionally determined, time-invariant, parameter. If electronic or other technologically improved clearing mechanisms were to be introduced, the assumption of time invariance would have to be abandoned.

Redeposit shares are likely to be a function of nominal interest rates paid on different assets, and, therefore, to vary through time. Results from empirical studies of household portfolios usually support a hypothesis that the share of time and savings deposits is an increasing function of the interest rate paid on such deposits.[6] An experiment that permits redeposit shares to vary with the savings deposit interest rate is reported in section 3. Other determinants of shares (or portfolio behavior) include transactions costs for savers, various forms of uncertainty, lifetime income profiles, bequest objectives, tax laws, and so on. None will be considered in the series of experiments that follow. This omission will not be serious given the limited objective of illustrating aggregation processes.

Once the possibility of portfolio choice is recognized, it is apparent that a complete model of credit creation must allow funds to flow into all intermediaries, not just commercial banks. Since simulation experiments below concern only commercial and savings banks, they must be interpreted cautiously in the context of the American economy.

The simulation experiments can be viewed as an application of the simple textbook bank credit creation algorithm. In section 2 a monetary authority is assumed to make a permanent one-time injection of a fixed amount of cash assets to *all* intermediaries, in this instance, commercial and savings banks. The monetary authority acts to insure that the sum of cash assets at all intermediaries is permanently augmented by $1,000 from an initial (pre-experiment) level. In section 3 the monetary authority pays no attention to savings bank liquidity. In this more conventional specification the authority acts to insure that commercial bank reserves are permanently augmented by exactly $1,000 from an initial level.

---

5. It is important to recognize that negative cash or reserves coefficients on year-ago time deposit levels in tables 6-2 and 6-6 place upper limits on time deposit redeposit shares, if monetary policy is to be conventionally represented. For example, in a system consisting only of commercial banks, the money stock expansion from a dollar cash injection becomes indefinitely large as the time deposit redeposit share approaches about two-thirds from below. In the following analysis it will be assumed that the time deposit redeposit share is less than 50 percent. Similar restrictions must be imposed for some savings bank simulations.

6. See, for example, studies by Feige [1964], Goldfeld [1966], and Hamburger [1968].

Since the turnover rate is not directly observable, its value has to be assumed in each trial of a simulation experiment. Restricting the turnover rate to be constant within an experiment proved convenient in section 2, but the rate is permitted to vary across trials in simulation experiments described in section 3. Since all mutual savings and most commercial bank deposit coefficients in the input-output model refer to monthly intervals, it was convenient to normalize all coefficients to monthly intervals. This necessitated pooling the first four coefficients in each column of tables 6-1, 6-2, 6-5, and 6-6, which refer to weekly or biweekly intervals, and calling the interval of the resulting coefficient a "month."[7] Coefficients actually used in simulation experiments are reported in the following two sections. The dimension of a turnover rate is the reciprocal of time. In conformity with conventional usage turnover is reported on an annual basis.

2. Asset Choices by Hypothetical Systems of Intermediaries

The relation between redeposit shares and the composition of credit flows within an economy is studied by examining results from four simulation experiments with different redeposit share specifications. The turnover rate is assumed to be twelve times per year.

For convenience, attention is restricted to commercial banks and to savings banks located in Connecticut and Massachusetts. Given the similarity of savings bank results in chapter 7, it did not seem illuminating to consider all four groups of banks here. Also, it is convenient to analyze only a small number of assets held by each type of intermediary. For commercial banks, cash, short-term United States government securities (less than one-year maturity), other United States government securities, mortgage loans, other loans, and all other assets are studied. For savings banks, assets examined include cash, United States government securities, mortgage loans, other loans, and all other assets.[8]

---

7. Since the four coefficients span a five-week interval, this interpretation is inaccurate. However, only very minor changes in aggregate time paths were obtained when this pooled coefficient was assumed to apply to the first eight weeks and other coefficients were shifted back one month. Apparently, the inaccuracy is of little consequence. A similar inaccuracy occurs when commercial bank and savings bank monthly coefficients are used together. Commercial bank monthly coefficients refer to the first differences of successive four-week averages. Savings bank figures instead are based on differences in successive end-of-calendar-month figures.

8. An attempt was made to examine asset categories that were broadly comparable across intermediaries. However, the composition of assets within these categories is not the same for different types of banks. This fact will be ignored in the text.

TABLE 12-1. COMMERCIAL BANK PARAMETERS USED IN SIMULATION EXPERIMENTS

Demand Deposit Coefficients

Month	Cash	Shorts	Other U.S. Govts.	Mortgage	Other Loans	Other Assets
t_0-t_1	.374	.284	.044	.032	.148	.118
t_1-t_2	.287	.345	.017	.017	.202	.132
t_2-t_3	.237	.343	.105	.044	.174	.098
t_3-t_4	.202	.342	.074	.034	.227	.121
t_4-t_5	.245	.348	.085	.029	.194	.099
t_5-t_6	.225	.308	.104	.061	.248	.054
t_6-t_7	.247	.177	.144	.049	.268	.116
t_7-t_8	.258	.150	.151	.051	.262	.129
t_8-t_9	.265	.237	.069	.060	.269	.101
t_9-t_{10}	.259	.105	.172	.078	.285	.101
$t_{10}-t_{11}$	.290	-.004	.157	.055	.319	.183
$t_{11}-t_{12}$	.298	.003	.173	.069	.321	.136
t_{12}	.267	.048	.142	.087	.350	.107
Item Number(s) in Table 5-1	1	44, 45, 46, 49	47, 48, 50, 51, 52, 53	27, 28, 29, 30	36, 37, 38, 39, 40, 41	Residual

Time Deposit Coefficients

Month	Cash	Shorts	Other U.S. Govts.	Mortgage	Other Loans	Other Assets
t_0-t_1	.200	.339	.076	.048	.245	.093
t_1-t_2	.041	.246	.073	.113	.247	.280
t_2-t_3	-.066	.073	.275	.037	.257	.424
t_3-t_4	-.122	.732	-.068	.120	.301	.037
t_4-t_5	.053	.303	-.033	.148	.217	.313
t_5-t_6	-.044	.110	.166	.162	.335	.272
t_6-t_7	.103	.068	.479	.157	.212	-.019
t_7-t_8	.009	.245	-.038	.253	.294	.237
t_8-t_9	-.072	.151	.244	.151	.169	.358
t_9-t_{10}	-.070	.104	.130	.282	.430	.123
$t_{10}-t_{11}$	-.010	.159	.208	.254	.039	.349
$t_{11}-t_{12}$	-.221	.125	.160	.271	.341	.324
t_{12}	-.134	.117	.197	.291	.242	.286
Item Number(s) in Table 5-1	1	44, 45, 46, 49	47, 48, 50, 51, 52, 53	27, 28, 29, 30	36, 37, 38, 39, 40, 41	Residual

TABLE 12-2. SAVINGS BANK PARAMETERS USED IN SIMULATION EXPERIMENTS

Month	Connecticut					Massachusetts				
	Cash	U.S. Govts.	Mortgage	Other Credit	Other Assets	Cash	U.S. Govts.	Mortgage	Other Credit	Other Assets
t_0-t_1	.089	.425	.131	.349	.005	.070	.621	.065	.222	.022
t_1-t_2	.112	.367	.236	.293	−.008	−.016	.843	.035	.117	.021
t_2-t_3	.069	.304	.378	.219	.031	−.055	.737	.229	.058	.030
t_3-t_4	.056	.168	.494	.245	.038	.013	.446	.513	.009	.020
t_4-t_5	.036	.146	.590	.229	−.001	−.037	.445	.605	−.040	.027
t_5-t_6	−.014	.111	.727	.208	−.032	−.068	.402	.653	−.018	.032
t_6-t_7	.010	−.083	.874	.215	−.016	.022	.235	.650	.096	−.002
t_7	.006	−.072	.998	.080	−.011	.010	.158	.802	.043	−.012
Item Number(s) in Table 5-6	1	2	5	4, 6	3, 7	1	2	5	4, 6	3, 7

NOTE: Coefficients in this table were derived from preliminary studies of mutual savings banks. They differ trivially from the final results reported in tables 7-2 and 7-3.

Coefficients used in simulation experiments are reported in tables 12-1 and 12-2; they are constructed from coefficients reported in tables 6-1, 6-2, 7-2, and 7-3 or from analogous coefficients in certain unreported regressions. The top row in each table shows the fraction of a deposit *inflow* that appears in each asset during the month in which the inflow occurred. The bottom row shows the equilibrium fraction of the *level* of deposits that a bank will allocate to each asset. Table 12-3 shows assumed redeposit shares for each of the four simulation experiments. In experiments one, two, and four, and most of their counterparts in section 4, it is assumed that the monetary authority initially makes the injection into commercial bank demand deposits. Thereafter they are redeposited in the shares shown in table 12-3. The injection in experiment three flows directly into savings banks.

TABLE 12-3. ASSUMED REDEPOSIT SHARES FOR SIMULATION EXPERIMENTS

	Commercial Banks		Savings Banks	
Experiment	*Demand*	*Time*	*Connecticut*	*Massachusetts*
one	.90	.10	0	0
two	.50	.50	0	0
three	0	0	.50	.50
four	.80	.10	.05	.05

To illustrate how a simulation might run, consider experiment one. After receiving the exogenous demand deposit injection of $1,000, the banking system desires to hold $374 in cash assets and allocates the rest in the proportions indicated by the first row of demand deposit coefficients in table 12-1. At the end of a month the system's deposits have risen to $1,626, that is, $1,000 exogeneous and $626 created by the system. Of the created deposits, $62.60 flows into time accounts and $563.40 goes into demand accounts. The system then invests the initial $1,000 in the proportions given by the second row of demand deposit coefficients, the created $563.40 in the proportions given by the first row of demand deposit coefficients, and the $62.60 in the proportions given by the first row of time deposit coefficients, and so on.

Table 12-4 reports the simulated time paths of the displacement for different commercial bank assets in response to a permanent cash injection of $1,000. The first half of the table concerns experiment one; it indicates, with the assumed turnover rate of twelve, that the system will realize 90 percent of its equilibrium credit expansion at the end of three

TABLE 12-4. SIMULATED TIME PATHS FOR BANK ASSETS: PURE COMMERCIAL BANKING SYSTEM
(Experiments One and Two)

	Experiment One						Experiment Two					
Month	Cash	Shorts	Other U.S. Govts.	Mortgage	Other Loans	Other Assets	Cash	Shorts	Other U.S. Govts.	Mortgage	Other Loans	Other Assets
1	374	284	44	32	148	118	374	284	44	32	148	118
4	611	827	181	88	509	324	489	788	247	114	581	448
7	803	983	341	164	796	394	637	1,120	386	270	985	637
10	917	845	478	248	987	443	756	1,098	636	448	1,230	753
13	975	465	567	313	1,191	520	774	872	772	643	1,521	924
16	986	304	595	373	1,312	516	785	819	905	824	1,741	1,080
19	986	254	599	403	1,375	510	794	872	999	970	1,947	1,205
22	989	246	603	417	1,406	506	825	908	1,111	1,090	2,120	1,309
25	994	246	608	423	1,420	506	850	915	1,206	1,201	2,277	1,405
28	997	241	612	426	1,429	508	867	911	1,292	1,303	2,415	1,497
31	998	234	615	429	1,436	509	878	913	1,366	1,395	2,541	1,579
34	999	229	616	431	1,440	509	891	918	1,434	1,476	2,652	1,651
37	999	227	617	432	1,442	509	903	924	1,494	1,549	2,753	1,715
40	1,000	226	617	433	1,444	509	914	928	1,548	1,613	2,843	1,773
43	1,000	226	617	433	1,445	509	922	930	1,596	1,672	2,923	1,825
46	1,000	225	617	433	1,445	509	931	932	1,640	1,724	2,995	1,871
49	1,000	225	617	433	1,445	509	938	935	1,678	1,770	3,059	1,913
Equilibrium	1,000	224	618	434	1,446	509	1,000	957	2,010	2,170	3,613	2,271

NOTE: All assets are measured in dollars. The time paths are in response to a $1,000 cash injection. The assumed turnover rate is 12. In experiment one, redeposit shares are assumed to be 90 percent demand deposits and 10 percent time deposits; in experiment two, redeposit shares are assumed to be 50 percent demand deposits and 50 percent time deposits.

quarters. However, individual assets reach this degree of convergence with very different lags, suggesting that the impact of the injection on real sectors may differ considerably from this systemwide average. After three quarters the desired cash holdings constitute 90 percent of the injection. Mortgage loans and short-maturity securities, on the other hand, do not reach this degree of convergence until around the end of six quarters. The remaining assets converge between three and six quarters. It is important to note that "other assets" and especially short-maturity securities do not converge monotonically to their equilibrium levels. In section 4 it will be argued that this fact may have caused a number of early econometric investigators to estimate unrealistically long lags for some policy instruments.

The second half of table 12-4 illustrates that the response path of this banking system to a permanent cash injection is quite sensitive to the public's portfolio behavior. When the public allocates its receipts equally between demand and time accounts, the system adjusts more slowly than in experiment one, where the public allocated most funds to demand accounts. This difference in speed occurs because the credit multiplier is larger when the redeposit shares are equal and, therefore, a given initial injection must circulate more times before equilibrium is attained. Since the turnover rate is a constant, more time must pass before the system reaches, say, 90 percent of its equilibrium level. In experiment two, total bank credit expansion had not reached 90 percent of equilibrium at the end of sixteen quarters.

In addition, the shapes of adjustment paths for different assets changed markedly with the redeposit share. In experiment two, short-maturity securities reached 90 percent of equilibrium first, at the end of six quarters; its path lost most of the very pronounced hump evident in experiment one. After twelve quarters desired system cash holdings exceeded 90 percent of the original injection. All other adjustment paths appear to be monotonic, and none of the remaining assets reached 90 percent of its equilibrium level during the simulation interval of sixteen quarters. From these two experiments, it appears that it is quite critical to study commercial bank portfolio responses to demand and time deposit flows separately and to incorporate descriptions of the public's portfolio allocations to these flows when estimating aggregate money supply functions.

Table 12-5 suggests how permanent cash injections might affect a financial system that had no commercial banks.[9] The public is assumed

9. Since the observed savings bank behavior occurred in a world in which commercial banks were present, results in table 12-5 should be interpreted with considerable care. It is doubtful that savings bank behavior would be unaffected by the disappearance of commercial banks.

TABLE 12-5. SIMULATED TIME PATHS FOR BANK ASSETS: PURE MUTUAL SAVINGS BANK SYSTEM
(Experiment Three)

	Connecticut					Massachusetts				
Month	Cash	U.S. Govts.	Mortgage	Other Credit	Other Assets	Cash	U.S. Govts.	Mortgage	Other Credit	Other Assets
1	45	213	66	175	3	35	311	32	111	11
4	135	519	548	464	31	4	1,100	391	161	40
7	138	550	1,441	712	4	−24	1,469	1,156	185	58
10	146	454	2,616	777	−6	−12	1,631	2,100	226	41
13	147	351	3,749	857	−22	−2	1,776	3,012	270	27
16	149	246	4,854	920	−35	10	1,902	3,901	311	10
19	151	145	5,912	983	−48	23	2,023	4,751	352	−6
22	153	47	6,927	1,042	−60	34	2,137	5,567	391	−21
25	154	−47	7,899	1,100	−72	46	2,247	6,348	428	−35
28	156	−136	8,831	1,155	−83	57	2,353	7,097	464	−49
31	157	−222	9,723	1,207	−94	67	2,454	7,814	499	−62
34	159	−304	10,578	1,258	−104	78	2,550	8,501	532	−75
37	160	−383	11,397	1,306	−114	87	2,643	9,159	563	−87
40	161	−459	12,182	1,352	−124	97	2,732	9,789	594	−99
43	163	−531	12,934	1,397	−133	105	2,817	10,393	623	−110
46	164	−600	13,654	1,439	−142	114	2,898	10,972	651	−121
49	165	−667	14,344	1,480	−150	122	2,976	11,526	677	−131
Equilibrium	382	−4,388	60,454	4,836	−685	618	9,552	48,576	2,588	−733

NOTE: All assets are measured in dollars. The time paths are in response to a $1,000 cash injection. The assumed turnover rate is 12. The redeposit shares are assumed to be 50 percent to Connecticut banks and 50 percent to Massachusetts banks.

to deposit 50 percent of its receipts in a Connecticut mutual savings bank and the rest in a Massachusetts bank. Therefore, total asset increments are always equal in the two sets of banks. With an assumed annual turnover rate of twelve, no asset for either type of bank neared its equilibrium level during the simulation interval. The explanation for this long lag is analogous to that proposed when comparing results from the two previous experiments; the credit multiplier is much larger in the pure savings bank system than in either of the commercial bank systems. Evidently, monetary policy would be a dull tool in economies where all intermediaries have small desired equilibrium cash/asset ratios.

Negative equilibria for United States government securities (in the case of Connecticut banks) and for other assets are a consequence of the lack of invariance, which was extensively discussed in chapter 7. They reflect misspecification and will not be considered further. The remaining results from this input-output formulation suggest that state laws, like the deposit tax in Massachusetts, can strikingly affect the magnitudes of credit flows into different real sectors. In equilibrium, Connecticut banks place a much larger share of their portfolios in private-sector loans than do their Massachusetts counterparts. To the extent that these ad hoc legal distortions are not offset by other intermediaries and corresponding changes in the public's saving behavior, such regulations seem to impart indefensible asymmetries in national credit markets.

Table 12-6 concerns a mixed financial system in which both commercial and savings banks attract funds from the public. Adjustment paths are reported for a selected set of assets. The total amount of credit created by the system, and indeed by commercial banks alone, exceeds the credit created by banks in the first experiment, but otherwise the systems described in experiments one and four are quite similar.[10] The system desires to hold 90 percent of the initial injection of cash assets shortly after the end of the third quarter. After seven quarters short-maturity government securities and other assets have also reached this degree of convergence. The shapes of most systemwide asset adjustment paths are also very similar to those reported for experiment one.

The major effect of introducing savings banks into the structure of experiment one was to cause a 75 percent expansion in the volume of

10. The reason that commercial banks themselves are able to create more credit when savings banks are introduced to the model of experiment one is a consequence of the fact that demand deposits themselves are the major absorber of cash in that system. The share of all funds being redeposited in commercial bank demand deposits is less in experiment four, and the expansion effect from fewer demand deposits swamped the "substitution effect" from funds flowing into savings banks.

TABLE 12-6. SIMULATED TIME PATHS FOR BANK ASSETS: MIXED COMMERCIAL AND SAVINGS BANK SYSTEM
(Experiment Four)

| | Commercial Banks | | | | Mutual Savings Banks | | | | | |
| | | | | | Connecticut | | | Massachusetts | | |
Month	Cash	Shorts	Mortgage	Other Loans	Cash	U.S. Govts.	Mortgage	Cash	U.S. Govts.	Mortgage
1	374	284	32	148	0	0	0	0	0	0
4	578	788	84	489	7	28	21	−1	58	9
7	768	938	159	767	6	29	62	−3	72	54
10	888	826	243	958	4	10	115	−1	56	94
13	953	487	310	1,166	2	−3	147	0	40	119
16	972	336	371	1,293	2	−8	163	1	33	131
19	976	280	405	1,364	1	−10	169	1	31	136
22	982	264	422	1,402	1	−11	173	2	31	139
25	988	257	430	1,422	1	−12	176	2	30	142
28	992	250	436	1,435	1	−12	178	2	30	143
31	994	242	440	1,444	1	−13	180	2	29	144
34	995	237	442	1,450	1	−13	181	2	29	145
37	996	234	444	1,453	1	−13	181	2	29	146
40	996	232	445	1,456	1	−13	181	2	29	146
43	996	232	445	1,457	1	−13	182	2	29	146
46	997	231	446	1,458	1	−13	182	2	29	146
49	997	231	446	1,458	1	−13	182	2	29	146
Equilibrium	997	229	447	1,460	1	−13	182	2	29	146

NOTE: All assets are measured in dollars. The time paths are in response to a $1,000 cash injection. The assumed turnover rate is 12. Redeposit shares are assumed to be 80 percent demand deposits, 10 percent time deposits, and 5 percent to Connecticut banks and 5 percent to Massachusetts banks.

mortgage loans. As a first approximation it can be concluded that this expansion was not at the expense of other forms of credit, since total system holdings of major categories of assets rose.[11]

In summarizing this section, three major results should be emphasized. First, both the equilibrium credit multiplier and the length of the lagged response to a cash injection are critically sensitive to equilibrium cash ratios that intermediaries choose to maintain. Second, the shapes of aggregate adjustment paths vary considerably across a single intermediary's assets and are not necessarily of the same functional form as their micro-counterparts. Finally, the functional form of adjustment paths for a given asset varies across intermediaries, and aggregate (systemwide) portfolio behavior cannot be predicted a priori without a specification of redeposit (portfolio) behavior by the public.[12]

3. On the Estimation and Validation of Deposit Supply Functions

In this section the simulation approach is applied to generate time series of aggregate commercial bank deposits for the period January 1960 through December 1970 from the history of total member bank reserves. With some important qualifications, the generated series may be compared with actual deposit data and the success of the model judged in terms of how strongly generated and actual deposit series are correlated.[13]

As a first step it is necessary to report structural coefficients that relate a bank's reserves to a history of its demand and time deposits. The equilibrium reserves coefficient on time deposits was negative in table 6-6, but not in table 6A-4, where bank effects were not removed. Structural coefficients were taken from both tables to guard against the possibility that perverse results would be obtained from the negative time deposit coefficient. The coefficients are constructed in the same manner as before and are reported in table 12-7.

11. The same conclusion would not obtain if the redeposit shares had gone from (90, 10, 0, 0) to (90, 0, 5, 5) instead of to (80, 10, 5, 5), because in that case total commercial bank credit would have declined, and individuals borrowing primarily from commercial banks would have suffered.

12. A similar finding was previously reported for a quite different model by Brainard and Tobin [1963]. They assumed that portfolio behavior by both intermediaries and the public was a function of market interest rates. This assumption is not necessary to show the pervasive effect of portfolio choices by the public on aggregate asset demand functional forms.

13. The aggregate data are published monthly in the *Federal Reserve Bulletin* and are not seasonally adjusted. Deposit data refer to all commercial banks and include large denomination negotiable certificates of deposit. They are reported in a table entitled "Components of Money Stock Measures and Related Items." Reserves are from a table entitled "Reserves and Borrowings of Member Banks." Both series are measured in billions of dollars.

TABLE 12-7. COMMERCIAL BANK RESERVE PARAMETERS USED IN SIMULATION
EXPERIMENTS

Month	Bank Effects Removed		No Bank Effects Removed	
	Demand	Time	Demand	Time
t_0-t_1	.168	.096	.152	−.067
t_1-t_2	.129	−.025	.131	−.011
t_2-t_3	.137	−.083	.088	−.212
t_3-t_4	.079	.018	.091	−.043
t_4-t_5	.113	−.127	.111	−.115
t_5-t_6	.117	.040	.095	.003
t_6-t_7	.138	.090	.128	−.046
t_7-t_8	.124	−.013	.152	.036
t_8-t_9	.125	−.040	.126	−.091
t_9-t_{10}	.096	−.168	.079	−.204
$t_{10}-t_{11}$	.151	.064	.196	.037
$t_{11}-t_{12}$	.144	−.148	.149	−.142
t_{12}	.106	−.053	.091	.034

NOTE: These parameters are from the results reported in tables 6-5 and 6A-4.

Simulation experiments were performed with turnover rates ranging from twelve to approximately sixty times per year. The set of turnover rates considered in the experiments is reported across the top of table 12-8.[14] In different experiments this array is searched in an attempt to obtain a good estimate of the rate at which deposits turn over in the United States economy. Figure 12-1 shows the relation between selected assumed turnover rates and adjustment paths for aggregate commercial bank deposits.

Similarly, within each experiment an aggregate deposit series is generated for each of a number of different commercial bank redeposit shares. To restrict computer expenses, a relatively coarse array of redeposit shares, ranging from 50 percent to 100 percent in demand deposits, was studied. This array, also reported in table 12-8, was used in two different classes of

14. With a turnover rate of twelve the system has effective use of new deposits once per month, i.e. it can place 100 percent of its undesired cash holdings in earning assets each period. Turnover rates higher than twelve were approximated by linear interpolation. For example, for a turnover rate of twenty-four, it was assumed that the system had effective use of new deposits two times per period. Thus, when calculating deposits for turnover rates of twelve and twenty-four, the system was assumed to place 100 percent and 200 percent, respectively, of its undesired cash holdings in earning assets in each period. This crude interpolation introduces considerable noise or "chatter" in deposit series at high rates of turnover, and largely fails at a turnover rate of sixty.

experiments. The first class is analogous to that just described for generating estimates of the turnover rate; it is assumed that the redeposit share is an institutionally fixed constant. In the second class, the redeposit share is assumed to be a function of the interest rate paid on time deposits. Figure 12-2 shows the relation between selected redeposit shares and adjustment paths for aggregate commercial bank deposits.

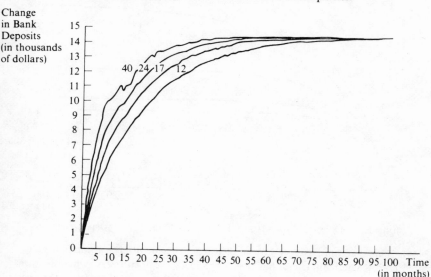

Change in Bank Deposits (in thousands of dollars)

FIGURE 12-1. DEPOSIT ADJUSTMENT PATHS FOR SELECTED TURNOVER RATES

NOTE: This diagram has been constructed from the coefficients in the first half of table 12-7, where bank effects have been removed, and for the case when 75 percent of receipts are assumed to be redeposited in demand accounts and 25 percent in time accounts. It is assumed that the banking system receives a permanent reserve injection of $1,000.

Which of the many possible simulated time series of bank deposits best approximates actual aggregate bank deposits in the United States?[15] An obvious choice is that simulated deposit series which is most highly correlated with the actual time series of aggregate bank deposits. This should be thought of as a maximum-likelihood approach for selecting estimates of the two aggregation parameters depicted in figures 12-1 and

15. Abstracting from cases where redeposit shares are a function of interest rates, so far the text has outlined 180 different time series. There are ten cells in the array of redeposit shares and nine cells in the array of turnover rates; the experiments are based on coefficients that (*a*) ignore and (*b*) remove individual bank effects.

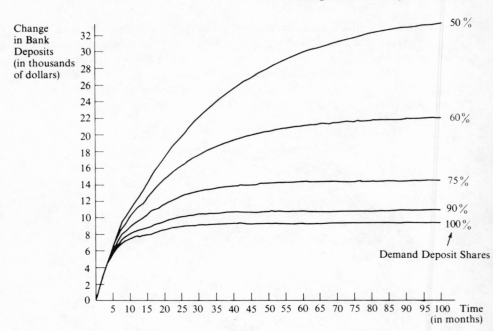

FIGURE 12-2. DEPOSIT ADJUSTMENT PATHS FOR SELECTED REDEPOSIT SHARES

NOTE: This diagram has been constructed from the coefficients in the first half of table 12-7, where bank effects have been removed, and for the case when the turnover rate is assumed to be twenty-four. It is assumed that the banking system receives a permanent reserve injection of $1,000.

12-2.[16] The pair of parameter values that yields the highest correlation between the simulated and actual deposit series would maximize the likelihood of observing the actual deposit series, if error terms in the aggregate relation are assumed to be independent and normally distributed.

As often happens in applied econometrics, these assumptions are not likely to be satisfied. Reserve requirements vary across member banks at a point in time and have changed over time. Since the simulation parameters should vary in response to reserve requirement changes, the use of a single set of parameters introduces errors of an unknown severity. Further, over time (1) new assets and liabilities are introduced, (2) markets are

16. It should be emphasized that the simple textbook credit creation algorithm, as developed here, places severe restrictions on the set of lag distributions that are appropriate for estimating aggregate deposit functions. Once an individual bank's portfolio adjustment pattern is known, only a speed (turnover) parameter and a distributive (redeposit share) parameter are necessary to close the system.

distorted by new legal environments and changes in regulations, and (3) technological innovations in check clearing have occurred; all such changes should cause the values of the two parameters to vary over time.

In addition, the distinction between member and nonmember bank deposits is rather inconsequential in the minds of the public and certainly in the views of modern quantity theorists. Unfortunately, reserves held by nonmember banks are neither homogeneous nor conveniently tabulated at the aggregate level. In order to establish some loose connection between the results of this section and deposit supply models, all commercial bank deposits will be related to reserves of Federal Reserve System member banks. This assumption is probably quite strong, since other investigators—for example, Goldfeld [1966, pp. 147–48]—have reported that deposits of nonmember banks are quite difficult to describe.

With these assumptions, correlations between the synthetic (simulated) and actual deposit series can be evaluated; they are reported in table 12-8.[17] Apart from the last column, which refers to the very crudely interpolated turnover rate of sixty, the "likelihood" surface is remarkably flat. Whether or not bank effects are removed, a slight peak occurs at a turnover rate of forty times per year. When bank effects are removed, this maximum has an associated redeposit share of approximately 100 percent demand deposits (and 0 percent time deposits). When no bank effects are removed, the peak occurs at 70 percent demand and 30 percent time deposits. In both cases, however, the surfaces are so flat that no strong conclusion about redeposit shares should be drawn.

The major conclusion from table 12-8 concerns lags in the deposit supply function. Aggregate data apparently are not capable of discriminating between one hypothesis holding that this function has a very long lag and another that it has a very short lag. This conclusion is very disturbing in view of the willingness of many economists to make very specific policy prescriptions about how the Federal Reserve should act in some relatively short, say, six-month, period. Table 12-8 suggests that there is no empirical basis for placing confidence in their prescriptions.

It is also interesting to examine correlations between synthetic and actual deposit series in subperiods. Table 12-9 reports correlations estimated from these series in two nonoverlapping sixty-six–month time intervals when bank effects are removed. Since many market interest rates were relatively low during the first interval and established one-hundred–year highs in the second, if a strong relation exists between either turnover

17. In constructing synthetic series, monthly reserves data beginning in October 1951 were employed. A 100-month history of reserves was used to generate a money stock estimate on each date in each series.

or redeposit share and interest rates, it should be evident in this table. In both periods, at the maxima the turnover rate was twelve times per year. Although the likelihood surface in both periods was characteristically flat, there is no reason to reject the hypothesis that turnover is independent of interest rates. At the maxima the redeposit share was 75 percent demand deposits in the first subperiod and 100 percent in the second. Given the flatness of the surface, this difference does not seem substantive either.

TABLE 12-8. CORRELATIONS BETWEEN LEVELS OF SYNTHETIC AND ACTUAL DEPOSIT SERIES

Share to Demand Accounts	Annual Turnover Rate[a]								
	12	13.5	15	17	20	24	30	40	60
	Bank Effects Removed								
100%	.975	.976	.977	.977	.978	.978	.979	.979	.979
95	.975	.975	.976	.977	.977	.978	.978	.979	.979
90	.974	.975	.975	.976	.977	.977	.978	.979	.978
85	.973	.974	.975	.975	.976	.977	.977	.978	.978
80	.972	.973	.974	.974	.975	.976	.977	.978	.977
75	.971	.971	.972	.973	.974	.975	.976	.977	.976
70	.969	.970	.971	.972	.973	.974	.975	.976	.973
65	.967	.968	.969	.970	.971	.973	.974	.975	.956
60	.964	.965	.966	.968	.969	.971	.972	.974	.857
50	.955	.956	.958	.960	.962	.964	.966	.968	.159
	No Bank Effects Removed								
100%	.973	.974	.975	.976	.976	.977	.977	.978	.939
95	.974	.974	.975	.976	.976	.977	.978	.978	.927
90	.974	.974	.975	.976	.977	.977	.978	.979	.910
85	.974	.974	.975	.976	.977	.977	.978	.979	.885
80	.974	.974	.975	.976	.977	.978	.978	.979	.852
75	.974	.975	.975	.976	.977	.978	.979	.979	.806
70	.974	.975	.975	.976	.977	.978	.979	.979	.748
65	.974	.975	.976	.976	.977	.978	.978	.979	.678
60	.974	.975	.976	.976	.977	.978	.978	.978	.598
50	.974	.975	.976	.977	.977	.976	.974	.970	.462

NOTE: The series are monthly data for January 1960 through December 1970, seasonally unadjusted. Largest correlation in each table is underscored.
[a] Turnover rates are approximate because of the nonstationarity of the calendar. They can be interpreted as saying that withdrawals are redeposited every 30, 27, 24, 21, 18, 15, 12, 9, and 6 days, respectively.

TABLE 12-9. CORRELATIONS BETWEEN LEVELS OF SYNTHETIC AND ACTUAL
DEPOSIT SERIES: SUBPERIODS

Share to Demand Accounts	Annual Turnover Rate[a]								
	12	13.5	15	17	20	24	30	40	60
	January 1960 through June 1966								
100%	.984	.983	.982	.980	.978	.975	.972	.967	.959
95	.985	.984	.983	.981	.979	.977	.973	.969	.961
90	.986	.985	.984	.983	.981	.978	.975	.971	.963
85	.987	.986	.985	.984	.983	.980	.977	.973	.965
80	.987	.987	.986	.985	.984	.982	.980	.976	.967
75	<u>.987</u>	.987	.987	.987	.985	.984	.982	.978	.969
70	.987	.987	.987	.987	.987	.986	.984	.981	.959
65	.985	.986	.987	.987	.987	.987	.985	.983	.795
60	.982	.983	.985	.986	.987	.987	.987	.985	.028
50	.962	.966	.971	.975	.978	.981	.984	.985	−.303
	July 1966 through December 1970								
100%	<u>.974</u>	.974	.974	.974	.974	.974	.973	.973	.972
95	.974	.974	.974	.974	.974	.974	.973	.973	.972
90	.974	.974	.974	.974	.974	.974	.973	.973	.972
85	.974	.974	.974	.974	.974	.974	.973	.973	.973
80	.974	.974	.974	.974	.974	.974	.973	.973	.973
75	.974	.974	.974	.974	.973	.973	.973	.973	.972
70	.973	.973	.973	.973	.973	.973	.973	.973	.972
65	.973	.973	.973	.973	.973	.973	.973	.973	.965
60	.973	.973	.973	.973	.973	.973	.973	.973	.921
50	.972	.972	.972	.972	.972	.973	.973	.973	.566

NOTE: The data are monthly, seasonally unadjusted. Parameters used to generate
the synthetic series were estimated from data with bank effects removed. Largest
correlation in each table is underscored.

[a] Turnover rates are approximate because of the nonstationarity of the calendar.
They can be interpreted as saying that withdrawals are redeposited every 30, 27, 24,
21, 18, 15, 12, 9, and 6 days, respectively.

One criticism that might be directed toward this analysis is that the
method generates good estimates of the average turnover and redeposit
share parameters, but not necessarily the more relevant marginal parameters. In an attempt to examine this issue, correlations were also computed for first differences of actual and synthetic series. If the average and
marginal parameters are identical, the estimates from analyzing levels and
first differences should be similar.

In Table 12-10 correlations between first differences of actual and synthetic series can be seen to have a maximum value at a turnover rate of twelve times per year, whether or not bank effects are removed. Indeed, it seems likely that the surface would peak at an even lower turnover rate, although this possibility was not explored. The value of the redeposit share at the maximum was quite sensitive to whether or not bank effects were removed. When bank effects were removed, the peak occurred when 50 percent of receipts were allocated each to demand and time accounts;

TABLE 12-10. CORRELATIONS BETWEEN FIRST DIFFERENCES OF SYNTHETIC AND ACTUAL DEPOSIT SERIES

Share to Demand Accounts	Annual Turnover Rate[a]								
	12	13.5	15	17	20	24	30	40	60
	Bank Effects Removed								
100%	.137	.133	.128	.122	.114	.104	.092	.078	.071
95	.139	.134	.128	.124	.115	.106	.094	.081	.074
90	.143	.138	.131	.124	.117	.107	.095	.083	.075
85	.145	.138	.136	.126	.120	.108	.097	.085	.073
80	.149	.143	.138	.131	.123	.114	.101	.088	.065
75	.154	.149	.142	.137	.127	.117	.104	.090	.056
70	.159	.155	.148	.140	.131	.122	.108	.095	.032
65	.165	.161	.155	.147	.139	.129	.116	.099	−.016
60	.172	.167	.162	.155	.148	.135	.123	.105	−.058
50	.185	.182	.178	.174	.168	.159	.149	.113	−.125
	No Bank Effects Removed								
100%	.155	.150	.145	.139	.129	.116	.100	.081	.031
95	.152	.148	.141	.134	.126	.113	.097	.075	.030
90	.149	.144	.138	.132	.123	.111	.092	.071	.030
85	.146	.141	.133	.127	.120	.108	.091	.066	.031
80	.142	.135	.129	.122	.114	.102	.088	.063	.032
75	.138	.132	.123	.116	.107	.098	.083	.059	.034
70	.131	.125	.117	.107	.097	.088	.075	.058	.037
65	.126	.118	.109	.098	.087	.075	.063	.052	.040
60	.120	.111	.098	.085	.071	.055	.045	.042	.044
50	.107	.093	.074	.052	.026	−.005	−.029	−.006	.052

NOTE: The data are monthly, January 1960 through December 1970, seasonally unadjusted. Largest correlation in each table is underscored.

[a] Turnover rates are approximate because of the nonstationarity of the calendar. They can be interpreted as saying that withdrawals are redeposited every 30, 27, 24, 21, 18, 15, 12, 9, and 6 days, respectively.

otherwise, the peak occurred when nearly 100 percent of receipts were placed in demand accounts. No explanation for this difference is apparent. Finally, in studying first differences, the surface has more curvature than was true for deposit levels.

The conclusion is that for the whole period, marginal and average turnover rates differ and that marginal turnover rates are very low. This in turn suggests that reserve injections are transmitted into aggregate deposit changes with a sizeable lag. Unlike the analysis of levels, the sharper features of the surface now suggest that lag structures might be identified from first differences of aggregate data, but this observation requires additional study. If the lag is as long as these results indicate, it is doubtful that the money stock could be varied to eliminate short-term economic fluctuations without inducing wild movements in interest rates and possibly destabilizing the economy.

The relation between aggregate bank deposits and interest rates was investigated in three stages. First, the redeposit share was related to a series of time deposit interest rates.[18] Then a redeposit share, determined by the interest rate on a date, was used together with each of the turnover rates and the history of reserves to generate a level of bank deposits on that date. Finally, the correlation between the actual deposit series and the synthetic series associated with each turnover rate was computed. The turnover rate yielding the highest correlation defined the aggregate supply function.

The relation between redeposit share and interest rates was assumed to be linear in logarithms. It was estimated from 144 successive monthly observations commencing in January 1959. The result was

$$\text{Ln} \frac{T}{D + T} = -1.6337 + .7328 \, \text{Ln} \, r \qquad S_\varepsilon = .066$$
$$(.0356) \quad (.0282) \qquad R^2 = .826$$

where

T = aggregate commercial bank time deposits,
D = aggregate commercial bank demand deposits, and
r = interest rate paid on time deposits (percent per annum).

Residuals estimated for this equation exhibit some serial correlation, but do not indicate that the relation was grossly misspecified. Unfornately, during the 132-month period, the share of time deposits in total

18. The deposit interest rate series was compiled at midmonth by the Federal Reserve Bank of Chicago from a sample of Seventh District member banks. Its regional character is undesirable, but it is the best series on time deposit interest rates known to the authors. Because of its timing, the series was always lagged one month in the present study.

deposits was rarely less than 40 percent. Consequently, the equation never predicted a value of the redeposit share that had more than 60 percent of receipts being redeposited in demand accounts. This implies that only a small fraction of possible synthetic series was ever used.[19] For the 132-month period, and apart from the poorly interpolated sixty times-a-year turnover case, the likelihood surface was essentially flat whether or not bank effects were removed. When bank effects were removed, the correlations were between .916 and .920; when not removed, they ranged from .978 to .984.

As in table 12-8, which did not consider interest rates, the conclusion is that the present analysis has not identified the lag between changes in reserves and changes in bank deposits. Intuitively, the reason for this failure is that different lag structures are all linear functions of the same time series of reserves, and weights do not differ that greatly for the turnover rates being examined. The difficulty in identifying lag structures in economic time series is well known [Griliches, 1967]; however, it had been hoped that the extensive restrictions imposed from the cross-section structure and the aggregation algorithm would shed more light than they did on the impact of reserves changes.[20]

4. MACRO-POLICY AND AGGREGATE BANK PORTFOLIO BEHAVIOR

The failure to identify a robust lag structure for the deposit supply function, in the preceding section and elsewhere, severely limits the policy lessons that can be drawn from this analysis. Lag structures, together with the set of information available to monetary authorities, determine what, if any, policy actions should be adopted on a date. In the absence of known lag structures, it is difficult to evaluate a sequence of policy actions. This section, therefore, discusses a number of issues that involve policy formation and stabilization, but it provides no touchstone.

Before turning to these topics, it is helpful briefly to survey other evidence about lag structures. Figure 12-3 shows that deposit turnover, measured by debit statistics, has varied considerably through time and

19. In principle, it would have been possible to expand the array within the range of redeposit share values of, say, 45 percent to 60 percent. However, in view of the facts that (1) the model would blow up for low values of the redeposit share when bank effects are removed, and (2) when no bank effects were removed the likelihood surface was essentially flat, this modification did not seem promising.

20. There is a possibility of gaining information about the lag structure by studying changes in different aggregate bank assets simultaneously.

that it varies among banks. The turnover rate studied in the preceding section is an average rate and therefore a function both of intertemporal variations in individual bank debit/deposit ratios and the relative growth rates of banks with different debit/deposit ratios. So, it is not altogether surprising that a sharp estimate of the turnover rate failed to emerge from section 3.

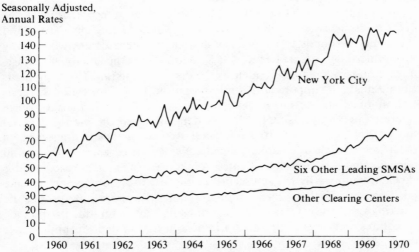

FIGURE 12-3. DEMAND DEPOSIT TURNOVER AT SELECTED BANKING CENTERS
(JANUARY 1960–JUNE 1970)
SOURCE: *Federal Reserve Bulletin*, various issues.

Similarly, during the decade commencing in January 1960, flow-of-funds statistics [Board of Governors of the Federal Reserve System, February 1968] indicate that different nonbank financial intermediaries grew at very different rates. This strongly suggests that redeposit shares were not constant across intermediaries. There is no reason to think that the share of bank deposits that savers hold as time deposits is independent of the composition of their nonbank financial assets. Again, the result in section 3 that a good estimate of the redeposit parameter failed to emerge was perhaps to be expected.

a. Lags in the "demand" for money

Many other investigators have studied money in relation to interest rates, income, wealth, and the reserve base. It is not productive to review this extensive literature, since the vast majority of these studies cannot be

meaningfully compared. Almost all studies differ in their underlying
theoretical specifications. In addition, many different estimation techniques have been employed; some investigators use single-equation
estimating methods to study demand and/or supply functions, while
others employ simultaneous equation methods to examine very intricate
models. Finally, most investigators have estimated relationships from
data pertaining to different time spans.

However, the model of section 2 does afford an interpretation of one
of the most surprising results in this literature—the finding that the demand
for money responds to changes in short-term interest rates with a very
pronounced lag [e.g. de Leeuw, 1965]. This finding appears to be a consequence, in part, of failing to identify the demand function. Two arguments
can be made in support of this interpretation. First, figure 12-4 suggests
how an open market sale might be expected to affect both the short-term
interest rate and the supply of bank deposits when the money demand
function is free of lags. If the Federal Reserve makes a single sale of
securities at time t_1, banks immediately will experience a decline in
deposits and a rise in interest rates. As the banking system reacts to this
shock, it temporarily will sell securities in order to restore its cash reserve
position; this further drives up interest rates. As more time passes, the
banking system slowly succeeds in curbing its loan commitments and then
reacquires securities so that the ratio of securities to deposits approaches
its preshock value.

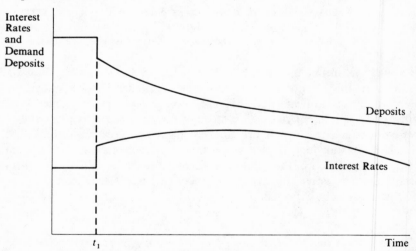

FIGURE 12-4. TIME TRAJECTORIES OF INTEREST RATES AND DEMAND DEPOSITS IN
RESPONSE TO AN OPEN MARKET SALE

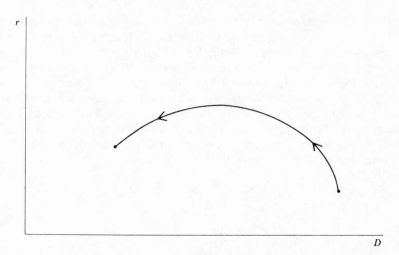

FIGURE 12-5. HYPOTHETICAL TIME SERIES OF INTEREST RATES AND DEPOSITS

The relation between deposits and interest rates is not monotone, as can be seen in figure 12-5, which was constructed from figure 12-4. It will be poorly represented by simple exponential distributed lag formulations; estimated lags will be exaggerated. The important point is that open market transactions themselves induce a negative relation between money and interest rates, and it is misleading to interpret such technical relations as describing only the public's demand for money. The public will *demand* higher interest rates before absorbing the securities, and banks will *supply* the public with fewer deposits *and* temporarily more securities.

The second argument about lack of identification applies both to earlier studies and to the approach of the present chapter. It derives from the fact that the Federal Reserve itself attempts to maintain "orderly" financial markets. For present purposes, an orderly market is defined to be a market in which either the quantity or the price changes by no more than a limit value, $\overline{\Delta Q}$ or $\overline{\Delta P}$, respectively, in some time interval. In practice, the Federal Reserve attempts to mitigate day-to-day variations in short-term rates of interest.[21] Figure 12-6 suggests that even if banks

21. The Federal Reserve's concern with interest rates can be attributed to the fact that it has very poor information about the quantity of money in the economy on any day, but it has continuous accurate information on interest rates. Indeed, revisions of money stock series are quite large over a number of weeks. Given the difference in the qualities of the two series, maintaining orderly markets can be achieved only by monitoring and responding to interest rates.

and the public responded instantaneously, some time would be required before the Federal Reserve would allow a shift from supply schedule 1 to supply schedule 2 to occur. When lagged behavior by banks is present, the form of the lags can be altered by Federal Reserve policy. With an orderly money market interest rate objective, the Federal Reserve is likely to make reserve injections endogenous by responding to bank behavior. Apparently no investigators have removed distortions introduced by the Federal Reserve, and in that sense they have failed to identify behavioral relations by the public or the banks, respectively. Estimated lag structures include behavior by the monetary authority, the banks, and the public.

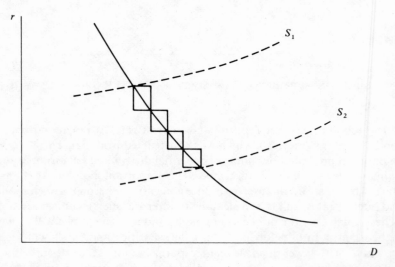

FIGURE 12-6. THE EFFECT OF MAINTAINING ORDERLY MARKETS IN A STATIC MODEL

b. Simulation experiments and some policy issues

In order to use simulation results to study policy questions, it is still necessary to assume values for redeposit share and turnover parameters. In view of the lack of robust empirical estimates of these parameters, the following should be interpreted qualitatively and not as predictions about actual time paths. Five experiments are described and concern (1) an interpretation of the "liquidity trap" episode toward the end of the Great Depression, (2) the trade-off between size of an open-market transaction and time proximity to a mortgage loan target, and (3) two variations of a proposal by Milton Friedman that the money stock should grow at a constant geometric rate. A turnover rate of twelve is assumed in all five experiments.

The first two experiments, which are reported in tables 12-11 and 12-12, utilize redeposit share assumptions that were previously considered in section 2.[22] In the first, 90 percent of receipts are redeposited in demand

TABLE 12-11. COMMERCIAL BANK RESPONSES TO MASSIVE MONETARY INJECTIONS: PURE COMMERCIAL BANK SYSTEM

Month	Cash	Deposits	Shorts	Cash + Shorts Deposits	Cash Deposits
1	$ 374	$1,000	$ 284	.658	.374
4	1,460	5,183	1,638	.598	.282
7	3,503	13,871	4,370	.568	.253
10	6,010	24,931	7,256	.532	.241
13	7,425	32,285	7,940	.476	.230
16	8,329	35,958	6,314	.407	.232
19	8,727	37,493	4,340	.349	.233
22	8,833	38,140	3,045	.311	.232
25	8,875	38,590	2,543	.296	.230
28	8,909	38,933	2,398	.290	.229
31	8,942	39,171	2,345	.288	.228
34	8,969	39,315	2,288	.286	.228
37	8,984	39,390	2,236	.285	.228
40	8,991	39,430	2,199	.284	.228
43	8,995	39,452	2,178	.283	.228
46	8,997	39,467	2,168	.283	.228
49	8,998	39,476	2,163	.283	.228
Equilibrium	$9,000	$39,496[a]	$2,158[a]	.283	.228

NOTE: The time paths are in response to an initial demand deposit injection of $1,000 plus additional exogenous injections of $1,000 in each of eight consecutive months. Redeposit shares are assumed to be 90 percent demand deposits and 10 percent time deposits. The assumed turnover rate is 12.
[a] Extrapolated approximation.

22. The experiments could also have been performed using the deposit supply formulation of section 3 with results similar to those reported in the text.

accounts, and 10 percent in time accounts. In the second, 80 percent go to demand accounts, 10 percent to time accounts, and 10 percent to savings bank accounts. The experiments illustrate how these hypothetical systems respond to repeated deposit injections by the monetary authority. They suggest that commercial bank portfolio behavior during the years 1936–40 was not especially different from bank practice in years immediately following 1960 and can be understood without imposing any assumptions

TABLE 12-12. COMMERCIAL BANK RESPONSES TO MASSIVE MONETARY INJECTIONS:
MIXED COMMERCIAL AND SAVINGS BANK SYSTEM

Month	Cash	Deposits	Shorts	Cash + Shorts	Cash
				Deposits	Deposits
1	$ 374	$ 1,000	$ 284	.658	.374
4	1,346	4,829	1,525	.595	.279
7	3,253	12,983	4,077	.565	.251
10	5,638	23,585	6,863	.530	.239
13	7,074	31,049	7,699	.476	.228
16	8,040	35,147	6,362	.410	.229
19	8,513	37,147	4,595	.353	.229
22	8,687	38,152	3,350	.316	.228
25	8,771	38,815	2,795	.298	.226
28	8,829	39,280	2,577	.290	.225
31	8,877	39,597	2,474	.287	.224
34	8,912	39,797	2,393	.284	.224
37	8,934	39,915	2,330	.282	.224
40	8,946	39,985	2,285	.281	.224
43	8,953	40,027	2,258	.280	.224
46	8,957	40,053	2,242	.280	.224
49	8,959	40,070	2,233	.279	.224
Equilib-rium	$8,965[a]	$40,109[a]	$2,211[a]	.279	.224

NOTE: The time paths are in response to an initial demand deposit injection of $1,000 plus additional exogenous injections of $1,000 in each of eight consecutive months. Redeposit shares are assumed to be 80 percent demand deposits, 10 percent time deposits, 5 percent to a Connecticut savings bank, and 5 percent to a Massachusetts savings bank. The assumed turnover rate is 12.

[a] Extrapolated approximation.

about the elasticity of interest rate expectations.[23] Two facts about the earlier period set the stage for this demonstration. First, with the exception of 1937, total reserves *and deposits* of the banking system grew at very rapid rates. Second, short-term securities paid very low interest rates; these rates probably did not cover transactions costs when securities were held for only a few weeks. Consequently, it is likely that short-term securities and cash were nearly perfect substitutes, and possible that cash actually dominated prime short-term securities in bank portfolios.

In each experiment, after an initial demand deposit injection of $1,000, banks' capacity to lend was exogenously expanded by an additional $1,000 in each of eight consecutive months. As reported in tables 12-11 and 12-12, these injections produced a perceptible increase in the ratio of cash to deposits for about one year. However, given the rate at which deposits were growing in the latter half of the Depression (10 to 20 percent per annum), this cash effect is not sufficient to account for the observed large increases of excess reserves in the banking system.

The series of injections produced a considerably more pronounced increase in cash plus short-term government securities as a percentage of deposits. During the year after initiating the simulation, this percentage averaged about 57 percent in each experiment; it remained above equilibrium during the second year as well. The experiments imply that a banking system with no growth in deposits should be observed in the long run to have cash plus short-term securities as a percentage of total deposits equal to 28 percent; for a system with deposits growing at 10 percent per annum, this percentage should be 31 percent; and for a system with deposits growing at 20 percent per annum, this percentage should be 34 percent.

Table 12-13 reports information about member bank reserves and financial assets during the Depression. Since short-maturity government securities were held by banks in negligible quantities during the late years of the Depression [Board of Governors of the Federal Reserve System, 1943, p. 109], portfolio percentages in the preceding paragraph may be compared roughly with total reserves as a percentage of the sum of reserves, loans, and investments in table 12-13. Between December 1936 and December 1937 this sum fell 2 percent, and the reserves percentage was 22 percent. In successive years thereafter the sum grew 7 percent, 11 percent, and 16 percent per annum, and the corresponding year-end reserves percentages were 27 percent, 31 percent, and 35 percent. Despite

---

23. A somewhat similar interpretation of bank behavior during the Depression has been suggested by Morrison [1966].

the crudeness of the comparison, the similarity between the actual experience and the simulation results is remarkable.[24]

TABLE 12-13. YEAR-END MEMBER BANK RESERVES, LOANS, AND INVESTMENTS
(in billions of dollars)

Year	Total Reserves	Loans	U.S. Govt. Securities	Other Securities	Sum
1933	3.8	12.8	7.3	5.1	29.0
1934	5.4	12.0	10.9	5.2	33.6
1935	7.8	12.2	12.3	5.5	37.8
1936	9.1	13.4	13.5	6.1	42.1
1937	9.4	14.0	12.4	5.4	41.2
1938	12.1	13.2	13.2	5.6	44.2
1939	15.4	14.0	14.3	5.7	49.3
1940	19.9	15.3	15.8	6.0	57.0

SOURCE: E. A. Goldenweiser, *American Economic Policy* (New York: McGraw-Hill,
1951), pp. 328–57.

The third experiment considers the relation between the date an action
is taken and the size of a deposit injection necessary to achieve a desired
increment to mortgage loans on some specified future date. It is assumed
that monetary authorities desire to make a single transaction on the action
date that will suffice to promote a $1 billion increase in mortgage lending
on, say, December 31 of the next year.[25] In this experiment 80 percent of
receipts are assumed to be redeposited in demand accounts, 10 percent
in time accounts, and 10 percent in savings bank accounts. From table 12-6
it can be seen that open market purchases of about $31 billion would be
required to hit this target in one month. If the target were to be reached
in four months, a purchase of about $8.8 billion would be required. After
seven months a purchase of about $3.6 billion, after ten months a purchase
of about $2.2 billion, and after fifty months a purchase of about $1.3

24. In view of the collapse of the banking system in 1933, it is not likely that the simulation
experiments would track aggregate bank deposits before 1937. Total reserves of the banking
system as a fraction of deposits did not begin to approach 1960 reserve requirements until
1936. Also between 1936 and 1940, actual bank loans were much smaller relative to security
holdings than was predicted in simulation experiments. Evidently the structure of interest
rates and/or Depression loan-loss experience led banks to avoid private sector advances
during that period.
25. For simplicity, the authorities are assumed to be unconcerned with the level of mortgage lending before and after this hypothetical date. Brito and Hester [1974] study control
problems in which the authorities seek to stabilize some variable continuously in a simple
financial system.

billion would be necessary. Obviously, forecasting the demand for and supply of mortgage loans and other illiquid assets is necessary if targets for such variables are to be hit without large open market transactions.

Experiments four and five concern a strategy for controlling the money stock often associated with the name of Milton Friedman. The monetary authorities are assumed to desire that commercial bank deposits grow at some constant geometric rate, say, 0.33 percent per month. In experiment four they start with an initial nonexpanding commercial bank deposit stock of $160 billion and cause it to increase by exactly 0.33 percent per month by engaging in open market operations. Unlike preceding experiments, open market operations produce simultaneous flows into demand, time, and savings accounts.[26] The redeposit shares are those of the mixed commercial-savings bank system just considered.

The first half of table 12-14 shows changes in various financial assets from their pre-experiment stationary levels. After a series of damped oscillations associated with initiating the experiment, all financial assets tend toward an equilibrium position where their proportions are invariant.[27] This "moving" equilibrium differs from the stationary equilibrium portfolio that would obtain in the absence of deposit growth; the difference is a function of the desired growth rate. For example, mortgage loans are 20.6 percent of commercial bank deposits in the moving equilibrium, but in the stationary equilibrium this percentage is 21 percent. Similarly, short-term government securities held by commercial banks are 6.2 percent of their deposits in the moving equilibrium and 5.6 percent in the stationary equilibrium. These differences are negligible for moderate variations in the deposit growth rate.

Experiment five examines the consequences of applying the constant geometric growth rule imperfectly and illustrates how erratic policies tend to influence different assets in bank portfolios. In this example monetary authorities are assumed to be ignorant of lags in bank portfolio adjustment and to make open market transactions infrequently—that is, once every five months. In determining open market transactions, they make a purchase or sale in the next period that would have been just

26. Previously, injections initially appeared as demand deposits and then flowed into other accounts according to redeposit share specifications. Note that in order for monetary authorities to be able to determine deposits exactly, they must have complete and current knowledge about the cash positions of banks. This requirement is relaxed in the next experiment.

27. This happens because the structure is a linear difference equation system having a stable equilibrium; autonomous cash injections by the authorities eventually grow at the same rate as deposits. As Brito and Hester [1974] show, the difference equation equilibrium may not be stable when monetary authorities have incomplete information about bank behavior and/or cash positions.

TABLE 12-14. FINANCIAL CHANGES IN RESPONSE TO INTRODUCTION OF GEOMETRIC GROWTH OF BANK DEPOSITS
(in millions of dollars)

Month	Steady Reserve Growth					Erratic Reserve Growth				
	Commercial Bank Deposits	Savings Bank Deposits	Total Mortgage[a]	Shorts[b]	Other[c] Loans	Commercial Bank Deposits	Savings Bank Deposits	Total Mortgage[a]	Shorts	Other Loans
1	533	59	24	155	85	0	0	0	0	0
4	2,144	238	141	709	420	0	0	0	0	0
7	3,771	419	358	1,140	807	5,534	614	330	1,735	1,018
10	5,414	602	652	1,415	1,256	4,615	512	691	1,605	1,236
13	7,074	786	968	1,476	1,777	2,065	230	750	−238	745
16	8,750	972	1,314	1,580	2,337	12,284	1,364	1,084	2,532	2,842
19	10,443	1,160	1,664	1,685	2,903	20,931	2,326	2,043	5,951	4,616
22	12,153	1,350	2,017	1,791	3,475	729	81	1,918	−1,677	1,785
25	13,880	1,542	2,373	1,898	4,052	16,460	1,828	1,673	77	3,284
28	15,625	1,736	2,734	2,006	4,635	43,562	4,840	3,712	12,093	10,263
31	17,387	1,932	3,097	2,115	5,224	−4,593	−510	4,078	−3,637	1,771
34	19,167	2,130	3,465	2,226	5,819	−45,855	−5,094	836	−23,116	−5,118
37	20,964	2,329	3,836	2,337	6,420	87,517	9,724	4,033	22,655	15,984
40	22,780	2,531	4,211	2,450	7,027	5,086	566	7,979	13,095	10,785
43	24,614	2,735	4,589	2,563	7,640	—	—	—	—	—
46	26,466	2,941	4,972	2,678	8,259	—	—	—	—	—
49	28,337	3,149	5,358	2,794	8,885	—	—	—	—	—

[a] At both commercial and mutual savings banks.
[b] At commercial banks.
[c] Commercial and industrial plus consumer loans at commercial banks.

sufficient to hit their target value (growing at 0.33 percent per month) at the time of the decision.

As is evident in the second half of table 12-14, this policy is a disaster; deviations from the base period levels of different financial assets exhibit growing cyclical instability. The reason is that with a turnover rate of twelve, the banking system multiplies these periodic deposit flows at a rate that is not consistent with long-term exponential growth of deposits. In this hypothetical nonstochastic world, it is not feasible for monetary authorities to make the money supply closely follow an exponential growth path.[28] In order for monetary authorities to avoid destabilizing financial markets, they must react very weakly to deviations between actual and desired deposit levels. For example, on transaction dates they should not attempt to close more than perhaps 5 percent of the gap between desired and actual levels through direct purchases or sales. A mild policy stance like this implies that they (and their monetarist critics) must be willing to tolerate quite extended periods of time when the money stock is either above or below its desired level, if policy is not to be destabilizing.[29]

Individual bank assets fluctuate quite differently in response to this policy, although all experience growing oscillations. Easily the most volatile are cash (not shown in table 12-14) and commercial bank short-term government securities. This happens because their adjustment paths are "peaked" and because banks hold small amounts of them in equilibrium relative to their adjustment path peaks. These assets respond very strongly to individual monthly deposit inflows. Mortgage and other bank loans with rising adjustment paths are likely to exhibit less volatility.[30] Some support for this conclusion is evident in the table.

To conclude the discussion of experiments four and five, it appears that a precise application of the geometric growth of deposits rule leads to aggregate bank portfolios that are only slightly different from the stationary cases heretofore called equilibrium portfolios. However, if deposits are not frequently controlled and/or if information about aggregate deposits

28. We are indebted to Professor D. L. Brito for valuable discussions of this example.

29. The system is explosive in this experiment because it is allowed to build up momentum between transaction dates. The system can be similarly explosive if monetary authorities are responding continuously to ancient or inaccurate data about the level of deposits.

30. If a series of independent deposit shocks, drawn from a distribution with a positive mean and a finite variance, is applied to the system under study, loans and long-term securities will tend to have a smaller coefficient of variation than, say, short-term securities. This can be seen by recognizing that the ancient level of deposits can be rewritten as a sum of prior deposit changes. Then the amount of any asset can be written as a weighted average of past deposit flows where (1) the weights are constructed from its adjustment path coefficients, (2) the standard deviation is an increasing function of the weights, and (3) the mean is independent of the weights.

is obtained with a lag, rote adherence to such a rule can get an economy
into serious trouble. The trouble is both that total bank deposits may
develop instability and that credit flows to different sectors may become
indefensibly erratic. It can be avoided if monetary authorities can be
persuaded not to attempt to reach their target deposit growth path pre-
cipitously.

Postscript

The drafting of this monograph spanned seven years. During this period banking changed greatly, and our own understanding of banks and their problems grew considerably. We attempted to maintain continuity of argument by sticking to our original plan. Consequently, a number of recent econometric and theoretical contributions have been ignored. A brief summary of what has been learned and a listing of those topics that appear to be most deserving of future study follows.

1. WHAT HAS BEEN LEARNED?

We undertook this study to analyze bank data that were available and that represented a very rich resource for (1) testing hypotheses about bank behavior, (2) estimating lags that are associated with monetary policy instruments, and (3) studying the ways in which financial intermediaries interact.

Arguments about bank behavior posed in chapters 2, 3 and 4 were supported by results described in chapters 6 through 11. Lagged responses by commercial banks to deposit shocks largely confirmed theoretical predictions and were found to be intertemporally invariant. Skepticism about the meaning and importance of *market* interest rates as opposed to *net* rates of return in describing variations in bank portfolios was reinforced by evidence from statistical cost accounting, reported in chapter 10. While gross rates of return differed among assets, net rates of return on different bank assets were very similar. Finally, banks that were unusually profitable, after adjusting for variations in portfolio composition, were observed to exhibit portfolio adjustment paths that are much closer to those predicted theoretically than are those of less profitable banks. The conclusion is that costs of adjustment to shocks are very important in accounting for variations in bank portfolios and profits. Variations in net interest rates may also play a role in explaining variations in bank portfolios, but if our findings are accepted, they play a secondary role within a given financial institution. Interest rate variations probably play a very important indirect role in determining how funds flow among intermediaries, as is noted below.

When mutual savings banks were studied, there was evidence that costs of adjustment were again an important determinant of variations in portfolios. However, results varied considerably across different subsamples of savings banks, and the portfolio equations were not time invariant. In part, intersample variations could be attributed to differences in supervisory agency environments. The observed interbank portfolio differences and the lack of invariance also appear to be attributable to the indefiniteness that characterizes the objective function of a mutual organization. Samples of commercial and mutual savings banks were observed over the same time period and were largely drawn from the same geographic area. It is therefore unlikely that factor costs or rates of return on comparable assets differed for these two intermediaries. What did differ were their organization charters and the set of regulations by which they were supervised.

Great difficulty was encountered in attempting to identify lags that described the response of the banking system to policy actions. A deposit shock to an individual bank was found to have measurable effects on different assets in a commercial bank's portfolio for approximately one year. Since lags are also associated with interbank flows of funds, it is likely that the aggregate portfolio of all commercial banks in a system would respond with a distributed lag that is considerably longer than a year. In simulation experiments, it was noted that lags tended to be longer when deposit turnover was slower and when the marginal share of deposits reappearing in bank time accounts was larger. We were, however, not able to estimate reliably the speed with which a banking system would convert a reserve injection into a near equilibrium level of bank deposits. Point estimates described in the last chapter suggested that the lags are quite long—on the order of a few years for 90 percent of the effects of a shock to be realized.

Introduction of a second intermediary, mutual savings banks, to the commercial banking system appeared to affect the demand for certain financial assets (like mortgage loans) markedly and might also alter the speed with which the combined financial system adjusts to policy-induced shocks. Since neither deposit turnover nor portfolio behavior by individual depositors was examined thoroughly, the effects of adding new financial intermediaries could not be analyzed completely in this study. To the extent that additional numbers of depository institutions are included, it seems likely that longer systemwide adjustment patterns would be observed. Moreover, if interest rate movements cause deposits to flow from one type of account to another or across intermediaries, very different shapes of systemwide adjustment paths are likely to be observed for different assets.

A finding of methodological interest is that it is possible to formulate rather elaborate "expectational" models of firm behavior that significantly explain variations in bank portfolios. Individual deposit forecasting equations were estimated for each bank, and they were quite successful. However, the forecasts produced from these equations undoubtedly differed from forecasts that sample banks actually made. The very complicated adaptive-expectations model of portfolio behavior described in chapter 9, which used the equation forecasts, was slightly less successful in describing variations in bank portfolios than was the much simpler and less plausible input-output model of chapter 6. The conclusion is *not* that simplicity is a virtue, but rather that intricate models that involve unobserved variables almost necessarily incorporate errors in variables and are extremely difficult to validate. Economists should make very modest claims about the role of expectations in empirical models until expectations can in fact be identified.

Finally, a few comments on the usefulness of large cross-section studies like this one can be offered. The present study has been both more time consuming for us and more informative to us than we had reason to expect. We were inexperienced and inefficient in assembling large data files from different sources. However, even an experienced investigator would have been appalled by the number of inconsistencies and pathological situations that we encountered in merging these comparatively clean data. The numbers aside, we have argued strongly that microeconomic data are the essential element in advancing economic science. Since almost all reasoning that underlies modern economic analysis has a microeconomic rationalization, it is critically important that hypotheses be tested at the micro-level, where they can be directly examined with large numbers of observations.

It is true that careful analysis of large cross-section data files is incredibly expensive. As institutions and technologies change, the social value of such analyses depreciates. It is therefore very important that anyone contemplating a large cross-section study be able to defend the lasting scientific value of the answers that he seeks.

By way of contrast, aggregate time series are constructed in ways that largely ignore both institutional and technological change. Investigators rarely explain how aggregation occurs, particularly when lags are present. These data are invaluable when forecasting and when piecing macro-models together, but they are quite incapable of verifying the fine points of economic theory.

2. What Should Be Done Next?

This study raised more questions than it answered—as it should have. The following seem most important:

1. What determines the speed at which financial assets turn over and what effect will automated clearing and expanding third-party transfers have on this parameter (or vector of parameters)?
2. What determines redeposit shares and how will the development of financial conglomerates affect shares in the future?
3. How will portfolio behavior differ from that described in this volume when the model is modified to let deposits be endogenously controlled by banks through bidding with interest rates—particularly if Regulation Q is dismantled?
4. What do mutual organizations maximize?

Selected Bibliography

Aigner, D. J., and C. M. Sprenkle. 1968. A simple model of information and lending behavior. *Journal of Finance* 23 (March): 151–66.

Aigner, D. J., and C. M. Sprenkle. 1969. A note on the optimal financing of inventory holdings. *Workshop series 6845*, Social Systems Research Institute, University of Wisconsin (mimeographed).

Allen, R. G. D. 1967. *Macro-Economic Theory: A Mathematical Treatment.* St. Martin's Press, New York.

Almon, S. 1965. The distributed lag between capital appropriations and expenditures. *Econometrica* 33 (January): 178–96.

American Bankers Association. 1962. *The Commercial Banking Industry.* Monograph prepared for the Commission on Money and Credit. Prentice-Hall, Englewood Cliffs, N.J.

Arrow, K., T. Harris, and J. Marschak. 1951. Optimal inventory policy. *Econometrica* 19 (July): 250–72.

Aschheim, J. 1959. Open-market operations versus reserve-requirement variation. *Economic Journal* 69 (December): 697–704.

Baumol, W. J. 1952. The transactions demand for cash: an inventory theoretic approach. *Quarterly Journal of Economics* 66 (November): 545–56.

Baumol, W. J. 1967. *Business Behavior, Value and Growth*, revised ed. Harcourt, Brace, and World, New York.

Beckhart, B. H., ed. 1959. *Business Loans of American Commercial Banks.* Ronald Press, New York.

Berle, A. A., Jr., and G. C. Means. 1933. *The Modern Corporation and Private Property.* Macmillan, New York.

Besen, S. M. 1965. An empirical analysis of commercial bank lending behavior. *Yale Economic Essays* 5 (Fall): 283–315.

Board of Governors of the Federal Reserve System. 1943. *Banking and Monetary Statistics.* Washington, D.C.

Board of Governors of the Federal Reserve System. 1959. *The Federal Funds Market.* Washington, D.C.

Board of Governors of the Federal Reserve System. 1968. *Flow-of-Funds Accounts 1945–1967.* Washington, D.C.

Borch, K. 1969. A note on uncertainty and indifference curves. *Review of Economic Studies* 36 (January): 1–4.

Brainard, W. C. and J. Tobin. 1963. Financial intermediaries and the effectiveness of monetary controls. *American Economic Review* 53 (May): 383–400.

Brainard, W. C., and J. Tobin. 1968. Pitfalls in financial model building. *American Economic Review* 58 (May): 99–122.

Brito, D. L. 1970. On the limits of economic control. Unpublished doctoral dissertation. Rice University, Houston, Texas.

Brito, D. L., and D. D. Hester. 1974. Stability and control of the money supply. *Quarterly Journal of Economics* 88 (May): 278–303.

Brunner, K. 1961. A schema for the supply theory of money. *International Economic Review* 2 (January): 79–109.

Brunner, K., and A. H. Meltzer. 1964. Some further investigations of demand and supply functions for money. *Journal of Finance* 19 (May): 240–83.

Bryan, W. R. 1967. Bank adjustments to monetary policy: alternative estimates of the lag. *American Economic Review* 57 (September): 855–64.

Bryan, W. R. and W. T. Carleton. 1967. Short-run adjustments of an individual bank. *Econometrica* 35 (April): 321–47.

Carson, D., and I. O. Scott, Jr. 1963. Commercial bank attributes and aversion to risk. In D. Carson, ed. *Banking and Monetary Studies*. Irwin, Homewood, Illinois: 420–33.

Chow, G. C. 1966. On the long-run and short-run demand for money. *Journal of Political Economy* 74 (April): 111–31.

Chambers, D., and A. Charnes. 1961. Inter-temporal analysis and optimization of bank portfolios. *Management Science* 7 (July): 393–410.

Chandler, L. V. 1964. *The Economics of Money and Banking*, 4th ed. Harper and Brothers, New York.

Charnes, A., and S. C. Littlechild. 1968. Intertemporal bank asset choice with stochastic dependence. *Systems Research Memorandum No. 188*. Northwestern University, Evanston, Illinois (mimeographed).

Charnes, A., and S. Thore. 1966. Planning for liquidity in financial institutions: the chance-constrained method. *Journal of Finance* 21 (December): 649–74.

Christ, C. F. 1963. Interest rates and 'portfolio selection' among liquid assets in the U.S. *Measurement in Economics: Studies in Mathematical Economics and Econometrics in Memory of Yehuda Grunfeld*. Stanford University Press, Stanford, Calif.: 201–18.

Cohen, K. J., and F. S. Hammer. 1967. Linear programming and optimal bank asset management decisions. *Journal of Finance* 22 (May): 147–65.

De Leeuw, F. 1965. A model of financial behavior. In J. Dusenberry et. al. *The Brookings Quarterly Econometric Model of the United States*. Rand McNally, Chicago: 464–530.

De Leeuw, F., and E. Gramlich. 1968. The Federal Reserve-MIT econometric model. *Federal Reserve Bulletin* 54 (January): 11–40.

Edgeworth, F. Y. 1888. The mathematical theory of banking. *Journal of the Royal Statistical Society* 51, Part I (March): 113–27.

Eisner, R., and R. H. Strotz. 1963. Determinants of business investment. *Impacts of Monetary Policy*. A series of research studies prepared for the Commission on Money and Credit. Prentice-Hall, Englewood Cliffs, N. J.: 59–233.

Eppen, G. D., and E. F. Fama. 1968. Solutions for cash-balance and simple dynamic-portfolio problems. *Journal of Business* 41 (January): 94–112.

Federal Home Loan Bank Board. 1968. "News" (November). Washington, D.C.

Federal Reserve Bank of Boston. 1960–62. *Functional Cost Analysis—Average Participating Bank*. Boston, Mass.

Federal Reserve Bank of Boston. 1963. Time deposits in New England. *1962 Annual Report*. Boston, Mass.

Federal Reserve Bank of Kansas City. 1957. Deposit instability in individual banks. *Monthly Review* (September): 3–11.

Feige, E. L. 1964. *The Demand for Liquid Assets: a Temporal Cross-Section Analysis*. Prentice-Hall, Englewood Cliffs, N.J.

Feldstein, M. S. 1969. Mean-variance analysis in the theory of liquidity preference and portfolio selection. *Review of Economic Studies* 36 (January): 5–12.

Fieldhouse, R. C. 1964. Certificates of deposit. In Federal Reserve Bank of New York, *Essays in Money and Credit*. New York: 42–46.

Friedman, M., and A. J. Schwartz. 1963. *A Monetary History of the United States 1867–1960*. Princeton University Press, Princeton, N.J.

Friedman, M., and A. J. Schwartz. 1970. *Monetary Statistics of the United States*. National Bureau of Economic Research, New York.

Goldenweiser, E. A. 1951. *American Economic Policy*. McGraw-Hill, New York.

Goldfeld, S. M. 1966. *Commercial Bank Behavior and Economic Activity*. North-Holland, Amsterdam.

Goldfeld, S. M., and E. J. Kane. 1966. The determinants of member bank borrowing: an econometric study. *Journal of Finance* 21 (September): 499–514.

Gould, J. P. 1968. Adjustment costs in the theory of investment of the firm. *Review of Economic Studies* 35 (January): 47–56.

Gramley, L. E. 1962. *A Study of Scale Economies in Banking*. Federal Reserve Bank of Kansas City, Kansas City, Mo.

Green, H. A. John. 1964. *Aggregation in Economic Analysis: An Introductory Survey*. Princeton University Press, Princeton, N.J.

Griliches, Z. 1967. Distributed lags: a survey. *Econometrica* 35 (January): 16–49.

Griliches, Z., and N. Wallace. 1965. The determinants of investment revisited. *International Economic Review* 6 (September): 311–29.

Hall, G. R., and C. F. Phillips, Jr. 1964. *Bank Mergers and the Regulatory Agencies*. Board of Governors of the Federal Reserve System, Washington, D.C.

Hamburger, M. J. 1968. Household demand for financial assets. *Econometrica* 36 (January): 97–118.

Haydon, R. B., and J. H. Wicks. 1966. A model of commercial bank earning assets selection. *Journal of Financial and Quantitative Analysis* 1 (June): 99–113.

Hendershott, P. H. 1968. Recent development of the financial sector of econometric models. *Journal of Finance* 23 (March): 41–66.

Hester, D. D. 1962. An empirical examination of a commercial bank loan offer function. *Yale Economic Essays* 2 (Spring): 3–57.

Hester, D. D. 1964. *Indian Banks: Their Portfolios, Profits, and Policy*. Bombay University Press, Bombay.

Hester, D. D. 1965. A model of portfolio behavior applied to mutual savings banks. Paper read at the First World Congress of the Econometric Society (mimeographed).

Hester, D. D. 1967a. Stock and mutual associations in the savings and loan industry. Research paper prepared for the Federal Home Loan Bank Board, Washington, D.C.

Hester, D. D. 1967b. Comment on competition and efficiency in the banking system —empirical research and its policy implications. *Journal of Political Economy* 75, Part II (August): 479–81.

Hester, D. D. 1969. Financial disintermediation and policy. *Journal of Money, Credit, and Banking* 1 (August): 600–17.

Hester, D. D., and J. L. Pierce. 1967a. Dynamics of portfolio adjustments by financial intermediaries: cross-section estimation and macro-simulation (mimeographed).

Hester, D. D., and J. L. Pierce. 1967b. Deposit forecasting and portfolio behavior. Paper read at the December meetings of the Econometric Society (mimeographed).

Hester, D. D., and J. L. Pierce. 1968. Cross-section analysis and bank dynamics. *Journal of Political Economy* 76, Part II (July/August): 755–76.

Hester, D. D., and J. L. Pierce. 1970. Commercial bank portfolio behavior and the money supply function. Paper read at the Second World Congress of the Econometric Society (mimeographed).

Hester, D. D., and J. F. Zoellner. 1966. The relation between bank portfolios and earnings: an econometric analysis. *Review of Economics and Statistics* 48 (November): 372–86.

Hodgman, D. R. 1963. *Commercial Bank Loan and Investment Policy*. University of Illinois Press, Urbana, Illinois.

Hurwicz, L. 1950. Least-squares bias in time series. In T. C. Koopmans, ed. *Statistical Inference in Dynamic Econometric Models*. Cowles Commission Monograph No. 10. Wiley, New York: 365–83.

Jolivet, V. M. 1966. The control of savings and loan associations. *Journal of Financial and Quantitative Analysis* 1 (December): 58–71.

Jorgenson, D. W. 1966. Rational distributed lag functions. *Econometrica* 34 (January): 135–49.

Kane, E. J., and B. G. Malkiel. 1965. Bank portfolio allocation, deposit variability, and the availability doctrine. *Quarterly Journal of Economics* 79 (February): 113–34.

Karlin, S. 1958. One stage inventory models with uncertainty. In K. Arrow, S. Karlin, and H. Scarf, eds. *Studies in the Mathematical Theory of Inventory and Production*. Stanford University Press, Stanford, Calif.: 109–34.

Kendall, L. T. 1962. *The Savings and Loan Business: Its Purposes, Functions, and Economic Justification*. Monograph prepared for the Commission on Money and Credit. Prentice-Hall, Englewood Cliffs, N.J.

Koyck, L. M. 1954. *Distributed Lags and Investment Analysis*. North-Holland, Amsterdam.

Kuh, E. 1959. The validity of cross-sectionally estimated behavior equations in time series applications. *Econometrica* 27 (April): 197–214.

Lintner, J. 1962. Dividends, earnings, leverage, stock prices and the supply of capital to corporations. *Review of Economics and Statistics* 44 (August): 243–69.

Lintner, J. 1965. The valuation of risk assets and the selection of risky investments in stock portfolios and capital budgets. *Review of Economics and Statistics* 47 (February): 13–37.

Lucas, R. E., Jr. 1967. Optimal investment policy and the flexible accelerator. *International Economic Review* 8 (February): 78–85.

Malkiel, B. G. 1966. *The Term Structure of Interest Rates: Expectations and Behavior Patterns.* Princeton University Press, Princeton, N.J.

Markowitz, H. M. 1959. *Portfolio Selection: Efficient Diversification of Investments.* Cowles Foundation Monograph No. 16. Wiley, New York.

Marschak, J. 1960. Remarks on the economics of information. *Contributions to Scientific Research in Management.* University of California Press, Los Angeles: 79–98.

Marschak, J., and R. Radner. 1972. *Economic Theory of Teams.* Cowles Foundation Monograph No. 22. Yale University Press, New Haven, Conn.

McGuire, J. W., J. S. Y. Chiu, and A. O. Elbing. 1962. Executive incomes, sales and profits. *American Economic Review* 52 (September): 753–61.

Meigs, A. J. 1962. *Free Reserves and the Money Supply.* University of Chicago Press, Chicago.

Meiselman, D. 1962. *The Term Structure of Interest Rates.* Prentice-Hall, Englewood Cliffs, N.J.

Meyer, J. R., and G. Kraft. 1961. The evaluation of statistical costing techniques as applied in the transportation industry. *American Economic Review* 51 (May): 313–34.

Meyer, J. R., and E. Kuh. 1957. *The Investment Decision: An Empirical Study.* Harvard University Press, Cambridge, Mass.

Modigliani, F., and M. H. Miller. 1958. The cost of capital, corporation finance and the theory of investment. *American Economic Review* 48 (June): 261–97.

Modigliani, F., R. H. Rasche, and J. P. Cooper. 1970. Central bank policy, the money supply, and the short-term rate of interest. *Journal of Money, Credit, and Banking* 2 (May): 168–218.

Morrison, G. R. 1966. *Liquidity Preferences of Commercial Banks.* University of Chicago Press, Chicago.

Morrison, G. R., and R. T. Selden. 1965. *Time Deposit Growth and the Employment of Bank Funds.* A study prepared for the Association of Reserve City Bankers, Chicago.

Mundlak, Y. 1961. Aggregation over time in distributed lag models. *International Economic Review* 2 (May): 154–63.

Murphy, N. B. 1968. Large firms and their banks. *New England Business Review.* Federal Reserve Bank of Boston (December): 18–22.

National Association of Mutual Savings Banks. 1962. *Mutual Savings Banking: Basic Characteristics and Role in the National Economy.* Monograph prepared for the Commission on Money and Credit. Prentice-Hall, Englewood Cliffs, N.J.

National Association of Mutual Savings Banks. 1963. *Facts and Figures.*

National Association of Mutual Savings Banks. 1965. *National Fact Book.*

Nerlove, M. 1967. Experimental evidence on the estimation of dynamic economic relations from a time series of cross sections. *Economic Studies Quarterly* 18 (December): 42–74.

Nerlove, M. 1968. Factors affecting differences among rates of return on investments in individual common stocks. *Review of Economics and Statistics* 50 (August): 312–31.

Nicols, A. 1967. Stock versus mutual savings and loan associations: some evidence of differences in behavior. *American Economic Review* 57 (May): 337–46.

Orcutt, G. H. 1962. Microanalytic models of the United States economy: need and development. *American Economic Review* 52 (May): 229–40.

Orcutt, G. H., H. W. Watts, and J. B. Edwards. 1968. Data aggregation and information loss. *American Economic Review* 58 (September): 773–87.

Orr, D., and W. G. Mellon. 1961. Stochastic reserve losses and expansion of bank credit. *American Economic Review* 51 (September): 614–23.

Parks, R. H. 1958. Income and tax aspects of commercial bank portfolio operations in Treasury securities. *National Tax Journal* 11 (March): 21–34.

Pierce, J. L. 1964. The monetary mechanism: some partial relationships. *American Economic Review* 54 (May): 523–31.

Pierce, J. L. 1965. A cross-section analysis of commercial bank portfolio management. Paper read at the December meetings of the Econometric Society (mimeographed).

Pierce, J. L. 1966. Commercial bank liquidity. *Federal Reserve Bulletin* 52 (August): 1093–101.

Pierce, J. L. 1967. An empirical model of commercial bank portfolio management. In D. D. Hester and J. Tobin, eds. *Studies of Portfolio Behavior.* Wiley, New York: 171–90.

Polakoff, M. E. 1960. Reluctance elasticity, least cost, and member bank borrowing: a suggested integration. *Journal of Finance* 15 (March): 1–18.

Poole, W. 1968. Commercial bank reserve management in a stochastic model: implications for monetary policy. *Journal of Finance* 23 (December): 769–91.

Porter, R. C. 1961. A model of bank portfolio selection. *Yale Economic Essays* 1 (Fall): 323–59.

Rangarajan, C. 1966. Deposit variability in individual banks. *National Banking Review* 4 (September): 61–71.

Rangarajan, C., and A. K. Severn. 1965. The response of banks to changes in aggregate reserves. *Journal of Finance* 20 (December): 651–64.

Rasche, R. H., and H. T. Shapiro. 1968. The F.R.B.-M.I.T. econometric model: its special features. *American Economic Review* 58 (May): 123–49.

Robinson, J. 1951. The rate of interest. *Econometrica* 19 (April): 92–111.

Robinson, R. I. 1962. *The Management of Bank Funds.* McGraw-Hill, New York.

Samuelson, P. A. 1967. General proof that diversification pays. *Journal of Financial and Quantitative Analysis* 2 (March): 1–13.

Scott, K. E., and D. D. Hester. 1967. Conversion of mutual savings and loan associations to stock form: legal and economic issues. Research paper prepared for the Federal Home Loan Bank Board, Washington, D.C.

Shaw, E. S. 1962. *Savings and Loan Market Structure and Market Performance.* A research study prepared for the California Savings and Loan Commissioner, Los Angeles, California.

Struble, F. M., and C. H. Wilkerson. 1967. Deposit variability at commercial banks. *Monthly Review* of the Federal Reserve Bank of Kansas City (July–August): 27–34.

Struble, F. M., and C. H. Wilkerson. 1967. Bank size and deposit variability. *Monthly Review* of the Federal Reserve Bank of Kansas City (November–December): 3–9.

Swan, C. 1970. A model of portfolio adjustment applied to mutual savings banks. University of Minnesota (mimeographed).

Taylor, L. D., and T. A. Wilson. 1964. Three-pass least squares: a method for estimating models with a lagged dependent variable. *Review of Economics and Statistics* 46 (November): 329–46.

Teigen, R. L. 1964a. A structural approach to the impact of monetary policy. *Journal of Finance* 19 (May): 284–308.

Teigen, R. L. 1964b. Demand and supply functions for money in the United States: some structural estimates. *Econometrica* 32 (October): 476–509.

Telser, L. G. 1967a. Discrete samples and moving sums in stationary stochastic processes. *Journal of the American Statistical Association* 62 (June): 484–99.

Telser, L. G. 1967b. A critique of some recent empirical research on the explanation of the term structure of interest rates. *Journal of Political Economy* 75, Part II (August): 546–60.

Theil, H. 1954. *Linear Aggregation of Economic Relations.* North-Holland, Amsterdam.

Tinsley, P. A. 1967. An application of variable weight distributed lags. *Journal of the American Statistical Association* 62 (December): 1277–89.

Tinsley, P. A. 1971. A variable adjustment model of labor demand. *International Economic Review* 12 (October): 482–510.

Tobin, J. 1950. A statistical demand function for food in the U.S.A. *Journal of the Royal Statistical Society,* Series A, 113, Part II: 113–41.

Tobin, J. 1956. The interest-elasticity of transactions demand for cash. *Review of Economics and Statistics* 38 (August): 241–47.

Tobin, J. 1958. Liquidity preference as behavior towards risk. *Review of Economic Studies* 25 (February): 65–86.

Tobin, J. 1959. Manuscript on monetary theory (mimeographed).

Tobin, J. 1963. Commercial banks as creators of "money." In D. Carson, ed. *Banking and Monetary Studies.* Irwin, Homewood, Illinois: 408–19.

Tobin, J. 1965. The theory of portfolio selection. In F. H. Hahn and F. P. R. Brechling, eds. *The Theory of Interest Rates.* Macmillan, London: 3–51.

Tobin, J. 1969. Comment on Borch and Feldstein. *Review of Economic Studies* 36 (January): 13–14.

Tucker, D. P. 1966. Dynamic income adjustment to money supply changes. *American Economic Review* 56 (June): 433–49.

Tucker, D. P. 1968. Credit rationing, interest rate lags, and monetary policy speed. *Quarterly Journal of Economics* 82 (February): 54–84.

United States Government, 1963. *Report of the Committee on Financial Institutions to the President of the United States.* United States Government Printing Office, Washington, D.C.

United States Government, 1971. *Report of the President's Commission on Financial Structure and Regulation.* United States Government Printing Office, Washington, D.C.

Wallis, K. F. 1967. Lagged dependent variables and serially correlated errors: a reappraisal of three-pass least squares. *Review of Economics and Statistics* 49 (November): 555–67.

Working, H. 1960. Note on the correlation of first differences of averages in a random chain. *Econometrica* 28 (October): 916–18.

Zellner, A. 1968. Note on the effect of temporal aggregation on the estimation of a stock adjustment equation. University of Chicago (mimeographed).

Index

Cowles Foundation Monographs

1. Charles F. Roos, DYNAMIC ECONOMICS (out of print)
2. Charles F. Roos, NRA ECONOMIC PLANNING (out of print)
3. Alfred Cowles and Associates, COMMON-STOCK INDEXES (2nd edition)
4. Dickson H. Leavens, SILVER MONEY (out of print)
5. Gerhard Tintner, THE VARIATE DIFFERENCE METHOD (out of print)
6. Harold T. Davis, THE ANALYSIS OF ECONOMIC TIME SERIES (out of print)
7. Jacob L. Mosak, GENERAL-EQUILIBRIUM THEORY IN INTERNATIONAL TRADE (out of print)
8. Oscar Lange, PRICE FLEXIBILITY AND EMPLOYMENT
9. George Katona, PRICE CONTROL AND BUSINESS (out of print)
10. Tjalling C. Koopmans, ed., STATISTICAL INFERENCE IN DYNAMIC ECONOMIC MODELS (out of print)
11. Lawrence R. Klein, ECONOMIC FLUCTUATIONS IN THE UNITED STATES, 1921–1941 (out of print)
12. Kenneth J. Arrow. SOCIAL CHOICE AND INDIVIDUAL VALUES (2nd edition)
13. Tjalling C. Koopmans, ed., ACTIVITY ANALYSIS OF PRODUCTION AND ALLOCATION
14. William C. Hood and Tjalling C. Koopmans, eds., STUDIES IN ECONOMETRIC METHOD
15. Clifford Hildreth and F. G. Jarrett, A STATISTICAL STUDY OF LIVESTOCK PRODUCTION AND MARKETING
16. Harry M. Markowitz, PORTFOLIO SELECTION: Efficient Diversification of Investments
17. Gerald Debreu, THEORY OF VALUE: An Axiomatic Analysis of Economic Equilibrium
18. Alan S. Manne and Harry M. Markowitz, eds., STUDIES IN PROCESS ANALYSIS: Economy-Wide Production Capabilities (out of print)
19. Donald D. Hester and James Tobin, eds., RISK AVERSION AND PORTFOLIO CHOICE
20. Donald D. Hester and James Tobin, eds., STUDIES OF PORTFOLIO BEHAVIOR
21. Donald D. Hester and James Tobin, eds., FINANCIAL MARKETS AND ECONOMIC ACTIVITY
22. Jacob Marschak and Roy Radner, ECONOMIC THEORY OF TEAMS
23. Thomas J. Rothenberg, EFFICIENT ESTIMATION WITH A PRIORI INFORMATION
24. Herbert Scarf, THE COMPUTATION OF ECONOMIC EQUILIBRIA
25. Donald D. Hester and James L. Pierce, BANK MANAGEMENT AND PORTFOLIO BEHAVIOR

(*continued on next page*)

Orders for Monograph 8 should be sent to Principia Press of Trinity University, 715 Stadium Drive, San Antonio, Texas.

Orders for Monographs 3 and 19 should be sent to the Cowles Foundation, Box 2125 Yale Station, New Haven, Conn. 06520.

Orders for Monographs 12, 13, 14, 16, 17, 21, 22, 23, and 24 should be sent to Yale University Press, 92A Yale Station, New Haven, Conn. 06520, or 20 Bloomsbury Square, London WC1A 2NP, England.

Orders for Monographs 15 and 20 should be sent to John Wiley & Sons, Inc., 605 Third Avenue, New York, N.Y. 10016.